Foundations of WF

An Introduction to Windows Workflow Foundation

Brian R. Myers

Apress®

Foundations of WF: An Introduction to Windows Workflow Foundation

Copyright © 2007 by Brian R. Myers

ISBN-13 (pbk): 978-1-59059-718-7

ISBN-10 (pbk): 1-59059-718-4

Printed and bound in the United States of America 9 8 7 6 5 4 3 2 1

Lead Editor: Jonathan Hassell
Technical Reviewer: Jim Flanagan
Editorial Board: Steve Anglin, Ewan Buckingham, Gary Cornell, Jason Gilmore, Jonathan Gennick,
    Jonathan Hassell, James Huddleston, Chris Mills, Matthew Moodie, Dominic Shakeshaft, Jim Sumser,
    Keir Thomas, Matt Wade
Project Manager: Tracy Brown Collins
Copy Edit Manager: Nicole Flores
Copy Editor: Susannah Pfalzer
Assistant Production Director: Kari Brooks-Copony
Production Editor: Laura Esterman
Compositor: Susan Glinert
Proofreader: Nancy Sixsmith
Indexer: Becky Hornyak
Cover Designer: Kurt Krames
Manufacturing Director: Tom Debolski

Distributed to the book trade worldwide by Springer-Verlag New York, Inc., 233 Spring Street, 6th Floor, New York, NY 10013. Phone 1-800-SPRINGER, fax 201-348-4505, e-mail orders-ny@springer-sbm.com, or visit http://www.springeronline.com.

For information on translations, please contact Apress directly at 2560 Ninth Street, Suite 219, Berkeley, CA 94710. Phone 510-549-5930, fax 510-549-5939, e-mail info@apress.com, or visit http://www.apress.com.

The source code for this book is available to readers at http://www.apress.com in the Code/Download section.

To my nieces (Erica, Natalie, and Sarah) and nephews (Ryan and Aaron)—
there is no limit to what you can achieve

Contents at a Glance

Contents

About the Author

BRIAN MYERS is a software engineer and database administrator for a large manufacturing company. He's a Microsoft Certified Solution Developer for .NET, a Microsoft Certified Application Developer for .NET, and a Microsoft Certified Professional. He holds an associate's degree in microcomputer applications development from the Pennsylvania College of Technology and a bachelor's degree in information systems from Pennsylvania State University. Along with his professional accreditations, he is also an Eagle Scout.

He has more than eight years of experience as a software developer, mostly with Microsoft technologies. Prior to taking his current position in June 2004, he worked for a consulting company for six years, handling various development projects as a developer and project manager.

Brian has also written articles for http://www.ASPToday.com, and he teaches courses in .NET development and SQL Server.

About the Technical Reviewer

JIM FLANAGAN is a software consultant with Transfer Technology, specializing in Web database applications in both SQL Server and Oracle. He has more than 24 years of computing industry experience and resides in Annville, Pennsylvania.

Acknowledgments

This is my second book, and I've already thanked a lot of people in the acknowledgments for my previous book. However, I need to thank my wife, Catharine Miller, for again encouraging me to write this book and always supporting what I do.

I want to thank Apress and Jon Hassell for giving me the chance to write this book. I also want to thank Sofia Marchant and Tracy Brown Collins, my project managers at Apress. Finally, from Apress, I want to thank Susannah Pfalzer, who did the copy editing, and Laura Esterman, for production.

I also want to thank my technical reviewer, Jim Flanagan. Jim and I worked together for six years, and I have a lot of respect for his work. He is very intelligent and talented. I was happy he agreed to provide the technical review for this book.

Introduction

For many years, I've been writing software applications that are based on workflow. In each of those applications, I needed to write code to handle the workflow actions. Even after writing some reusable code, substantial code needed to be created. Now Microsoft has released Windows Workflow Foundation, which will make creating workflow code much easier. WF, as it is known, provides out-of-the-box activities that can be added to a workflow application. With only minor changes to the properties of these activities, WF can provide a fully functional workflow for your application. You can also create your own activities to extend the out-of-the-box activities, and you can even embed a Workflow Designer into a Windows-based application and allow users to create workflow.

This book will explain the basics of workflow, and also show you most of the out-of-the-box activities that are provided with WF. Each chapter covers at least one out-of-the-box activity, and each chapter includes not only an explanation of the activity, but also a practical example of the activity. Finally, this book will provide you with a real-world example of creating an ASP.NET application integrated with a workflow created with WF.

If you've created workflow applications in the past, you'll want to look at WF and what it has to offer. This book will be a great start to using WF and will get you ready to create workflow applications faster than in the past.

CHAPTER 1

■ ■ ■

Introduction to Workflow and Windows Workflow Foundation

In this chapter, you'll learn what workflow is and get introduced to a new .NET technology known as Windows Workflow Foundation (WF). I'll explain the different types of workflow and provide reasons for using each type of workflow. I'll define workflow activities and provide a list of workflow activities within WF.

What Is Workflow?

In the business world, workflow is how an item is moved from one person to another through a process. That process is the business process, and it defines the steps necessary to complete a piece of work. Steps in the process can be required or optional. For example, a business process for a vacation request might be that the employee must provide some information, such as the dates requested, to his or her supervisor. Then, the employee's supervisor must determine if the employee has vacation time to use, and if the date or dates requested are available for vacation. The supervisor must provide the date information to the human resources department. Finally, the human resources department verifies that all policies have been followed, and provides the information to accounting at the appropriate time so payroll adjustments can be made.

Notice that I didn't mention technology in my explanation of the business process. Business processes should be defined absent of technology. However, you can see there's a flow to the work. Also, notice that at several points in the flow, decisions need to be made. For example, the supervisor must make sure the employee has vacation time to use, and the company might have specific requirements about the number of employees that can be on vacation at the same time within a department. Because the flow can't move from one step to the next without some criteria being met, this is a state-based workflow. A state-based workflow means that each step of the flow has criteria that must be met before the flow can continue to the next step. A state-based workflow waits on external entities to perform some action before moving to the next step.

This example of workflow has a large amount of potential branching. Within a workflow, branching is when a decision needs to be made, such as when the supervisor must determine if the employee has enough vacation time to use, and if company policies related to staff size within a department will be met. In this case, two decisions need to be made: first, if the employee has vacation time to use, and second, if policies have been met. For each branch in a workflow, there must be at least two alternatives. You can't have a workflow just stop at a decision point.

For example, the supervisor can't determine that the employee doesn't have enough vacation time and simply stop the workflow. Some step must still be taken to let the employee know the vacation request has been denied. So in the supervisor step, the branching involved would be as follows: if the employee has vacation time then approve, and if the employee doesn't have vacation time, don't approve the request and send it back to the employee.

Another type of workflow is sequential. Sequential workflow is a workflow whose steps are performed one right after the other, but might include branching. In this case, *sequential* refers more to continuous operation, instead of the order in which actions are performed. The traditional concept of sequential in programming is without branching, but when related to workflow, sequential means continuous, instead of without branching. Steps in a Sequential workflow don't wait for an external entity to perform the next step. You can think of the Sequential workflow as close to continuous. There might be some external entity's action required to begin the flow, but once the flow is started, little if any external action is needed. Technology must be applied to a business process. For example, you might have a process that automatically updates a sales order as complete, and sends an e-mail notice to the customer and the sales person when a sales order is shipped. An external entity must start the process by saying that the sales order has shipped, but then some system would mark the sales order as complete, determine the customer's e-mail address, determine the sales person's e-mail address, and then send the e-mail. Once an external entity initiates the flow, the flow continues until an exception is encountered or the flow is completed.

When to Use Which Workflow Type

Sequential workflow within WF follows the traditional thinking of workflow. That is, the workflow is in control. As long as the process is simple and rarely goes outside the bounds, then a Sequential workflow will work. For example, an employee performance review workflow might have an employee's supervisor create a review and send the review to the employee. The employee sends the review back to the supervisor, and the supervisor sends the review to the employee. The supervisor is involved twice, but there's little room for deviation from the flow. This is a good example of a Sequential workflow. Again, remember that just because the flow is sequential doesn't mean it can't have branching and looping.

On the other hand, State Machine workflow deals with different states. A process that can have many different iterations is a candidate for a State Machine workflow. A help desk system would be a good candidate for a State Machine workflow. For example, a user creates a ticket and that ticket goes into a queue. The state of the ticket is pending. The help desk manager reviews the queue and sets a priority. Also, the help desk manager then assigns the ticket to a technician. The state of the ticket is now assigned. The technician says to begin work on the ticket. The state is now Working. However, the technician must wait for information from another vendor. The state goes to pending vendor. After some time, the vendor returns information. However, the technician doesn't have time to work on the ticket, so he assigns it to another technician. The state is back to assigned. The technician begins and completes the work and the ticket is closed. The state is now closed. Performing this type of process with a Sequential workflow would require a lot of while loops and if branching, because there are so many possible statuses and not every ticket would use each state. Most tickets wouldn't use the pending vendor status, but some tickets might.

Why Use Workflows?

Why might you even want to use workflows? I can, and have, created a help desk application with the same complexities mentioned earlier as an ASP.NET application with Visual Basic. The biggest reason to create workflow, especially with WF, is that you're creating a model. Most projects that facilitate a business process have some type of model associated with them. This model might be use cases and UML diagrams, or it might be as simple as a flow chart. These are models—ways to look at the process. With WF, the model and the workflow are the same thing. You use pieces of the business process to make a workflow, and you piece together the business process, which makes a model. Before WF, you'd create UML diagrams that showed how classes were to interact, and with some tools you could get the diagrams to create class definitions automatically, along with method and property definitions. With WF, when you're laying out the business process—that is, modeling the business process—you're also building the application. WF also has other facilities that help take care of a great deal of the plumbing related to workflow. For example, you can persist workflow data, so that even during a reboot, running processes can be started from the point they stopped. Finally, WF allows processes to change on the fly. You can change the process while instances of the process are running, and the instances will adhere to the new process.

Introducing Windows Workflow Foundation

Windows Workflow Foundation (WF) is a technology that Microsoft has packaged with the .NET Framework for Microsoft Vista. WF is part of the programming model for Microsoft Vista, the next release of the Windows operating system. The new name for that programming model is WinFX, and it's a significant expansion of the Microsoft .NET Framework that was first released several years ago. Although WF is part of the WinFX programming model for Windows Vista, it can be run on clients that have Windows Server 2003 SP1, Windows XP SP2, Windows XP Home Edition, or Windows XP Media Center Edition. To develop workflow applications, you must be using Visual Studio 2005—any version except Express. You can build workflow applications using VS2005 by adding the Visual Studio 2005 Extensions for Windows Workflow Foundation.

Architecture of Windows Workflow Foundation

WF itself is a programming model, along with an engine and a set of tools for building workflow-enabled applications. The programming model is made up of exposed APIs that other programming languages can use to interact with the workflow engine. These APIs are encapsulated within a namespace called `System.Workflow.` That namespace will be part of the WinFX programming model, but can also be installed as an add-on to the existing .NET Framework 2.0.

   The easiest way to interact with the new APIs and namespace is through the Workflow Designers, which you can add onto VS2005. You must download and install WF (more on this in the next section) unless you're using Windows Vista as your operating system. When you download and install the foundation, WF gets bolted onto the .NET Framework 2.0 and VS2005. Within VS2005, you'll have new project types and will be able to import and use the `System.Workflow` namespace. The new Workflow Designer projects allow you to design workflow visually using the same drag-and-drop methods you use for creating Windows or Web-based applications. Within the designers, you build workflow much like you'd create a flowchart with a tool such as

Microsoft Visio. WF also allows you to package the designers for reuse. For example, you could build a Windows application that allows business people to create their own workflow libraries.

The design tools that become part of VS2005 make up the first component of the overall WF. The next component is the actual workflow. Workflow is made up of a group of activities. These activities facilitate a business process or part of a business process. Activities are a central idea within the concept of workflow and the WF. A single workflow within WF is made up of one or more activities. In the context of the WF, *activities* are the actual work units necessary to perform a workflow. A number of out-of-the-box activities are provided as part of the WF. These out-of-the-box activities are part of the WF base activity library. You aren't restricted only to these activities; you can create custom activities and create your own library (as will be done in Chapter 8). You create the custom activities using the VS2005 Workflow Designers.

The next component of the WF is the WF runtime engine. The WF runtime engine executes workflow, made up of activities, and created with the VS2005 Workflow Designers. The runtime engine also includes services such as scheduling, state management, and rules. The scheduling service schedules the execution of activities within a given workflow. The state management service allows the state of a workflow to be persisted, instead of storing that state in another mechanism, such as a database. The rules service executes Policy activities. I'll further explain Policy activities in the section entitled "Out-of-the-Box Activities" and in more depth in Chapter 5. For now, realize that you can create workflows that are based on business rules and that perform some action when those rules are satisfied. The rules service handles all this.

The last component of WF is a host process. WF itself doesn't have an executable environment. Instead, another process must host the runtime engine and workflows. This host process may be a Windows application or an ASP.NET application. During development, this host process is VS2005. The soon-to-be-released Microsoft Office 12 can also be a host for a workflow created with WF.

Getting Started with WF and VS2005

Before you can create or use workflows, you must first install the Windows Workflow Foundation or be running Windows Vista. Even if you're running Windows Vista as an operating system, you must install the Workflow Designers for VS2005. If you're running an operating system other than Windows Vista, you need to install the Visual Studio 2005 Extensions for Windows Workflow Foundation. This installation package includes the VS Workflow Designers, the WF SDK, and the WF runtime components. The installation is self-explanatory, so I won't walk through it here. When the package is installed, two new programs will appear in the Add/Remove Programs within the Control Panel. The first is the Visual Studio 2005 Extensions for Windows Workflow Foundation. These are the Workflow Designers that are part of VS2005. The other program is the Windows Workflow Foundation, which is an add-on to the .NET Framework 2.0 and contains the components mentioned earlier.

As soon as the Visual Studio 2005 Extensions for Windows Workflow Foundation is installed, you can open VS2005 and find new projects.

When you open VS2005, click File ➤ New ➤ Project. When the New Project window appears, click the plus sign next to your favorite programming language, such as VB. Notice when the project types list is expanded, there's a new project type called Workflow. When you click the Workflow project type, you'll see the new project templates (see Figure 1-1).

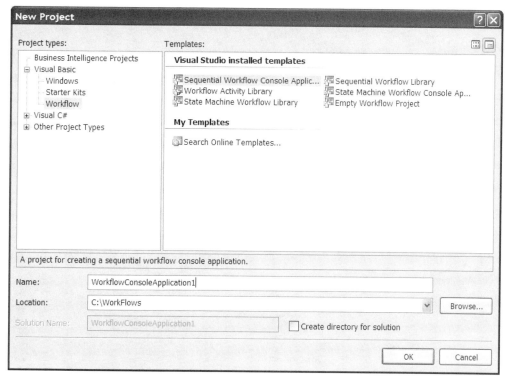

Figure 1-1. *New workflow project templates*

The Sequential Workflow Console Application and State Machine Workflow Console Application provide the workflow model for the two types of workflow that can be created within WF: sequential and state machine. In the first section of this chapter, I explained what workflow was, and discussed Sequential workflow and State Machine workflow. WF implements these workflows using these models. First you need to select a workflow model, then you need to add activities to that model. In the section entitled "Out-of-the-Box Activities" you'll find a list of all the out-of-the-box activities and a brief explanation of each. Most of this book will expand that brief explanation and provide examples for each of the base activities.

There isn't much difference between each of the project templates. In this section, I'll explain the differences between the templates, and then show you how to create one project using each template (except for the empty workflow project template). The projects created in this section will be used in Chapter 2 to demonstrate how to create and execute a simple workflow project of each type.

The first project will be the Sequential Workflow Console Application. Create a new Sequential Workflow Console Application by creating a new workflow project within VS2005 and selecting the Sequential Workflow Console Application project template from the Workflow project type under VB (in Chapter 2 you'll create the C# projects). Create a new folder on your computer called WorkFlows, which is simply for organization. However, the WF beta doesn't allow saving into the default directory, so you need to create a folder into which to put the workflow. Create the project as VBFirstSequentialWFConsoleApplication within that WorkFlows folder. Your New Project window should look like Figure 1-2.

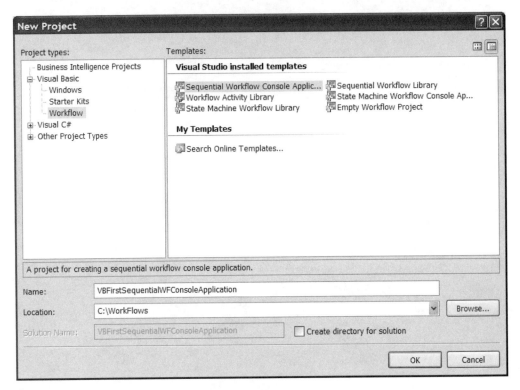

Figure 1-2. *Create VBFirstSequentialWFConsoleApplication*

With that VS2005 instance still open, open a new instance of VS2005. Create a new project, but this time create a Sequential Workflow Library project called VBFirstSequentialWFLibrary, as shown in Figure 1-3.

Make the VS2005 instance with the first application (VBFirstSequentialWFConsoleApplication) active. Click the Solution Explorer. You'll notice there's a file called Workflow1.vb and a file called Module1.vb, as shown in Figure 1-4.

The reason the workflow file has a .VB extension just like classes do is because both workflows and activities are classes. Chapter 2 will further cover the fact that workflows and activities are classes and behave like classes (have events, for instance). If you make the other instance of VS2005 active, you'll notice there's only a Workflow1.vb file. The reason for this is that the first application is the console application. The Module1.vb file contains a `Sub Main` procedure that's used to start the workflow. Again, Chapter 2 will further cover Module1.vb and `Sub Main`.

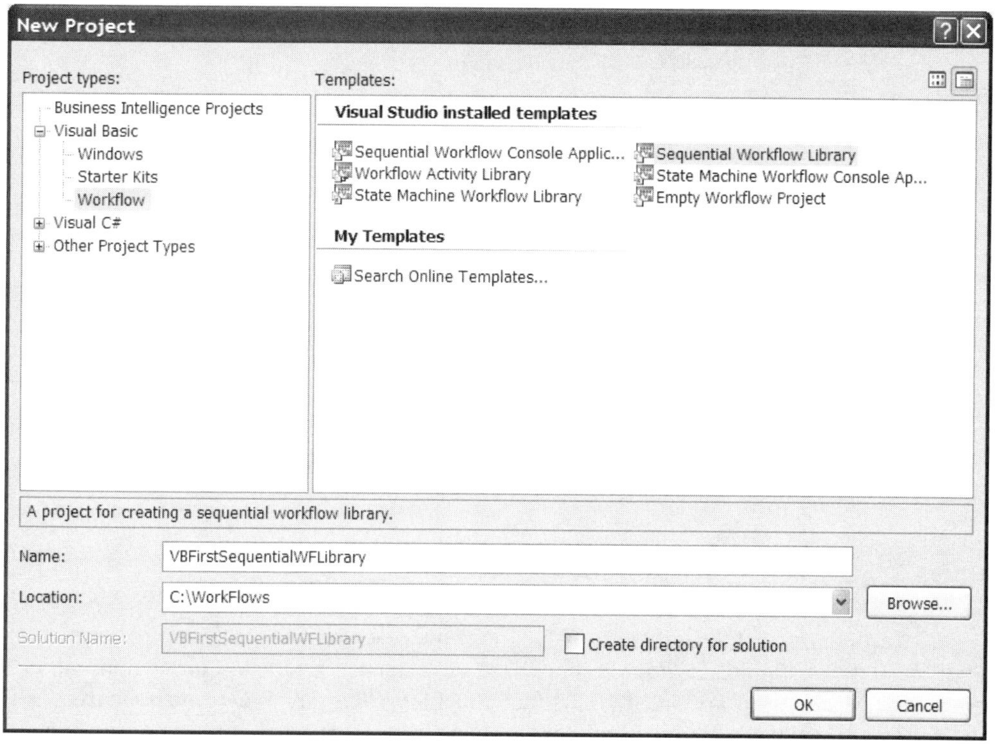

New Project   ? ☒

Project types:

- Business Intelligence Projects
- Visual Basic
  - Windows
  - Starter Kits
  - Workflow
- ⊞ Visual C#
- ⊞ Other Project Types

Templates: ⊞ ▭

Visual Studio installed templates

- Sequential Workflow Console Applic...
- Workflow Activity Library
- State Machine Workflow Library
- Sequential Workflow Library
- State Machine Workflow Console Ap...
- Empty Workflow Project

My Templates

- Search Online Templates...

A project for creating a sequential workflow library.

Name: VBFirstSequentialWFLibrary

Location: C:\WorkFlows   ▾   Browse...

Solution Name: VBFirstSequentialWFLibrary   ☐ Create directory for solution

OK   Cancel

Figure 1-3. *Create VBFirstSequentialWFLibrary*

Figure 1-4. *Sequential Workflow Console Application in the Solution Explorer*

The Toolbox within VS2005 for a workflow project is different from a typical project using the selected language. Instead of controls such as text boxes or grid views , the Toolbox contains a control for each of the activities from the WF Basic Activity Library (the out-of-the-box activities). The formal design area is where the controls from the Toolbox will be placed. The design area is the area with the Sequential workflow starting point already defined, waiting for the next activity to be placed next in the flow, as shown in Figure 1-5.

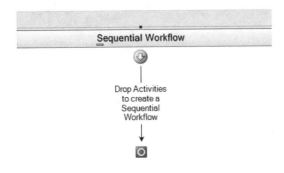

Figure 1-5. *Sequential Workflow design area*

To further prepare for Chapter 2 and creating your first workflow projects, create a new State Machine workflow console application called VBFirstStateMachineWFConsoleApplication, and a State Machine Library called VBFirstStateMachineWFLibrary. When you open the projects, you'll notice the same differences in the Solution Explorer between the console application and the library. Also compare the Toolbox of a State Machine workflow to that of a Sequential workflow project. A few differences will be discussed and shown in Chapter 2. Finally, notice that the design area is different for the State Machine workflow, as shown in Figure 1-6. There's no starting point, just a container for the first state.

Figure 1-6. *State Machine workflow design area*

Close all the projects that are open. The final project to create is the Workflow Activity Library project. Call this project VBFirstWorkflowActivityLibrary. When you open this project, again you'll notice a different design area, as shown in Figure 1-7. This design area allows you to create new activities from the existing out-of-the-box activities. These are called *composite activities*. The Workflow Activity Library project is similar to creating a class library. This allows you to customize existing activities and create your own, to be reused within other projects.

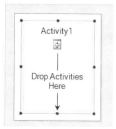

Figure 1-7. *Activity Library design area*

Out-of-the-Box Activities

The preceding section showed how to create each of the new types of workflow projects. However, without an understanding of the out-of-the-box activities, you won't be able to create effective workflow projects. This section will describe all the out-of-the-box activities and indicate which chapter within this book to find out more information about this activity.

- *Code activity:* The Code activity allows you to add your own VB or C# code to the workflow. This is a simple form of the custom activity. The actual code resides in a "code beside" file and gets compiled with the workflow. Any code entered here executes synchronously, so the workflow must wait for it to complete. More information about this activity will follow in Chapter 2.

- *Compensate activity:* This is an error activity, and can only be added to an exception handler activity. You use this activity to undo actions already performed by the workflow after an error has occurred. This is the equivalent of rolling back a transaction. For more information about the Compensate activity, read Chapter 7.

- *Conditional Activity Group:* This is a conditional activity that executes other activities based on a condition that applies to the Conditional Activity Group (CAG) or to the activity that's linked to the CAG. Use this grouping of activities to execute a set of activities based on criteria specified for each activity in the group, until some condition is met for the group as a whole. This would allow a group of activities to be executed in parallel, because they each have their own criteria for defining when the activity is complete. You can use a WhenCondition on an activity within the group and an UntilCondition on the group as a whole. All activities continue to execute, if a WhenCondition is provided for the activities, unless the UntilCondition on the group is met. When the UntilCondition on the group is satisfied, the entire group will stop executing. For more information about the CAG, refer to Chapter 3.

- *Delay activity:* This is a flow activity that allows you to build interval-based pauses into your workflow. With this activity, you can set a duration so that the workflow will pause before continuing to execute. For more information about the Delay activity, refer to Chapter 4.

- *EventDriven activity*: This is a flow activity that contains other activities that are to be executed when an event occurs. The event is subscribed to by child activities, such as the Delay activity, which wait for external events to happen. For more information about the EventDriven activity, refer to Chapter 4.

- *Fault Handler activity*: This is an error handling activity. The Fault Handler activity performs much like the `Catch` block in code. A workflow can have many of these activities to handle the various types of exceptions that could occur within the workflow. The Fault Handler activity can contain other activities that are fired when an exception is encountered, including a Compensate activity. For more information about the Fault Handler activity, refer to Chapter 7.

- *IfElse activity*: This is a conditional activity. Use the IfElse activity to execute a branch of activities based on a condition. The first branch must have a condition, but the last branch doesn't require a condition (this is the else part of the activity). The execution is the same as an If Else statement: the first successful branch execution ends the execution of the activity. For more information about the IfElse activity, refer to Chapter 3.

- *Invoke Web Service activity*: This activity invokes a Web service using a proxy class, and can pass and receive parameters. When invoking a Web service with this activity, you specify a method of the Web service to invoke. For more information about the Invoke Web Service activity, refer to Chapter 6.

- *Listen activity*: This activity is a composite activity (made up of a minimum of two activities). Each activity that makes up the Listen activity must be an EventDriven activity. The first event raised by an EventDriven activity is executed, and the other EventDriven activity or activities within the Listen activity isn't executed. You can't use a Listen activity in a State Machine workflow. For more information about the Listen activity, refer to Chapter 7.

- *Parallel activity*: This activity is a composite activity, made up of two or more Sequence activities. The Parallel activity allows the execution of more than one activity at the same time. The activity isn't complete until all Sequence activities that make up the Parallel activity have completed. You need to be careful with the Parallel activity, as more than one Sequence activity within the Parallel activity might attempt to access the same data and could cause conflicts. For more information about the Parallel activity, refer to Chapter 4.

- *Policy activity*: You can use the Policy activity to represent a collection of rules. A rule has a condition and action or actions that should be taken when that condition is met. The Policy activity allows you to set up a rules-based workflow that can have many conditions, instead of using a series of IfElse activities. For more information about the Policy activity, refer to Chapter 5.

- *Replicator activity*: The Replicator activity is a conditional activity that's similar to the For Each statement. The Replicator activity creates a number of instances of a single activity while running. All instances must complete before the Replicator activity can complete. For more information about the Replicator activity, refer to Chapter 5.

- *Sequence activity.* This is a flow activity and a composite activity. This activity provides an easy way to link activities together that are to be executed in sequence. All activities in the sequence are executed before the sequence is complete. For more information about the Sequence activity, refer to Chapter 4.

- *SetState activity.* This activity is a flow activity that's used to specify a transition to a new state within a State Machine workflow. For more information about the SetState activity, refer to Chapter 4.

- *State activity.* This is a flow activity. This activity represents a state (the main component of a State Machine workflow) within a State Machine workflow. The State activity makes up the building block of the State Machine workflow. When an event is handled within a State Machine workflow, a different state activity is entered to handle that state. For more information about the State activity, refer to Chapter 4.

- *StateInitialization activity.* This activity is a flow activity and a composite activity. This activity is part of a State activity, and is made up of other activities that are to be executed when the State activity is first entered. This activity doesn't need to respond to events. For more information about the StateInitialization activity, refer to Chapter 4.

- *Suspend activity.* This is a flow activity. The Suspend activity pauses the operation of a workflow to allow intervention to occur if an error condition requiring special attention is encountered. When this activity is executed, an error is logged. A workflow that has been paused can still receive messages, but those messages are queued. For more information about the Suspend activity, refer to Chapter 4.

- *Terminate activity.* This is a flow activity. This activity immediately ends a workflow's operation if an error condition is met. Unlike the Suspend activity, which only pauses the workflow when a serious error occurs, this activity stops the workflow. This activity also logs an error. For more information about the Terminate activity, refer to Chapter 4.

- *Throw activity.* This is an error handling activity. Use this activity to throw an exception from within a workflow or another activity. The action of this activity is the same as the Throw statement within a Catch block in code. For more information about the Throw activity, refer to Chapter 7.

- *Transaction Scope activity.* This is a flow activity. This activity provides transaction support, and exception and event handling. All activities that make up a transaction are placed within this activity. For more information about the Transaction Scope activity, refer to Chapter 7.

- *While activity.* This is a conditional activity. This activity executes another activity until a condition is met. The condition that needs to be met can be a rule condition (see the "Policy activity" bullet point) or a code condition. For more information about the While activity, refer to Chapter 3.

Conclusion

This chapter introduced you to workflow, and showed you how you can use the new WF to develop workflow-based applications. This chapter also discussed the new project type within VS2005 for workflow, and defined each of the out-of-the-box-activities that are part of the Windows Workflow Activity Library.

The next chapter will expand on the workflow projects that were created in this chapter. You'll learn how to use the VS2005 Workflow Designers and how to create a simple workflow project.

CHAPTER 2

▪▪▪

First Workflow

This chapter will show you the code that's generated when a new workflow project is created, as well as demonstrate how workflow and activities are created as classes. After I introduce you to the code that's generated, you'll create a simple Sequential workflow and State Machine workflow. You'll create both these workflows in both VB and C#, and I'll show you how to debug the workflows using a console application.

Workflow and Activities As Classes

All workflows and the activities that make up the workflow are classes, because .NET is based on OOP principles. If you're unfamiliar with OOP concepts, a class is a code structure that attempts to model the real world. In this case, a workflow class attempts to model a real workflow, and an Activity class models an activity within a workflow. In both cases, the class exposes properties (variables) and methods (functions or subs) that allow other code to interact with the class, either workflow or activity. As mentioned in Chapter 1, Workflow is a new namespace added to the .NET Framework. This namespace is under the System namespace. Workflows and activities are classes; to demonstrate this, open the VBFirstSequentialWFConsoleApplication project that was created in Chapter 1. After you open the project, open the Object Browser (use the View menu and select Object Browser). Three assemblies make up the Workflow namespace and functionality. They are Activities, ComponentModel, and Runtime, as shown in Figure 2-1. Each of these assemblies is composed of namespaces and classes.

⊞ ·⬚ System.Workflow.Activities
⊞ ·⬚ System.Workflow.ComponentModel
⊞ ·⬚ System.Workflow.Runtime

Figure 2-1. *Workflow assemblies*

To see the underlying assembly and its path, click one of the assembly names, and the path appears in the window to the right. Expand the Activities assembly to find the namespaces within the assembly, as shown in Figure 2-2.

Figure 2-2. *Namespaces within the Activities assembly*

The first namespace is `Activities`. The `Activities` namespace contains all the classes that make up the out-of-the-box activities that are included. Expand the `Activities` namespace, and you'll see classes such as Code activity, Delay activity, and IfElse activity. These are the classes that make up those activities. Click the IfElse Activity, as shown in Figure 2-3.

Figure 2-3. *IfElse Activity class*

After clicking the class, you'll see the methods of that class in the right window of the Object Browser, as shown in Figure 2-4.

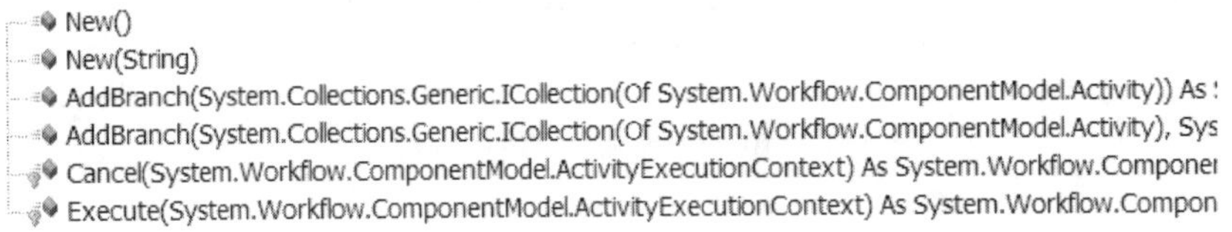

Figure 2-4. *Methods of the IfElse activity*

These methods allow you to add branches to an IfElse activity, and also allow you to execute the IfElse activity. Notice there's a class called IfElseBranchActivity. You can use this to create a branch of an IfElse activity. You'll see later that when using the Workflow Designer, this code is all added for you behind the scenes. You can choose to create workflows and work with activities without the designer, or you can choose to package the designer into your application to allow the end users to create their own workflow. You'd work with these classes to allow users to create their own workflow.

The next namespace under the Activities assembly is the `Activities.Rules` namespace. This namespace works with the Policy activity to create a rule-based workflow that executes differently based on business rules that are stored and evaluated. This namespace also works with the remaining namespace within the Activities assembly: the `Activities.Rules.Design` namespace. This namespace contains only two classes, and represents dialog boxes that allow a user to define the rules of a rule-based workflow.

The second assembly that makes up the workflow functionality is the ComponentModel assembly. This assembly has all the base classes that make up the classes within the `Activities` namespace, and also contains all the classes for the designers. You'll see there are five namespaces within this assembly. The first is `Markup`, which provides markup (XML functionality) that can be used within an application. The second namespace is `ComponentModel`. Expand this namespace within the Object Browser, and you'll notice what appear to be many base classes. One of the most important classes here is the Activity class. This class is worth taking a further look at, so expand it as shown in Figure 2-5.

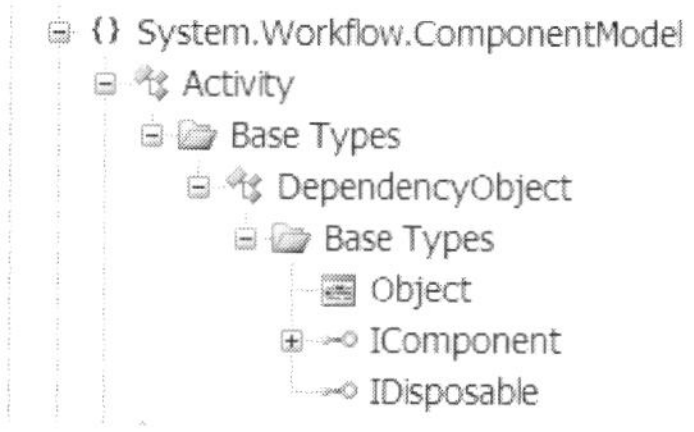

```
⊟ {} System.Workflow.ComponentModel
   ⊟ ◈ Activity
      ⊟ 📂 Base Types
         ⊟ ◈ DependencyObject
            ⊟ 📂 Base Types
               └─ 🖼 Object
               ⊞ ─○ IComponent
               └─○ IDisposable
```

Figure 2-5. *Activity class*

Notice the Activity class inherits from the DependencyObject class, which inherits from the Object class. This shows that the Activity class is a low-level class that's generic and used for many different purposes. Each of the Activity classes within the `Activities` namespace inherits from the Activity class. To see this, go back to the `Activities` namespace, expand the IfElse activity again, and expand the Base Types to see the Activity class that was just viewed under the `ComponentModel` namespace under the IfElse Activity class, as shown in Figure 2-6.

```
⊟ ◈ IfElseActivity
   ⊟ 📂 Base Types
      ⊟ ◈ CompositeActivity
         ⊟ 📂 Base Types
            ⊟ ◈ Activity
               ⊟ 📂 Base Types
                  ⊟ ◈ DependencyObject
                     ⊟ 📂 Base Types
                        └─ 🖼 Object
                        ⊞ ─○ IComponent
                        └─○ IDisposable
      └─○ IActivityEventListener(Of ActivityExecutionStat
```

Figure 2-6. *The Activity base class is inherited from, in order to make the IfElse Activity class*

Notice the IfElse activity inherits from the CompositeActivity class, which inherits from the Activity class, which inherits from the DependencyObject class, which finally inherits from the Object class.

The remaining namespaces within the ComponentModel assembly are the `Compiler`, `Design`, and `Serialization` namespaces. You can use these namespaces if you want to package a Workflow Designer within your application to allow end users to create their own workflow. Otherwise, these namespaces provide the base for the designers that are built into VS2005.

The last assembly that makes up the workflow functionality is the Runtime assembly. This assembly provides four namespaces that make up the runtime services for workflow. They are the Runtime, DebugEngine, Hosting, and Tracking namespaces. Each works with VS2005 to provide a runtime and hosting environment for your workflow. You could use these namespaces if you wanted to build your own host and runtime environment for your workflow.

Personally, I prefer to work with the design tools such as VS2005. I'm able to be much more productive by using the existing tools. However, I understand that sometimes you need to be able to get to the underlying functionality to customize it your own way. That's why it's such a good thing that the workflow assemblies expose so much functionality. If you want to create your own designers, you can do that. I'm just not interested in doing that.

Workflow Code in VB .NET

To see further that workflow and activities are code, close the Object Browser and view the code in the workflow file (called Workflow1.vb), as follows:

```
Imports System
Imports System.ComponentModel
Imports System.ComponentModel.Design
Imports System.Collections
Imports System.Drawing
Imports System.Workflow.ComponentModel.Compiler
Imports System.Workflow.ComponentModel.Serialization
Imports System.Workflow.ComponentModel
Imports System.Workflow.ComponentModel.Design
Imports System.Workflow.Runtime
Imports System.Workflow.Activities
Imports System.Workflow.Activities.Rules
Partial Public Class Workflow1
    Inherits SequentialWorkflowActivity
Public Sub New()
    MyBase.New()
    InitializeComponent()
End Sub
End Class
```

Notice all the Import statements, including the Import statements for the various namespaces within the workflow assemblies that were discussed earlier. Because workflow itself isn't executable and must be hosted, all these namespaces must be imported so the workflow can stand alone. Because this is a Sequential workflow (instead of a State Machine workflow), the class Workflow1 inherits from the SequentialWorkflowActivity class. To get an understanding of where the SequentialWorkflowActivity class fits into all the workflow assemblies, right-click SequentialWorkflowActivity and choose Goto Definition. This opens the Object Browser back up to the SequentialWorkflowActivity class. Notice it's part of the Activities namespace within the Activities assembly. You'll also find the StateMachineWorkflowActivity class within this namespace.

The project that was opened is a console application. This means there's already a host application built into this project. This host application has a module called Module1.vb by default. Close the Object Browser and open the Module1.vb file. The first part of the code file, as follows, shows the imports and the beginning of the Module1 code:

```
Imports System
Imports System.Collections.Generic
Imports System.Text
Imports System.Threading
Imports System.Workflow.Runtime
Imports System.Workflow.Runtime.Hosting
Module Module1
    Class Program
        Shared WaitHandle As New AutoResetEvent(False)
        Shared Sub Main()
            Dim workflowRuntime As New WorkflowRuntime()
            Dim Parameters As Dictionary(Of String, Object) =
                New Dictionary(Of String, Object)
            AddHandler workflowRuntime.WorkflowCompleted,
                AddressOf OnWorkflowCompleted
            AddHandler workflowRuntime.WorkflowTerminated, AddressOf
                OnWorkflowTerminated
            Dim workflowInstance As WorkflowInstance
            workflowInstance = workflowRuntime.CreateWorkflow
                (GetType(Workflow1),Parameters)
            workflowInstance.Start()
            WaitHandle.WaitOne()
        End Sub
```

Because Module1 is to be the hosting environment for the workflow, the Runtime and Hosting namespaces are imported into this module:

```
Imports System.Workflow.Runtime
Imports System.Workflow.Runtime.Hosting
```

The Sub Main code is created to open an entry point into this console application. This would be the entry point for the workflow, and where the process of executing the workflow would begin. You add two handlers to this code, one called OnWorkflowCompleted and one called OnWorkflowTerminated:

```
AddHandler workflowRuntime.WorkflowCompleted, AddressOf OnWorkflowCompleted
AddHandler workflowRuntime.WorkflowTerminated, AddressOf OnWorkflowTerminated
```

The two AddHandler lines of code point to two subs within the Program class that make up events that are raised by the workflow. Adding the handlers, and subsequently the subs, allows you to write code to be executed when workflow is completed or terminated:

```
Shared Sub OnWorkflowCompleted(ByVal sender As Object, ByVal e As
WorkflowCompletedEventArgs)
     WaitHandle.Set()
End Sub
Shared Sub OnWorkflowTerminated(ByVal sender As Object, ByVal e As
WorkflowTerminatedEventArgs)
     Console.WriteLine(e.Exception.Message)
     WaitHandle.Set()
End Sub
```

The next set of code lines creates an instance of the class WorkflowInstance. WorkflowInstance is a class within the Runtime namespace, and creates a running instance of the workflow for each new instance of this class:

```
Dim workflowInstance As WorkflowInstance
workflowInstance = workflowRuntime.CreateWorkflow(GetType(Workflow1))
```

Each time a user executes the workflow from the beginning, a new instance of the workflow is created, just as a new, unique instance of a class is created when the New keyword is used with a class name. This is the concept of *encapsulation*, which is central to object-oriented programming (OOP) and implemented here to make sure data from one instance of the workflow doesn't interfere with another instance. For example, say you have a workflow that allows an employee to request time off. Parameters that might be passed to the workflow are the date or dates requested off. If I request time off, a new workflow instance is created for me, and my requested date off is stored. If you also request time off, a new workflow instance is created for you, and your requested date off is stored. You don't want the two dates to get mixed up, or a supervisor down the line would approve a vacation request for the wrong date. After a generic workflow instance is created, a specific type of workflow is assigned to that instance by determining the type of the workflow. Finally, you start the workflow instance, and it waits:

```
workflowInstance.Start()
WaitHandle.WaitOne()
```

Workflow Code in C#

The preceding section showed the default Module1 and workflow code in VB .NET. This section will show the same code in C#. Because only the VB .NET projects were created in Chapter 1, the C# projects need to be created now. Create a new C# Sequential workflow console application called CFirstSequentialWFConsoleApplication, and create a new C# State Machine workflow console application called CFirstStateMachineWFConsoleApplication.

Open the C# Sequential workflow console application just created. Open the Solution Explorer, and you'll see the file name is different. In VB, the code file for establishing the console application was Module1.vb, but within a C# application it's called Program.cs. First, open the Workflow1.cs file view the code, which follows:

```
using System;
using System.ComponentModel;
using System.ComponentModel.Design;
using System.Collections;
using System.Drawing;
using System.Workflow.ComponentModel.Compiler;
using System.Workflow.ComponentModel.Serialization;
using System.Workflow.ComponentModel;
using System.Workflow.ComponentModel.Design;
using System.Workflow.Runtime;
using System.Workflow.Activities;
using System.Workflow.Activities.Rules;

namespace CFirstSequentialWFConsoleApplication
{
    public sealed partial class Workflow1: SequentialWorkflowActivity
    {
     public Workflow1()
        {
            InitializeComponent();
         }
     }
}
```

Although the language is different, this class uses the same namespaces and classes as the VB .NET code did. Within VB .NET, namespaces and classes are used within another class by adding the Imports statement; in C# the using statement is added. Other than the syntax being different, the beginning of the Workflow1 class is also different. First, the code that's created by the designer is now shown by default, which is the same as in VB .NET, but the designer-generated code is hidden differently in C#. If you expand the designer-generated code, you'll see the InitializeComponent function and code that sets the name of the workflow. Within VB .NET, the call to InitializeComponents is in the same place, but code for InitializeComponents is separate.

Open the Program.cs file and see the code is similar to that of the Module1.vb file. The objectives and order of the code is the same; obviously, the code used to accomplish each objective is different. The code for Program.cs follows:

```
using System;
using System.Collections.Generic;
using System.Text;
using System.Threading;
using System.Workflow.Runtime;
using System.Workflow.Runtime.Hosting;
using CFirstSequentialWFConsoleApplication.Properties;
```

```
namespace CFirstSequentialWFConsoleApplication
{
    class Program
    {
     static AutoResetEvent waitHandle = new AutoResetEvent(false);
     static void Main(string[] args)
     {
          WorkflowRuntime workflowRuntime = new WorkflowRuntime();

          workflowRuntime.WorkflowCompleted += OnWorkflowCompleted;

          workflowRuntime.WorkflowTerminated += OnWorkflowTerminated;

          {
              Console.WriteLine(e.Exception.Message);
              waitHandle.Set();
          };

          WorkflowInstance instance =
          workflowRuntime.CreateWorkflow(typeof(
              CFirstSequentialWFConsoleApplication.Workflow1));
          instance.Start();
          waitHandle.WaitOne();

    }
```

Again, you'll notice the "using" instead of "Imports":

```
using System.Workflow.Runtime;
using System.Workflow.Runtime.Hosting;
```

If you aren't familiar with C# code, the static void Main(string[] args) is the same as the Sub Main() declaration in VB .NET. The next lines of code create an instance of the WorkflowRuntime class and call it workflowRuntime:

```
static void Main(string[] args)
{
    WorkflowRuntime workflowRuntime = new WorkflowRuntime();
```

These three lines of code create the variable of type WorkflowRuntime and assign a new instance of the WorkflowRuntime type to that variable. The next line creates a new variable called waitHandle:

```
AutoResetEvent waitHandle = new AutoResetEvent(false);
```

In the VB .NET code, this was done in the variable declarations of the class instead of here, further into the code of Sub Main(). The next two lines create the delegates to handle when the workflow is completed and when the workflow is terminated. These are the same as adding a handler with AddHandler within the VB .NET code:

```
workflowRuntime.WorkflowCompleted += OnWorkflowCompleted;
workflowRuntime.WorkflowTerminated += OnWorkflowTerminated;
```

The next line writes out any exceptions that have occurred. The following line (waitHandle.Set();) doesn't have an equivalent in VB .NET. This line releases any threads that need to process:

```
{
    Console.WriteLine(e.Exception.Message);
    waitHandle.Set();
};
```

The final three lines are the same as the final three lines in VB .NET. An instance of the WorkflowInstance class is created and assigned to a variable, then the current workflow waits until all activities have completed:

```
WorkflowInstance instance =
workflowRuntime.CreateWorkflow(typeof(CFirstSequentialWFConsoleApplication.
Workflow1));
instance.Start();
waitHandle.WaitOne();
```

First Workflow in VB

This section will cover how to create your first workflow within VB. First we'll look at the Sequential workflow, followed by the State Machine workflow. For each workflow type, I'll walk you through how to add activities to a workflow and how to write code for activities within the workflow.

Sequential Workflow

With the built-in VS2005 Workflow Designers, creating a simple workflow is just a matter of drag and drop. Open the VBFirstSequentialWFConsoleApplication and open Workflow1 in design mode instead of viewing the code. The easiest activity to begin with is the Code activity, as it's something you're already familiar with. Take the Code activity from the Toolbox and drag it onto the designer between the green start arrow and the red stop block. When you drop the activity there, it will automatically take the name CodeActivity1 and have a red exclamation point at the top right corner of the activity control, as shown in Figure 2-7.

Click that exclamation point and an arrow appears. Click the arrow and you see a message stating "Property ExecuteCode is not set." This means that there's no code in the Code activity. Open the Properties window and set the Name of the Code activity to "Step1" and the description of the Code activity to "Step 1 in Process." You'll notice there's a property called ExecuteCode. This is the property that the Code activity control wants filled in. You can automatically get the handler code created by right-clicking the Code activity and choosing Generate Handlers. This opens the code window and creates the Step1_ExecuteCode sub, which handles the ExecuteCode event. This event will fire when the code is executed within the Code activity. The designer adds this handler automatically for you.

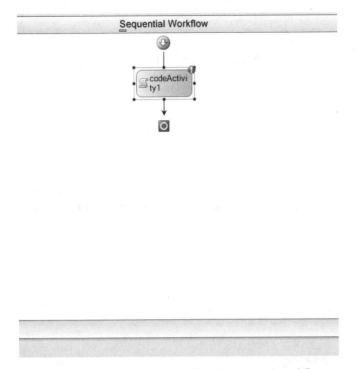

Figure 2-7. *Code activity control within Sequential workflow*

Again, you could add all the functionality that was just automatically created for you in code if you wanted to. To see how the handler was created, right-click the InitializeComponent() line of code within the New sub and choose Goto Definition. You don't want to change this code; the designer created it for you. The following line of code adds the handler ExecuteCode to the Step1 Code activity:

```
AddHandler Me.Step1.ExecuteCode, AddressOf Me.Step1_ExecuteCode
```

There's also the following line of code:

```
Private WithEvents Step1 As System.Workflow.Activities.CodeActivity
```

This creates a private variable called Step1, which is a CodeActivity class. Again, you could do all this with your own code, but it's much easier with the built-in designers.

To best demonstrate how this activity and the workflow work, add a line of code to the ExecuteCode sub that opens a message box with a prompt of "Step1":

```
Private Sub Step1_ExecuteCode(ByVal sender As System.Object, ByVal e As
System.EventArgs)
    MsgBox("Step1")
End Sub
```

Execute the application. You see the console window appear. The message box then appears. It might be hidden behind the console window, but it appears in your taskbar. Add a second Code activity control to the workflow after the Step1 Code activity. Give this Code activity control the name Step2 and the description "Step 2 in process." Add a handler like you did with the Step1 Code activity. Within the ExecuteCode handler for the Step2 Code activity, add a message box with a prompt of "Step2":

```
Private Sub Step2_ExecuteCode(ByVal sender As System.Object, ByVal e As
System.EventArgs)
    MsgBox("Step2")
End Sub
```

Finally, run the application. The Step1 message box appears first. If you don't click OK, the workflow will pause and wait until the message box is clicked. After the message box is clicked, the Step2 message box will appear. This shows that the workflow is sequential. No other external action was necessary to move the workflow from step one to step two.

The best way to see what's happening is to step through the code line by line using the debugger. Set a breakpoint on the line of code creating the specific workflow activities within the Sub Main of the Module1.vb file:

```
workflowInstance = workflowRuntime.CreateWorkflow(GetType(Workflow1))
```

Also, set a breakpoint on the second message box within the Workflow1 class. When you step through the code, you'll see the first code to be executed is the constructor (Sub New) of the Workflow1 class. While in the constructor, the Sub InitializeComponent is called. This sub creates all the necessary class instances to support the workflow. Although you created the workflow within the designer and you drew it out, this sub actually creates the instances and uses them. Once again, this shows that you can use the workflow namespaces and classes without the designers, but the designers build all this code for you.

This sub also adds the necessary handlers that the designer automatically generated earlier. When the code execution comes back to the Sub Main, the workflow is started, then the workflow waits. Once the workflow begins to wait, the first activity within the workflow begins, because this is a Sequential workflow. That workflow fires the execute code handler because the activity was a Code activity. The first message box appears. Then, when you click OK, the breakpoint within the Step2_ExecuteCode sub in the Workflow1 class is executed, and the breakpoint at the second message box is hit. Finally, after you click OK on the message box, the End Sub of the Sub Main back in Module1 is encountered. The flow of control is as follows:

1. Sub Main begins.

2. Handlers are added.

3. An instance of the Workflowinstance class is created.

4. The specific workflow is assigned to the Workflowinstance (sequential in this case):

   a. The Workflow1 class constructor is executed.

   b. All properties of all activities within Workflow1 are set.

5. Workflowinstance is started.

6. Sub Main waits for the activities within the workflow to finish.

7. Each activity within the workflow is processed—in this case, the ExecuteCode handler of each Code activity.

8. Sub Main completes.

Passing Parameters to VB .NET Workflow

One of the many workflows that needs to be implemented might need to have values passed into it. This might include needing to know the user name of a user, or to know a document name that is to be approved or not approved. The workflow can accept input parameters, which are defined within the workflow file as public write-only properties, or the workflow can provide back output parameters that are defined within the workflow file as read-only properties.

The first step is to define the parameters that you want passed to the workflow as public write-only properties. Add two private integer variables to the Workflow1 class, one called InputValue1, and one called InputValue2. Define two public write-only properties, one called Input1 and the other called Input2. Then define the output parameter by defining a private integer called OutputResult, and a public read-only property called OutputValue. Here's the resulting code:

```
Private InputValue1 As Integer
Private InputValue2 As Integer
Private OutputResult As Integer
Public WriteOnly Property Input1() As Integer
        Set(ByVal value As Integer)
            InputValue1 = value
        End Set
End Property
Public WriteOnly Property Input2() As Integer
        Set(ByVal value As Integer)
            InputValue2 = value
        End Set
End Property
Public ReadOnly Property OutputValue() As Integer
        Get
            Return OutputResult
        End Get
End Property
```

Next, add OutputResult = InputValue1 + InputValue2 to the Step1_ExecuteCode sub before the message box:

```
Private Sub Step1_ExecuteCode(ByVal sender As System.Object, ByVal e As
System.EventArgs)
    OutputResult = InputValue1 + InputValue2
    MsgBox("Step1")
End Sub
```

This line of code adds the local variables for the input parameters together and assigns the result to the local variable for the output parameter. Open the Module1.vb file and add a new dictionary object to the Sub Main. This dictionary object is called Parameters, and holds the parameters that are to be passed to the workflow. The line of code to do this is as follows:

```
Dim Parameters As Dictionary(Of String, Object) = New Dictionary(Of String, Object)
```

The beginning of Sub Main looks like the following code:

```
Shared Sub Main()
Dim workflowRuntime As New WorkflowRuntime()
Dim Parameters As Dictionary(Of String, Object) =New Dictionary(Of String, Object)
```

Next, before the CreateWorkflow statement, add two strings to the Parameters dictionary. The names must match the names of the public write-only properties that were created within the workflow file. The code to do this assignment is as follows:

```
Parameters.Add("("Input1",45)",
Parameters.Add("Input2", 45)
```

After adding the parameters, you must change the CreateWorkflow line of code as follows to add the parameters to the workflow:

```
workflowInstance = workflowRuntime.CreateWorkflow(GetType(Workflow1), Parameters))
```

The updated Sub Main will look like the following:

```
Shared Sub Main()
    Dim workflowRuntime As New WorkflowRuntime()
    Dim Parameters As Dictionary(Of String, Object) =
        New Dictionary(Of String, Object)
    AddHandler workflowRuntime.WorkflowCompleted,
        AddressOf OnWorkflowCompleted
    AddHandler workflowRuntime.WorkflowTerminated,
        AddressOf OnWorkflowTerminated
    Dim workflowInstance As WorkflowInstance
    Parameters.Add("Input1", 45)
    Parameters.Add("Input2", 45)
    workflowInstance = workflowRuntime.CreateWorkflow(
        GetType(Workflow1), Parameters)
    workflowInstance.Start()
    WaitHandle.WaitOne()
End Sub
```

Finally, you need to display the parameter returned when the workflow completes. For this, you need to add code to the OnWorkflowCompleted event handler. The OnWorkflowCompleted event handler has two parameters, one of which is e and is defined as WorkflowCompletedEventArgs. The parameter e has a property called OutputParameters that contains the values of any output parameters from the workflow. To see the value in these output parameters again, you have to specify the read-only property of the workflow with the correct name. The code to view the output parameters from a workflow is as follows:

```
MsgBox("Output parameter: " & e.OutputParameters("OutputValue").ToString).
```

The updated OnWorkflowCompleted sub looks like the following:

```
Shared Sub OnWorkflowCompleted(ByVal sender As Object, ByVal e As
WorkflowCompletedEventArgs)
    MsgBox("Output parameter: {0} " & e.OutputParameters("OutputValue").ToString)
    WaitHandle.Set()
End Sub
```

All the code is now in place to pass two input parameters, each with a value of 45, into the workflow, and for the workflow to add those two input parameters together and send the result back as an output parameter. Run the workflow and you'll get the same two message boxes as before—one for each step—and a message box at the end with a value of 90 in it.

State Machine Workflow

Keep the Sequential workflow example opened, and also open the VBFirstStateMachineWFConsoleApplication project. This is a console application with a State Machine workflow instead of the Sequential workflow that was shown previously. This section will show you the code and execution of a State Machine workflow within a console application, and also show the differences in code and property items between the Sequential workflow and the State Machine workflow.

The first thing you'll notice is that the Workflow Designer surface is a little different. There are no lines that show one activity linking to another. The reason for this is that state must change before control can move from one activity to another. Open the Module1.vb file from the Solution Explorer. You'll see that the code in this file is the same as the code in the Module1.vb file for the Sequential workflow. Because Module1.vb is used to create the console application that's hosting the workflow, this code won't change depending on the workflow type (Sequential or State Machine) that you're creating. A State Machine workflow is different from a Sequential workflow in that the first activity within a State Machine workflow must be a state. There must be a first state to begin the workflow, and the execution of the workflow is based on that first state. When you open the Workflow Designer, you'll see there's already a state on the designer surface. This will be the completion state, the last state in the workflow that lets the workflow know that all activities have been completed. Click this State activity and open the Properties window. Change the name to CompletedState and add a description of "This is the last state." To make this the completion state for the workflow, right-click the state and choose Set as Completed State.

After you set this state as the completed state, you'll see an exclamation point in the upper-right corner of the designer surface. If you click this, you'll get a message "InitialStateName Property must point to a valid StateActivity Activity." This message means that there's no initial State activity. You've set the default state that's automatically on the designer surface to be the completed state, but there is no initial state. So, drag over a new State activity from the Toolbox.

After you drag the new State activity to the designer surface, open the Properties window, change the name to FirstState, and change the description to "This is the first state." Next, right-click the state and choose Set as Initial State. By doing this, you're setting this state as the initial State activity that will be executed when the workflow is executed. The State activity requires another activity—either an EventDriven, StateInitialization, or StateFinalization activity—to be placed within the State activity. Therefore, the State activity is a composite activity because it's made up of one or more other activities.

Right-click the FirstState State activity and choose AddEventDriven. When you do this, the designer surface will change, as shown in Figure 2-8.

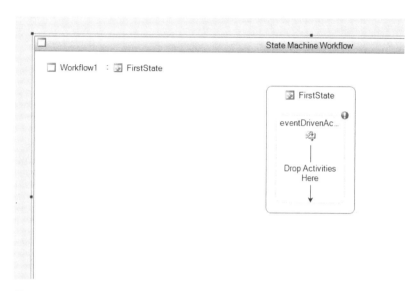

Figure 2-8. *State Composition View*

The State Composition View allows you to add EventActivity activities to the FirstState State activity. You can return to the State Composition View (the normal workflow design surface) by right-clicking anywhere on this design surface and choosing Back To State Composition View. Another way to return to the State Composition View is to click either the Workflow1 or FirstState links on the top left of this window. If you click the FirstState link at the top left, you'll return to the FirstState state, and if you click the Workflow1 link at the top left, you'll return to the overall workflow. They're one and the same for now because you have a small workflow, but this can be useful if you have a long workflow. If you're back in the State Composition View (the default workflow design surface), then you'll see the EventDriven activity added within the FirstState State activity, as shown in Figure 2-9.

If you double-click the eventDrivenActivity1 state within the FirstState State activity, you'll get back to the EventDrivenActivity. You'll see an exclamation point in the right corner of the EventDrivenActivity1 activity within the FirstState State activity. When you click the exclamation point, you'll see that a child activity must be present. For this first, simple State Machine workflow, drag and drop the Delay activity from the Toolbox. Make sure to drop it within the EventDrivenActivity1 activity. You'll use this Delay activity to pause a set period of time before changing states. All this workflow is going to do is wait a set period of time, move to the next state, pause a set period of time, and then move to the completed state.

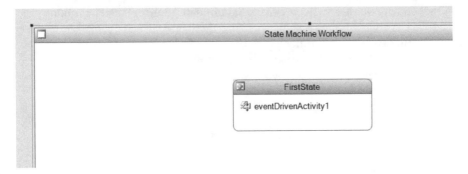

Figure 2-9. *EventDrivenActivity1 within the FirstState State activity*

Click the DelayActivity1 activity and open the Properties window. Find the Time Interval property—you'll see this is a drop-down list. You can either choose a time interval from here for the delay or you can customize the interval. Enter 00:00:30. This is a 30-second interval, and causes the workflow to pause at the FirstState State activity for 30 seconds before changing state. Now add another State activity with a name of SecondState and a description of "This is the second state." Add an EventDriven activity to this state and a Delay activity to the EventDrivenActivity that pauses 30 seconds. The workflow will look like Figure 2-10.

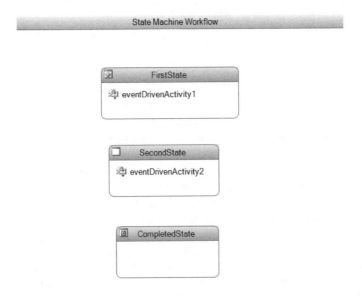

Figure 2-10. *Three State activities within the State Machine workflow*

The final task that needs to be done is to enable the states to be changed. The FirstState State activity will change states to the SecondState State activity, and the SecondState State activity will change states to the CompletedState State activity. The FirstState and SecondState State activities will each pause 30 seconds before changing states. You need to use the SetState activity to change state. Double-click the EventDrivenActivity1 activity within the FirstState State activity. Drag and drop a SetState activity after the Delay activity that's already within the EventDriven activity, so the EventDriven activity looks like Figure 2-11.

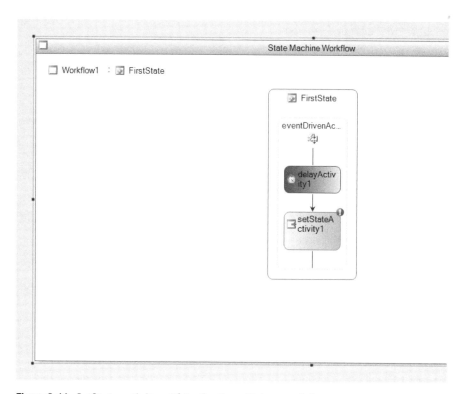

Figure 2-11. *SetState activity within the EventDriven activity*

The exclamation point in the upper-right corner of the SetState activity is there because you haven't set the target state for the state to be changed to. Click the SetStateActivity1 activity and open the Properties window. Find the TargetStateName property, which has a drop-down list. This drop-down list contains the names of all the State activities within this workflow. You can choose from this drop-down which State activity this State activity should change to when the SetState activity is fired. In this case, choose SecondState. Return to the State Composition View and double-click the EventDrivenActivity2 activity within the SecondState State activity. Add a SetState activity to the EventDriven activity and set the TargetStateName property to CompletedState. After you add the SetState activity, return to the State Composition View. You'll see that the State activities are all linked together now with a line and arrow that shows the flow of the state machine, as shown in Figure 2-12.

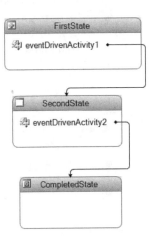

Figure 2-12. *State Machine workflow with flow shown*

Now that the first State Machine workflow is built, it's time to test it. First, open the Module1.vb file and add `msgbox("Workflow Complete")` after `WaitHandle.WaitOne()` within Sub Main:

```
Shared Sub Main()
    Dim workflowRuntime As New WorkflowRuntime()
    AddHandler workflowRuntime.WorkflowCompleted,
        AddressOf OnWorkflowCompleted
    AddHandler workflowRuntime.WorkflowTerminated,
        AddressOf OnWorkflowTerminated
    Dim workflowInstance As WorkflowInstance
    workflowInstance = workflowRuntime.CreateWorkflow(GetType(Workflow1))
    workflowInstance.Start()
    WaitHandle.WaitOne()
    MsgBox("Workflow Complete")
End Sub
```

When the workflow is done, this message box will appear to show you that the workflow has completed. Return to the State Composition View. From this view, you can set a breakpoint that allows you to step through each activity in the workflow. To do this, right-click the FirstState State activity and choose Breakpoint, then Insert Breakpoint. Debug the workflow, and the console window appears. The FirstState State activity is highlighted in yellow (this might take a few seconds). Hit the F11 key to step through.

The EventDrivenActivity1 activity is now being executed; more specifically, the DelayActivity within the EventDrivenActivity1 activity is being executed. When the DelayActivity is completed (the execution has paused for 30 seconds), the EventDrivenActivity1 activity will be highlighted in yellow to show it's the active activity. Hit the F11 key again and see the DelayActivity highlighted in yellow. Hit F11 again, and the SetState activity is highlighted. After you hit F11 two more times, the debugger goes back to the State Composition View and shows the FirstState activity as highlighted again. Hit the F11 key again, and the control moves to the SecondState activity—it's highlighted.

Step through the SecondState activity until you're back to the State Composition View again and the CompletedState is highlighted. Finally, when you hit F11 while the CompletedState activity is highlighted, a message box with "WorkflowComplete" appears. This shows the workflow has completed all the execution. You can use this debugger to verify that the activities are in the correct order. As the activities get more complex, make sure that all the variables and other states are set correctly at the correct time.

First Workflow in C#

The creation of a workflow from the standpoint of the Workflow Designers is the same for both VB .NET and C#. The only difference is the code that's created by the designers. I'm not going to show how to create both the Sequential and State Machine workflows again in C#. Instead, I'll show some of the differences between the code and the projects themselves.

Code Differences Between VB and C#

The obvious difference between workflow created in VB and workflow created in C# is that the file that's used to host the console application is called Program.cs instead of Module1.vb. Open Program.cs from the CFirstSequentialWFConsoleApplication project and move the following line of code to the class declaration area (between the class statement and the `static void Main` statement):

```
AutoResetEvent waitHandle = new AutoResetEvent(false);
```

Next, add `Static` to the beginning of that line. Remove the same line within `static void Main()`. Next, change the following lines of code:

```
workflowRuntime.WorkflowCompleted += delegate(object sender,
WorkflowCompletedEventArgs e) {waitHandle.Set();};
workflowRuntime.WorkflowTerminated += delegate(object sender,
WorkflowTerminatedEventArgs e)
```

Replace these lines with the following:

```
workflowRuntime.WorkflowCompleted += OnWorkflowCompleted;
workflowRuntime.WorkflowTerminated += OnWorkflowTerminated;
```

You're removing the preceding lines so you can better define what action to take when the workflow is completed or terminated. Remove the following lines:

```
{
    Console.WriteLine(e.Exception.Message);
    waitHandle.Set();
};
```

Add the following code to the bottom of the file to create the events that will handle when the workflow is completed and terminated:

```
static void OnWorkflowCompleted(object sender, WorkflowCompletedEventArgs e)
{
    Console.WriteLine("Completed");
}
static void OnWorkflowTerminated(object sender, WorkflowTerminatedEventArgs e)
{

}
```

The code in Program.cs looks like the following:

```
static void Main(string[] args)
{
    WorkflowRuntime workflowRuntime = new WorkflowRuntime();
    workflowRuntime.WorkflowCompleted += OnWorkflowCompleted;
    workflowRuntime.WorkflowTerminated += OnWorkflowTerminated;
    WorkflowInstance instance =
    workflowRuntime.CreateWorkflow(typeof(CFirstSequentialWFConsoleApplication.
    Workflow1), parameters);
    instance.Start();
    waitHandle.WaitOne();
}
static void OnWorkflowCompleted(object sender, WorkflowCompletedEventArgs e)
{
    Console.WriteLine("Completed");
}
static void OnWorkflowTerminated(object sender, WorkflowTerminatedEventArgs e)
{

}
```

Return to the workflow and the designer. View the workflow code and add the following lines to provide the subs to call when each step is executed, as was done in the VB code:

```
private void Step1_ExecuteCode(object sender, EventArgs e)
{
    OutputResult = InputValue1 + InputValue2;
    Console.WriteLine("Step1");
}
private void Step2_ExecuteCode(object sender, EventArgs e)
{
    Console.WriteLine("Step2");
}
```

Debug this workflow, and you'll see Step1, Step2, and Completed within the console window.

If you aren't familiar with C#, I recommend *A Programmer's Introduction to C# 2.0, Third Edition*, by Eric Gunnerson and Nick Wienholt (Apress, 2005). All the code samples in the remaining chapters will show both VB and C#, but little explanation will be provided for the C# unless it's necessary.

Passing Parameters to C# Workflow

Passing parameters to workflow created in C# is fundamentally the same as in VB .NET, but with different code syntax, of course. Open the project CFirstSequentialWFConsoleApplication first and then open the Workflow1.cs file to view the code. Add three private variables and three public properties, as was done in the VB example (Input1, Input2, OutputValue). The code would look like the following:

```
private int InputValue1;
private int InputValue2;
private int OutputResult;

public int Input1
{
set
    {
        InputValue1 = value;
    }
}

public int Input2
{
set
    {
        InputValue2 = value;
    }
}

public int OutputValue
{
get
    {
        return OutputResult;
    }
}
```

If you aren't familiar with C# coding, here's an overview of the code: because the two input variables are write-only, they only need the Set statements, and the output variable only needs the Get statement because it's a read-only property. After adding these properties and variables, add the following code to the Step1_ExecuteCode function before the console.write line of code:

```
OutputResult = InputValue1 + InputValue2;
```

This adds the two private variables. The completed Step1_ExecuteCode sub will look like the following lines of code:

```
private void Step1_ExecuteCode(object sender, EventArgs e)
{
    OutputResult = InputValue1 + InputValue2;
    Console.WriteLine("Step1");
}
```

Open the Program.cs file to add the necessary console application code. Just before creating the WorkflowInstance object, add the following two lines. These define and assign values to the two input parameters:

```
Dictionary<string, object> parameters = new Dictionary<string, object>();
parameters["Input1"] = 45;
parameters["Input2"] = 45;
```

Replace the Console.Writeline statement within the OnWorkflowCompleted() function with the following line of code:

```
Console.WriteLine(e.OutputParameters ["OutputValue"]);
```

This line of code writes out the value returned from the return parameter. The resulting Program.cs looks like the following:

```
static AutoResetEvent waitHandle = new AutoResetEvent(false);
static void Main(string[] args)
{
    WorkflowRuntime workflowRuntime = new WorkflowRuntime();
    workflowRuntime.WorkflowCompleted += OnWorkflowCompleted;
    workflowRuntime.WorkflowTerminated += OnWorkflowTerminated;
    Dictionary<string, object> parameters = new Dictionary<string, object>();
    parameters["Input1"] = 45;
    parameters["Input2"] = 45;
    WorkflowInstance instance =
    workflowRuntime.CreateWorkflow(typeof(
        CFirstSequentialWFConsoleApplication.Workflow1), parameters);
    instance.Start();
    waitHandle.WaitOne();
}
static void OnWorkflowCompleted(object sender, WorkflowCompletedEventArgs e)
{
    Console.WriteLine(e.OutputParameters["OutputValue"]);
}
static void OnWorkflowTerminated(object sender, WorkflowTerminatedEventArgs e)
{
}
```

Make sure you have the name of the parameter exactly correct—it's case sensitive. When you debug the workflow, you'll see the flag from each of the activities and then the value of the output parameter.

Real-World Example

Beginning with this chapter, through Chapter 9, you'll work on a real-world example. This example will help you take the instructions provided in each chapter and scale those to a larger, more meaningful application. This helps you better understand how to extend what you've learned in one chapter to what you've learned in previous chapters. Chapter 10 concludes with the creation of an Employee Performance Review application, which is a Web-based application that also uses WF.

The real-world example to be used in the next several chapters is that of a purchase order system. You'll learn how to use workflow to add purchase orders, to update purchase orders, and to use workflow to validate that a new purchase order meets various business rules before it's entered. For this example to work, you need Microsoft SQL Server (2000 or 2005), Microsoft SQL Desktop Engine, or Microsoft SQL Server Express.

If you aren't familiar with the commands and objects used for data access, the code has been included for you to use. You can find the code samples for this book in the Source Code area of the Apress website (http://www.apress.com). You might also want to check out *Pro ADO.NET 2.0* by Sahil Malik (Apress, 2005) for more ADO.NET information. Finally, for some of the chapter examples and for the Employee Performance Review application in Chapter 10, you might need access to a Web server running Internet Information Server (IIS). VS has a built-in Web server that you can use for local testing and development that might work just fine for you.

The first step is to determine what your system needs to know about a purchase order. We're going to start out simply, and add information as the chapters go on. For now, a purchase order needs the following:

- Purchase order number

- Part number

- Purchased date

- Expected date

- Buyer login

- Buyer name

- Quantity ordered

- Was it received?

- Quantity received

- Date received

Also note that the system generates the purchase order number when a new purchase order is entered. It's the next number in sequence, but it's a six-character number. This chapter is only concerned with adding a purchase order to the database using parameters that are passed into the workflow through the console. After considering what information needs to be gathered, you need to create a database. Create a database called Purchasing. You can accept all defaults for the location and file sizes. After you create the database, find the Chapter2 folder within the code for this book. Within the Chapter2 folder is another folder called SQL. Within that folder, find the appropriate CreateTable file (either 2000 or 2005) for your SQL Server and execute that file on the database. This creates the table tblPurchaseOrders.

Within the SQL folder in the Chapter2 folder, you'll also find a VB file called SQLDBAccess.vb. You'll use this file throughout the book to provide data access code, so you don't need to re-create that code in each chapter. If you're unfamiliar with OOP concepts, this is a class file, and will be used as a class. By using this file as a class, you can access its functionality many times.

Create a new VB Sequential Workflow Console Application called VBPurchaseOrderConsole. You'll also find this application already completed in the Chapter2\VBPurchaseOrderApplication folder. Change the name of the workflow file (workflow1.vb) to PurchaseOrderProcess.vb. Right-click the workflow and add the following private variables to be used by the public properties (which will receive the parameters):

```
Private StrPurchaseOrderNumber as string
Private StrPartNumber as string
Private DtePurchaseDate As Date
Private DteExpectedDate As Date
Private StrBuyerLogin As String
Private StrBuyerName As String
Private IntQuantityOrdered As Integer
```

Notice the received fields aren't included. The reason for this is that right now you're only dealing with adding a purchase order. Eventually you'll deal with what happened when a purchase order is received. After adding the private variables, add the following public properties that will receive the parmater values:

```
Public WriteOnly Property PartNumber() as String
    Set(ByVal value as String)
        StrPartNumber=value
    End Set
End Property
Public WriteOnly Property PurchaseDate() As Date
    Set(ByVal value As Date)
        DtePurchaseDate = value
    End Set
End Property
Public WriteOnly Property ExpectedDate() As Date
    Set(ByVal value As Date)
        DteExpectedDate = value
    End Set
End Property
Public WriteOnly Property BuyerLogin() As String
    Set(ByVal value As String)
        StrBuyerName = value
    End Set
End Property
Public WriteOnly Property BuyerName() As String
    Set(ByVal value As String)
        StrBuyerName = value
```

```
        End Set
End Property
Public WriteOnly Property QuantityOrdered() As Integer
        Set(ByVal value As Integer)
                IntQuantityOrdered = value
        End Set
End Property
```

Note in the preceding public properties that Purchase Order Number isn't present. The reason for this is that the system will generate the next purchase order number. The workflow will return that purchase order number. To do this, you need to add a read-only public property:

```
Public ReadOnly Property PurchaseOrderNumber() As String
        Get
                Return StrPurchaseOrderNumber
        End Get
End Property
```

Now that you've defined the private variables and public properties, it's time to add the SQLDBAccess.vb file. To do this, right-click the project in the Solution Explorer and choose Add, then Existing Item. Navigate to the Chapter2\SQL folder within the code folder and select SQLDBAccess.vb. To allow your workflow to use this class, add a line of code to the end of where the private variables are created:

```
Private clsDB as SQLAccess
```

The next step is to add the code to Sub Main to prompt for, accept, and pass the input parameters. Open the Module1.vb file and add the following code immediately within the Sub Main declaration:

```
Dim Parameters As New Dictionary(Of String, Object)
```

This declares a variable called Parameters that's of type Dictionary, which holds a list of strings. We do have variables that are string, date, and integer, but the string variables can be converted easily to the other types. Next, add the following lines, first to prompt for, and then to read the values into the parameters:

```
Console.Write("("Enter the Part Number")")
Parameters.Add("("PartNumber",",Console.ReadLine)
Console.Write("Enter the Purchase Date:")
Parameters.Add("PurchaseDate", Cdate(Console.ReadLine))
Console.Write("Enter the Expected Date:")
Parameters.Add("ExpectedDate", Cdate(Console.ReadLine))
Console.Write("Enter the Buyer Login:")
Parameters.Add("BuyerLogin", Console.ReadLine)
Console.Write("Enter the Buyer Name:")
Parameters.Add("BuyerName", Console.ReadLine)
Console.Write("Enter the Quantity Ordered:")
Parameters.Add("QuantityOrdered", Cint(Console.ReadLine))
```

Make sure the name parameter to the Add method is the same as the public property name. For example, the first parameter to be added is PartNumber, and PartNumber is a public property of the workflow. If the parameters don't match, the value can't be passed. Also make sure to include CDate when passing a date value, and CInt when passing an integer value; otherwise, you'll get an Invalid Value error. Finally, change the CreateWorkflow line to the following:

```
workflowInstance = workflowRuntime.CreateWorkflow(GetType(PurchaseOrderProcess),
     Parameters)
```

This passes the Parameters dictionary object to the workflow.

Following is the completed Sub Main code necessary to prompt for, read, and pass the necessary parameters for a purchase order:

```
Shared Sub Main()
    Dim Parameters As New Dictionary(Of String, Object)
    Console.Write("("Enter the Part Number")")
    Parameters.Add("("PartNumber",",Console.ReadLine)
    Console.Write("Enter the Purchase Date:")
    Parameters.Add("PurchaseDate", Cdate(Console.ReadLine))
    Console.Write("Enter the Expected Date:")
    Parameters.Add("ExpectedDate", Cdate(Console.ReadLine))
    Console.Write("Enter the Buyer Login:")
    Parameters.Add("BuyerLogin", Console.ReadLine)
    Console.Write("Enter the Buyer Name:")
    Parameters.Add("BuyerName", Console.ReadLine)
    Console.Write("Enter the Quantity Ordered:")
    Parameters.Add("QuantityOrdered", Cint(Console.ReadLine))
    Using workflowRuntime As New WorkflowRuntime()
    AddHandler workflowRuntime.WorkflowCompleted, AddressOf OnWorkflowCompleted
    AddHandler workflowRuntime.WorkflowTerminated, AddressOf OnWorkflowTerminated
    Dim workflowInstance As WorkflowInstance
    workflowInstance = workflowRuntime.CreateWorkflow(
        GetType(PurchaseOrderProcess), Parameters)
    workflowInstance.Start()
    WaitHandle.WaitOne()
    End Using
End Sub
```

The last change to be made to Module1.vb is to change the sub OnWorkflowCompleted. When the workflow is completed, the purchase order number is to be given back to the user. Change the OnWorkflowCompleted sub, as follows:

```
Shared Sub OnWorkflowCompleted(ByVal sender As Object, ByVal e As
    WorkflowCompletedEventArgs)
    MsgBox("Purchase Order Number is: " &
        e.OutputParameters("PurchaseOrderNumber").ToString)
WaitHandle.Set()
End Sub
```

Make sure the `WaitHandle.Set()` line is after the message box line; otherwise, your workflow will complete before the message box can appear. The last steps in this process are to add a Code activity to the workflow, and to add all necessary code to insert the purchase order, determine the purchase order number, and then provide that purchase order number to the user. To start, add a Code activity to the workflow and name the Code activity AddPurchaseOrder. Generate handlers for the Code activity.

Now, within the AddPurchaseOrder_ExecuteCode sub, you must build the SQL statement and execute it against the database to insert the purchase order record. Before you can interact with a database, you must determine the connection string that's necessary. Because this is a Windows-based application instead of a Web-based application, an app.config file can hold settings that you want to use later. Click the My Project link within Solution Explorer, which opens a form with several tabs down the left side. Click the Settings tab and a new page appears. However, this page only has a link that says "This project does not contain a default settings file. Click here to create one." Click this link to create the app.config file for this project. When the settings form appears, change the name value in the first row to ConnString and use the drop-down list under Type to change the type to ConnectionString (the last one in the list). Your settings form looks like Figure 2-13.

	Name	Type	Scope	Value
	ConnString	(Connec... ⌄	Application	
*		⌄	⌄	

Figure 2-13. *Application settings within My Project*

Click the ellipse at the right side of the Value column for the first row. This allows you to choose a data source. Choose Microsoft SQL Server and click Continue, as shown in Figure 2-14.

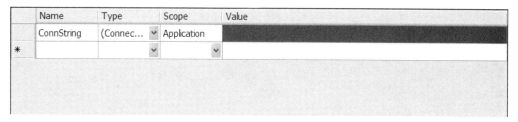

Figure 2-14. *Choose Microsoft SQL Server as the data source.*

When the Connection Properties form appears, you can enter **(local)** as the server name. Leave Windows Authentication checked. This assumes that the account you're logged into on your computer is a SQL Server user and can use the Purchasing database. Click the drop-down for Database Name and choose Purchasing. If you don't see the Purchasing database, either you didn't enter (local) correctly (this must match exactly), or your login doesn't have access to the Purchasing database. If you see other databases, but not Purchasing, then the latter is correct; if you don't see any database names, then you didn't enter the Server Name correctly. If you're encountering a problem with using (local), you can use the drop-down list under Server Name to find your server's name. The completed connection properties look like Figure 2-15.

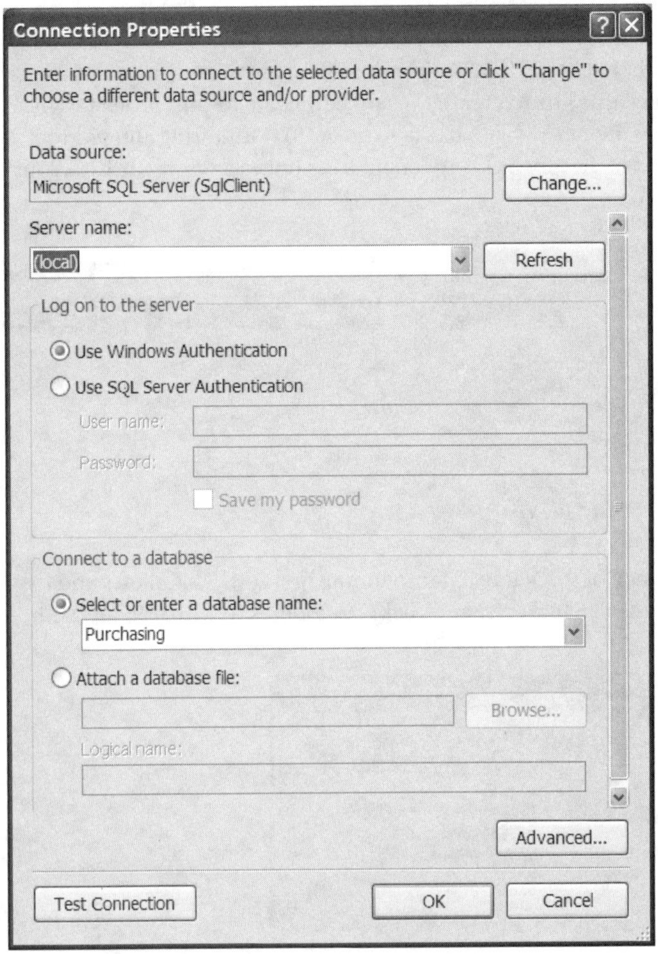

Figure 2-15. *Completed connection properties*

Now the connection string has been established. Click the Save button to save the project properties and close the project properties.

Next, view the code for the workflow and add a new sub called SQLInsertUpdate. This sub will do the work to insert the record and update the purchase order number. You'll call this from the ExecuteCode sub. Add the following code to this new sub (just type **Try** and the rest of the Catch will appear):

```
Dim StrSQL As String
Dim IntPurchaseOrderID As Integer
Try
     clsDB = New SQLAccess(My.Settings.ConnString.ToString)
     StrSQL = "Insert into tblPurchaseOrders(StrPartNumber,DtePurchaseDate,
     DteExpectedDate," & _
     "StrBuyerLogin,StrBuyerName,IntQuantityOrdered) values
         ('" & StrPartNumber & "','" & DtePurchaseDate & "', & _
         '" & DteExpectedDate & "','" & StrBuyerLogin & "'," & _
         "'" & StrBuyerName & "'," & IntQuantityOrdered & ") Select @@Identity"
     If clsDB.ExecuteSingleNumberReturnSQL(StrSQL) Then
         IntPurchaseOrderID = clsDB.NumberValue
     End If
```

This section of code first creates two variables to be used only within this sub. StrSQL holds the SQL statement, and the IntPurchaseOrderID returns the ID of the record just inserted. Because the tblPurchaseOrders table has an identity field as the first field, and this is the primary key, SQL Server automatically generates a new number for this field for each new row inserted. The Select @@Identity at the end of the SQL statement returns that inserted value back to this sub. The returned value is assigned to the IntPurchaseOrderID internal variable. The next step after inserting the record and getting the ID of the record is to use that ID to create the purchase order number, so that number can be returned to the user. Add the following lines of code to accomplish this:

```
Select Case IntPurchaseOrderID
Case Is < 10
StrPurchaseOrderNumber = "00000" & IntPurchaseOrderID
Case Is < 100
StrPurchaseOrderNumber = "0000" & IntPurchaseOrderID
Case Is < 1000
StrPurchaseOrderNumber = "000" & IntPurchaseOrderID
Case Is < 10000
StrPurchaseOrderNumber = "00" & IntPurchaseOrderID
Case Is < 100000
StrPurchaseOrderNumber = "0" & IntPurchaseOrderID
Case Else
StrPurchaseOrderNumber = CStr(IntPurchaseOrderID)
End Select
StrSQL = "Update tblpurchaseorders set StrPurchaseOrderNumber='" &
StrPurchaseOrderNumber & "' " & _
"where intpurchaseorderid = " & IntPurchaseOrderID
If Not clsDB.ExecuteNonQuerySQL(StrSQL) Then
     StrPurchaseOrderNumber = String.Empty
End If
```

This section of code determines the value of IntPurchaseOrderID—the ID returned when the record was inserted. This ID needs to have zeroes added to it until it's a six-character number, because the purchase order number must be six characters long. This code pads zeros to the ID until there are six characters, and then that value is assigned to the StrPurchaseOrderNumber private variable to be returned as an output parameter for the workflow.

The last step is to add SQLInsertUpdate to the AddPurchaseOrder_ExecuteCode sub. This calls the SQLInsertUpdate sub each time the AddPurchaseOrder Code activity is executed.

To test this process, execute the workflow. Provide valid values for each of the parameters when prompted. You'll receive a message box with the new purchase order number in it. Open your tblPurchaseOrders table within SQL Server and verify the record was added and that the purchase order number was updated.

I'm not going to provide the C# example for the real-world example in this or in other chapters. The main reason for this is that most of the Microsoft examples provided with the SDK are in C#. You can look at those examples to find out how to write the code in C#.

Conclusion

This chapter explained and showed that activities and workflows are simply classes, and can be interacted with just like other classes. This chapter also showed examples of VB and C# workflow projects, and how to pass parameters to each type of workflow. This chapter also set up the real-world example to be used in other chapters of this book. It also provided an example of how to insert a record into a database based on parameters passed into a workflow. The next chapter will address the first set of activities: conditional activities.

CHAPTER 3

∎∎∎

Conditional Activities

This chapter will introduce the conditional activities that you can use within a workflow. The conditional activities are activities that perform different actions based on criteria, or perform certain actions multiple times. After introducing each activity, I'll show an example of how to use that activity.

IfElse Activity

The IfElse activity allows you to set up branching within a workflow. Branching within a workflow performs some action (in this case, an activity) based on a condition. You define and evaluate that condition within an IfElseBranch activity within the IfElse activity. When the workflow encounters an IfElse activity, the leftmost IfElseBranch activity is evaluated first. If that branch returns True it's executed; otherwise, the next branch is executed. You don't need to set a condition on the second branch—it's considered the Else part. The IfElse activity requires one branch, but the second is optional. You can use the IfElse activity with one branch to be the same as an If . . . EndIf statement. Finally, both a Sequential and a State Machine workflow can use the IfElse activity.

IfElse Activity Within Sequential Workflow

Create a new VB Sequential Workflow Console Application called VBIfElseSequentialExample. Add a private variable to the workflow called IntInputValue, and a public write-only property called InputValue:

```
Private IntInputValue As Integer
    Public WriteOnly Property InputValue() As Integer
        Set(ByVal value As Integer)
        IntInputValue = value
        End Set
End Property
```

Open the Module1.vb file and add a dictionary called parms to add parameters, the same as was done in Chapter 2. The beginning of Sub Main looks like the following:

```
Shared Sub Main()
    Dim workflowRuntime As New WorkflowRuntime()
    AddHandler workflowRuntime.WorkflowCompleted, AddressOf OnWorkflowCompleted
    AddHandler workflowRuntime.WorkflowTerminated, AddressOf OnWorkflowTerminated
    Dim parms As Dictionary(Of String, Object) = New Dictionary(Of String, Object)
```

To make this and future examples a little more interactive, add the following two lines:

```
Console.WriteLine("Input value:")
parms.Add("InputValue", Cint(Console.ReadLine()))
```

The first line prompts the user for an input value, and the second line reads in the input and adds it to the dictionary with a key of InputValue. The Console.Readline waits for the user's input, so you don't need to worry about pausing. The CInt function call is required to convert the value read from the line on the console to an integer, because the public property InputValue is expecting an integer. If you don't have this CInt function call, the workflow will fail. Finally, add the parms parameter to the CreateWorkflow line:

```
workflowInstance = workflowRuntime.CreateWorkflow(GetType(Workflow1), parms)
```

Again, this passes the dictionary of parameters to the workflow. The completed Sub Main follows:

```
Shared Sub Main()
    Dim workflowRuntime As New WorkflowRuntime()
    AddHandler workflowRuntime.WorkflowCompleted, AddressOf OnWorkflowCompleted
    AddHandler workflowRuntime.WorkflowTerminated, AddressOf OnWorkflowTerminated
    Dim parms As Dictionary(Of String, Object) = New Dictionary(Of String, Object)
    Console.WriteLine("Input value:")
    parms.Add("InputValue", CInt(Console.ReadLine()))
    Dim workflowInstance As WorkflowInstance
    workflowInstance = workflowRuntime.CreateWorkflow(GetType(Workflow1), parms)
    workflowInstance.Start()
    WaitHandle.WaitOne()
End Sub
```

Next, drag and drop an IfElse activity from the Toolbox onto the Workflow1 Workflow Designer. Leave the IfElse activity name as the default, but change the left IfElseBranchActivity to Branch1 and the right to Branch2, so your Workflow Designer looks like Figure 3-1.

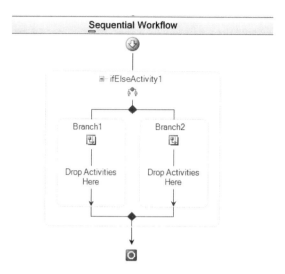

Figure 3-1. *New IfElse activity with Branch1 and Branch2*

Notice the exclamation point at the top right of the left branch. Remember the left branch is the default and must have an activity inside it. The right branch represents the Else and isn't required. Drop a Code activity within Branch1, and call the Code activity Branch1Code. Right-click the Branch1Code activity and choose Generate Handlers to create the sub to add your code to. Add a message box that says "Branch 1" within the Execute Code sub. When Branch1 (the left side of the IfElse) is evaluated as True, this Code activity will execute. Add a Code activity to Branch2, and call it Branch2Code. Generate Handlers for this Code activity and add a message box with "Branch 2" within the Execute Code sub. The code for these two subs follows:

```
Private Sub Branch1Code_ExecuteCode(ByVal sender As System.Object, ByVal e As
System.EventArgs)
     MsgBox("Branch 1")
End Sub
Private Sub Branch2Code_ExecuteCode(ByVal sender As System.Object, ByVal e As
System.EventArgs)
     MsgBox("Branch 2")
End Sub
```

Now you've added an activity to perform some action when a branch evaluates to True, but you still need to add a condition to each IfElseBranch activity. This condition is what's evaluated. To add this condition, you need to add a public sub to the workflow code for each branch that will be evaluated. View the code of the Workflow.vb file and add the following lines of code:

```
Public Sub Branch1Condition(ByVal sender As Object, ByVal e As ConditionalEventArgs)
    e.Result = IntInputValue > 50
End Sub
Public Sub Branch2Condition(ByVal sender As Object, ByVal e As ConditionalEventArgs)
    e.Result = IntInputValue > 25
End Sub
```

The declaration of each sub contains two parameters. The first isn't relevant, but is necessary. You use the second one (e) to let the workflow know if the branch should be executed or not. e.Result needs to evaluate to either a True or False condition. The workflow uses this result when evaluating each branch to determine if that branch should be executed. To finish this connection, you must tell the IfElseBranch activity to look at the appropriate sub when evaluating that branch. To do this, return to the Workflow Designer and click the Branch1 IfElseBranch activity and view the properties. From the drop-down list for the Condition property, choose System.Workflow.Activities.CodeCondition. The Condition property will then have a plus sign next to it; use this to expand the property to see another Condition property. For this property, enter **Branch1Condition**, as shown in Figure 3-2.

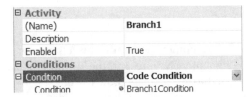

Figure 3-2. *Condition property for Branch1*

Repeat this for Branch2, setting the Condition property to Branch2Condition. By setting this property for each branch, you're telling the workflow engine where to look to evaluate which branch is True. Within each sub that you define as the condition, you can perform any code you want, as long as the e.Result line of code returns either a True or False. To best see what's going on, add a breakpoint to the whole IfElse activity (right-click the activity and choose Breakpoint). Debug the workflow and enter 45 for the input value. You'll notice as you step through that the IfElse activity goes right to Branch2. The workflow evaluated the condition on Branch1 and determined that to be False, then moved to Branch2. The "Branch 2" message box appears. Finally, debug the workflow again and enter **10** as the input value. When the breakpoint is activated and you step through, you'll notice that neither Branch1 nor Branch2 is executed; instead, the next step is to the end of the workflow. This is because neither branch evaluated as True.

Close this project and create a new C# Sequential Workflow Console Application called CIfElseSequentialExample. Open the Workflow.cs file and view the code. Add a private variable called IntInputValue and a public variable called InputValue with only a set statement (so it's write-only):

```
private int IntInputValue;
public int InputValue
{
    set
    {
        IntInputValue = value;
    }
}
```

Open the Program.cs file and add a dictionary called parms. Then add a parm called InputValue, and pass that parm dictionary when creating the workflow instance. The beginning of Main looks like the following:

```
static void Main(string[] args)
{
    WorkflowRuntime workflowRuntime = new WorkflowRuntime();
    AutoResetEvent waitHandle = new AutoResetEvent(false);
    workflowRuntime.WorkflowCompleted += delegate(object sender,
        WorkflowCompletedEventArgs e) {waitHandle.Set();};
    workflowRuntime.WorkflowTerminated += delegate(object sender,
        WorkflowTerminatedEventArgs e)
{
 Console.WriteLine(e.Exception.Message);
waitHandle.Set();
};
Dictionary<string, object> parms= new Dictionary<string, object>();
```

Also, add a console.readline similar to what was done in the VB example, so that both examples take interactive input from the user. To read the line from the console and make sure the data type is correct, use the following line of code:

```
parms["InputValue"] = System.Convert.ToInt32 (Console.ReadLine());
```

The completed Main follows:

```
static void Main(string[] args)
{
    WorkflowRuntime workflowRuntime = new WorkflowRuntime();
    AutoResetEvent waitHandle = new AutoResetEvent(false);
    workflowRuntime.WorkflowCompleted += delegate(object sender,
        WorkflowCompletedEventArgs e) {waitHandle.Set();};
    workflowRuntime.WorkflowTerminated += delegate(object sender,
        WorkflowTerminatedEventArgs e)
    {
        Console.WriteLine(e.Exception.Message);
        waitHandle.Set();
    };
```

```
        Dictionary<string, object> parms= new Dictionary<string, object>();
        Console.WriteLine("Input Value");
        parms["InputValue"] = System.Convert.ToInt32 (Console.ReadLine());
        WorkflowInstance instance =
            workflowRuntime.CreateWorkflow(typeof(
            CIfElseSequentialExample.Workflow1),parms);
        instance.Start();
        waitHandle.WaitOne();
}
```

Drag and drop an IfElse activity onto the Workflow Designer. Rename the left branch to Branch1. While you're on the Properties page of the left branch, also tie this into the condition. Within C#, this action is a little different, and actually easier. From the condition drop-down within the Properties window, choose System.Workflow.Activities.CodeCondition and enter **Branch1Condition** as the condition. Once you do this and move from that property, the Branch1Condition definition is automatically created for you, and that code appears. Then, just add the same condition for e.Result, as was done in the VB sample. Do the same with Branch2. To finish this example, add a Code activity to each branch, and set up each Code activity the same way as in the VB example. The rest of the code behind the workflow looks like the following:

```
private void Branch1Condition(object sender, ConditionalEventArgs e)
{
    e.Result = IntInputValue > 50;
}
private void Branch2Condition(object sender, ConditionalEventArgs e)
{
    e.Result = IntInputValue > 25;
}
private void Branch1Code_ExecuteCode(object sender, EventArgs e)
{
    Console.WriteLine("Branch1");
}
private void Branch2Code_ExecuteCode(object sender, EventArgs e)
{
    Console.WriteLine("Branch2");
}
```

Finally, just as in the VB example, add a breakpoint to the IfElse activity and debug the application, the first time with the value 45, and the second time with the value 10. You'll see the same results; when 45 is entered, Branch2 is executed, and when 10 is entered, neither is executed.

IfElse Activity Within State Machine Workflow

To begin this new project, create a new VB State Machine Workflow Console Application called VBIfElseStateMachineExample. As was done in Chapter 2, change the name of the state that's first displayed in the designer to CompletedState and set it as the Completed State. Next, view the code for the workflow and add a private variable called IntInputValue and a public write-only property called InputValue, as was done in the Sequential workflow example:

```
Private IntInputValue As Integer
Public WriteOnly Property InputValue() As Integer
    Set(ByVal value As Integer)
        IntInputValue = value
    End Set
End Property
```

You're going to be adding an IfElse activity to this workflow, so create the Branch1Condition and Branch2Condition subs the same way as was done for the Sequential workflow, using the same criteria statements:

```
Private Sub Branch1Condition(ByVal sender As System.Object, ByVal e As
    ConditionalEventArgs)
e.Result = IntInputValue > 50
End Sub
Private Sub Branch2Condition(ByVal sender As System.Object, ByVal e As
    ConditionalEventArgs)
e.Result = IntInputValue > 25
End Sub
```

Add another State activity with a name of FirstState, and set it as the initial state. You'll also need to add two other State activities, one of which will be executed for each different branch. Add a State activity called Branch1State and another called Branch2State.

Within the FirstState activity that was just added, drag a StateInitialization activity and leave the name as the default. Double-click the activity to drill down and be able to add other activities to it. Add an IfElse activity and view the properties of the left branch. Change the name to Branch1 and choose CodeCondition as the condition again. This time, because you already added the Branch1Condition and Branch2Condition subs, you'll see them in the second Condition drop-down. Choose the Branch1Condition for Branch1. Perform the same steps on the right branch with a name of Branch2 and Branch2Condition. Now the IfElse activities are all set up to evaluate which branch to follow.

The next step is to tell each branch what to do when it's evaluated as True. Add a SetState activity to each branch with a name of SetStateBranch1 and SetStateBranch2, and change the TargetState to the appropriate state, either Branch1State or Branch2State. The composite FirstState activity should look like Figure 3-3.

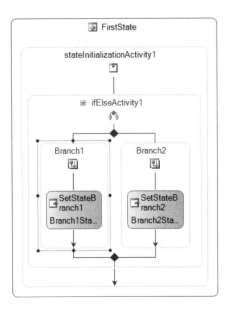

Figure 3-3. *FirstState activity*

Next, you need to add activities to the Branch1State and Branch2State activities. These states will be executed when the appropriate branch is executed within the just-completed FirstState activity. Within the Branch1State activity, add an EventDriven activity with a name of Branch1EventActivity. Within this activity, add a Delay activity called Branch1Delay that only delays for five seconds. After the Delay activity, add a Code activity with a name of Branch1Code. Generate the handlers for this Code activity and add a message box that states "Branch1." Finally, add a SetState activity called Branch1SetState with a target state of CompletedState. This SetState activity will move control to the CompletedState (the last state in the workflow) when executed. The Branch1State should look like Figure 3-4. Repeat the same process for Branch2State.

The remaining code in the Workflow.vb file is as follows:

```
Private Sub Branch1Code_ExecuteCode(ByVal sender As System.Object,
ByVal e As System.EventArgs)
    MsgBox("Branch1")
End Sub
Private Sub Branch2Code_ExecuteCode(ByVal sender As System.Object,
ByVal e As System.EventArgs)
    MsgBox("Branch2")
End Sub
```

The completed workflow should look like Figure 3-5.

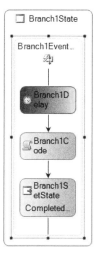

Figure 3-4. *Branch1State activity*

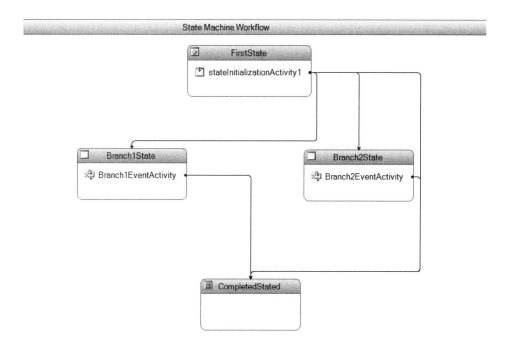

Figure 3-5. *VBIfElseStateMachine workflow*

The final step is to add the parameter code to the Module1.vb file so the user can interact with the console application and enter a value. Use the same code that was used for the Sequential workflow. Sub Main within Module1.vb will look like the following code:

```
Shared Sub Main()
    Dim workflowRuntime As New WorkflowRuntime()
    AddHandler workflowRuntime.WorkflowCompleted, AddressOf OnWorkflowCompleted
    AddHandler workflowRuntime.WorkflowTerminated, AddressOf OnWorkflowTerminated
    Dim workflowInstance As WorkflowInstance
    Dim parms As Dictionary(Of String, Object) = New Dictionary(Of String, Object)
    Console.WriteLine("Input value: ")
    parms.Add("InputValue", CInt(Console.ReadLine()))
    workflowInstance = workflowRuntime.CreateWorkflow(GetType(Workflow1), parms)
    workflowInstance.Start()
    WaitHandle.WaitOne()
End Sub
```

As with the Sequential workflow, add a breakpoint to the FirstState state activity and debug the workflow. The first time through, enter **45** as the input value. Notice the sequence of activities. Branch2 within the IfElse activity is executed, which sets the state to Branch2State. The Branch2State is executed, which first delays five seconds, then provides a message box with "Branch2" in it. Finally, the state is set to CompletedState and the workflow ends. As with the sequential example, debug the workflow again and enter **10** as the value. When you do this, notice that none of the branches are executed and the workflow never completes. This is the difference between Sequential and State Machine workflows. The Sequential workflow continues to the next step if neither of the branches evaluates to True. However, a State Machine workflow needs a SetState activity to be executed to move from state to state. Because neither branch within the IfElse activity was executed, neither SetState activity was executed.

To fix this situation, right-click the IfElse activity and choose Add Branch. This adds a branch to the right of Branch2. Call this Branch3; there's no condition for this branch. This branch is the Else part of the If Else statement. This branch is executed if none of the other branches evaluate to True. Within Branch3, add a SetState activity called SetStateBranch3, with a target state of CompletedState. When this branch is executed, because the others evaluated to False, the workflow state will be set to the CompletedState and the workflow will end. To test this, debug again and enter **10** again, and you'll see that the workflow moves to Branch3 and then to the CompletedState. Remember this example anytime you want to use an IfElse activity within a State Machine workflow. There must be a branch that's executed, no matter what the value is.

There are no significant code changes between the Sequential workflow and the State Machine workflow in these two examples, so I'm not going to show the C# code for the IfElse activity within a State Machine workflow.

While Activity

The While activity allows you to perform another activity multiple times, as long as a condition is evaluated to True. The While activity can only have one activity within it, so you might need to use composite activities to perform multiple tasks. The process the While activity goes though is first to evaluate the condition. If the condition is True, the activity within the While activity is executed; otherwise, the While activity completes.

While Activity Within Sequential Workflow

Create a new VB Sequential Workflow Console Application called VBWhileSequentialExample. Open the Workflow.vb file and view the code. Add a private integer variable called IntCounter and assign 0 to the variable using the following code:

```
Private IntCounter As Integer = 0
```

This not only creates the variable, but also initializes it to 0. Next, add a sub called WhileCondition that assigns the value of IntCounter to e.Result, then increments IntCounter:

```
Public Sub WhileCondition(ByVal sender As Object, ByVal e As ConditionalEventArgs)
    e.Result = IntCounter < 10
    IntCounter = IntCounter + 1
End Sub
```

This sub will be the condition for the While activity. The setup of this condition is the same as the condition for an IfElse activity. The preceding code first determines if the local variable IntCounter is less than 10, then also increments the variable by 1.

Next, view the Workflow Designer and add a While activity to the workflow. Leave the name the same, but change the Condition property to be CodeCondition, and choose WhileCondition from the second Condition property drop-down box. This sets up the While activity to look at the WhileCondition. Finally, add a Code activity to the While activity. Leave the name the same, but generate handlers. Within the code handler, add a message box that displays the value of the local variable IntCounter:

```
Private Sub codeActivity1_ExecuteCode(ByVal sender As System.Object,
ByVal e As System.EventArgs)
    MsgBox(IntCounter)
End Sub
```

Add a breakpoint to the While activity and debug the workflow. You'll see the While activity is entered first, and then the Code activity. Once inside the loop, the Code activity is the only activity being executed. The Code activity displays the counter each time, until the counter is 10. Although the condition states less than 10, the counter is incremented after that test so the condition stops at 9. However, there's another increment after the condition is met, which displays 10 as the final number.

The C# code is only slightly different from the VB code. Create a new C# Sequential Workflow Console Application called CWhileSequentialExample. View the code of the Workflow.cs file and add a new int variable called IntCounter that's initialized to 0:

```
private int IntCounter=0;
```

View the designer and drop a While activity onto the designer. Leave the name the same, but change the condition to a CodeCondition called WhileCondition. Remember, in C# if you enter the name of the condition within the properties, the template code is created for you. Add the assignment to e.Result and the increment, as follows:

```
private void WhileCondition(object sender, ConditionalEventArgs e)
{
    e.Result = IntCounter < 10;
    IntCounter++;
}
```

Add a Code activity and write to the console the value of IntCounter each time the Code activity is executed. Add a breakpoint to the While activity and debug the application. The console shows each increment of the variable until 10.

While Activity Within State Machine Workflow

Create a new VB State Machine Workflow Console Application called VBWhileStateMachineExample. View the code and create a private integer variable called IntCounter and initialize it to 0:

```
Private IntCounter As Integer = 0
```

Also, add the WhileCondition sub with the same code as the Sequential workflow example:

```
Public Sub WhileCondition(ByVal sender As Object, ByVal e As ConditionalEventArgs)
    e.Result = IntCounter < 10
    IntCounter = IntCounter + 1
End Sub
```

Name the default state CompletedState and set it as the CompletedState. Add a new State activity with a name of FirstState. Add a StateInitialization activity to the FirstState activity. Within the StateInitialization activity, add a While activity with a Condition property pointing to the WhileCondition sub that was created earlier. Within the While activity, add a Code activity and leave the default name. Generate the handlers for the Code activity and add a message box that displays the value of IntCounter:

```
Private Sub codeActivity1_ExecuteCode(ByVal sender As System.Object,
ByVal e As System.EventArgs)
    MsgBox(IntCounter)
End Sub
```

Finally, to avoid an issue with the state machine not completing, add another SetState activity after the While activity. This SetState activity should have the CompletedState as its target state. When the While activity is completed, this SetState activity will complete the workflow; otherwise, when the While activity is completed, the state machine would wait and never complete. The FirstState activity should look like Figure 3-6.

Add a breakpoint to the FirstState activity and debug the workflow. Each time the While activity is executed, the Code activity is executed. If you try to use a SetState activity within the While activity to set the state to another state that would have the Code activity in it, the Code activity will never be executed. If you want to execute an activity within the While activity of a state machine, that activity needs to be within the While activity.

As with the IfElse example, the code for a C# example of the state machine isn't significantly different from an example for a Sequential workflow, so I won't show that code.

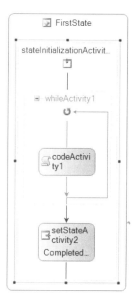

Figure 3-6. *FirstState activity with While activity inside*

Conditional Activity Group

The Conditional Activity Group (CAG) contains other activities. Each activity within the CAG contains a WhenCondition that determines whether that activity should be executed. Each time the CAG is executed, an UntilCondition is evaluated. If that condition is True, the CAG exists, and all activities that might be left will be cancelled. If that condition is False, then all activities within the CAG will be evaluated, and those whose WhenCondition evaluates to True will be executed. You can use this type of activity to execute multiple activities in parallel or in sequence by using the WhenCondition and UntilCondition.

Conditional Activity Group Within Sequential Workflow

Create a new VB Sequential Workflow Console Application called VBCAGSequentialExample. Add a CAG to the workflow and add a Code activity to the CAG. Give the Code activity a name of Code1 and generate the handlers. View the code of the workflow, add a private integer variable called IntCounter, and initialize it to 0:

```
Private IntCounter As Integer = 0
```

Within the Code1_ExecuteCode sub, add a message box with the following code:

```
msgbox("Code 1: Counter=" & IntCounter)
```

It will look like the following:

```
Private Sub Code1_ExecuteCode(ByVal sender As System.Object, ByVal e As
System.EventArgs)
    MsgBox("Code 1: Counter=" & IntCounter)
End Sub
```

This displays "Code 1" and the number stored in the variable. Run the workflow. Because there's no UntilCondition on the CAG activity, all activities are only executed once.

View the code of the workflow and add a Code1WhileCondition with the following code, then set the Condition property of the Code1 activity to be this condition:

```
Private Sub Code1WhileCondition(ByVal sender As System.Object, ByVal e As
ConditionalEventArgs)
    e.Result = IntCounter <4
    IntCounter = IntCounter+1
End Sub
```

This condition, and setting the property, causes the Code1 activity to execute each time the CAG executes and the IntCounter value is less than 4. Run the workflow again. Again, you get the same result: the Code1 message box only displays one time. This is because the overall CAG is only executing one time, because there's no UntilCondition on the CAG.

View the code for the workflow, and this time add an UntilCondition sub with the same type of definition that the WhileCondition subs have had:

```
Private Sub UntilCondition(ByVal sender As System.Object,
ByVal e As ConditionalEventArgs)
    e.Result = IntCounter = 4
End Sub
```

This code executes all activities within the CAG that meet their own WhileConditions until the private variable is equal to 4. Remember this is an Until statement, so you can't use "less than" in this case. You could have the criteria be IntCounter>4, which would execute the activities as long as IntCounter was less than or equal to 4:

```
Private Sub UntilCondition(ByVal sender As System.Object,
ByVal e As ConditionalEventArgs)
    e.Result = IntCounter>4
End Sub
```

After adding this code, be sure to set the UntilCondition of the CAG. Run the workflow, and you'll see the message box appear four times. Add a breakpoint to the CAG and watch the code go into the WhileCondition and UntilCondition each time until the private variable is 4.

Add another Code activity to the CAG and call it Code2. Generate the handlers and add a message box similar to that in Code1, except change the message to "Code 2":

```
Private Sub Code2_ExecuteCode(ByVal sender As System.Object,
ByVal e As System.EventArgs)
    MsgBox("Code 2: Counter=" & IntCounter)
End Sub
```

Run the workflow again. This time, you'll see the Code1 message box appear the first time; then the Code2 message box appears. However, the Code2 message box only appears one time. The reason for this is that there's no WhileCondition for Code2 yet.

Add the following WhileCondition and set the Condition property of Code2 to this condition:

```
Private Sub Code2WhileCondition(ByVal sender As System.Object,
ByVal e As ConditionalEventArgs)
    e.Result = IntCounter > 4
    IntCounter = IntCounter + 1
End Sub
```

Run the workflow again. This time, you won't see a Code2 message box, but notice that the counter is incremented by two. That's because the WhileCondition for code2 is being executed. However, the condition isn't being met (IntCounter>4), but the increment line of code is being executed. Remove the increment line from Code2WhileCondition and run again. Again, only the Code1 message boxes appear because the WhileCondition of Code2 isn't met. Change the UntilCondition to be e.result = IntCounter = 8:

```
Private Sub UntilCondition(ByVal sender As System.Object,
ByVal e As ConditionalEventArgs)
    e.Result = IntCounter = 8
End Sub
```

Run the workflow again. The Code1 message box appears the first four times; then the Code2 message box appears. This shows how you can use the CAG to create a sequence.

Conditional Activity Group Within State Machine Workflow

You can use the CAG in a similar manner in a State Machine workflow. Keep the Sequential workflow project open, as you can use the same code. Create a new VB State Machine Workflow Console Application called VBCAGStateMachineExample. Copy the code from Workflow.vb from the Sequential workflow to the Workflow.vb file of the State Machine workflow. There will be a lot of errors at first until all the workflow has been added.

Change back to the Workflow Designer and make the name of the default state activity CompletedState, and set it as completed state. Add a new State activity and call it FirstState. Within the FirstState activity, add a StateInitialization activity. Within the StateInitialization activity, add a CAG. Within the CAG, add two Code activities named Code1 and Code2, similar to what was done in the Sequential workflow example. Generate the handlers for both Code activities and set the WhenCondition for each Code activity to the appropriate WhenCondition code that was added. Finally, on the CAG, set the UntilCondition property to the UntilCondition code that was created. Again, don't forget to add a SetState activity after the CAG with a target of the CompletedState. Otherwise, the State Machine workflow won't complete. The FirstState activity should look like Figure 3-7.

Run the workflow, and you'll get the same result as the Sequential workflow. The Code1 message box appears four times, and the Code2 message box appears from five to eight times.

As with the other workflow examples, the code for C# is the same as for the Sequential and the State Machine workflows, so I won't show that code.

Figure 3-7. *CAG within FirstState activity*

Real-World Example

The previous chapter introduced the purchase order application by setting up the database, table, and code to add a purchase order. Now, you'll use the activities covered in this chapter (IfElse) to validate the data in the parameters, and you'll also use the While activity to display data. Begin by opening the VBPurchaseOrderConsole application created in the previous chapter.

Open Module1.vb and place a comment marker (single quote) next to the lines of code that prompt for and read the part number:

```
'Console.Write("Enter the Part Number:")
'Parameters.Add("PartNumber", Console.ReadLine)
```

Execute the workflow. The prompt for the part number won't appear, and no value will be added to the record for the part number. However, the record will be created and a purchase order number provided. All public properties of a workflow are optional, and therefore might not be provided by the outside application. For this reason, you'll use a series of IfElse activities to verify that all parameters have been provided and they're within a valid range. If a parameter is either not provided or not in the correct range, a message box will appear for the user. The purchase date must either be the current date or a future date, and the quantity ordered must be greater than zero.

The logic for this validation is as follows:

```
If PartNumber is empty then
    Display error message
Else
    If PurchaseDate is empty then
        Display error message
    Else
        If ExpectedDate is empty then
            Display error message
        Else
            If BuyerLogin is empty then
                Display error message
            Else
                If BuyerName is empty then
                    Display error message
                Else
                    If QuantityOrdered is empty then
                        Display error message
                    Else
                        If ExpectedDate<CurrentDate then
                            Display error message
                        Else
                            If QuantityOrdered>0 then
                                AddPurchaseOrder
                            Else
                                Display error message
                            End if
                        End if
                    End if
                End if
            End if
        End if
    End if
End if
```

Add an IfElse activity called CheckPartNumber. Name the left branch PartNumberPresent
and the right PartNumberMissing. Right-click the workflow and add the following code to the
end of the workflow code file:

```
Public Sub PartNumberPresentCondition(ByVal sender As Object,
ByVal e As ConditionalEventArgs)
    e.Result = StrPartNumber <> String.Empty
End Sub
Public Sub PartNumberMissingCondition(ByVal sender As Object,
ByVal e As ConditionalEventArgs)
    e.Result = StrPartNumber = String.Empty
End Sub
```

The first sub is used as the condition for the left branch (the default branch). This branch is executed if the part number has been provided. This condition verifies by comparing the values of the part number's private variable and the empty string. If the part number's private variable (StrPartNumber) has a value, this condition will return True, and the other activities within this branch will be executed. If StrPartNumber is blank, this condition will return False, and the right branch will be evaluated. The right branch will use the PartNumberMissingCondition sub, which would evaluate to True, and the activities in that branch will be executed. Set the Condition property of the PartNumberPresent branch to CodeCondition, and set the Condition to PartNumberPresentCondition. Set the Condition property of the PartNumberMissing branch to CodeCondition, and set the Condition to PartNumberMissingCondition. This ties the branches of the IfElse activity to the Condition subs.

To test this out, add a Code activity to each branch, leaving the default name. Generate handlers for each Code activity. For the left branch, add msgbox("Part Number Present") within the generated handlers. For the right branch, add msgbox("Part Number Missing") for the generated handlers. Execute the workflow and enter values for the prompts. You'll get the message that the part number is missing.

Delete the two Code activities that were just added to the IfElse activity, and delete the handler code with the message boxes that you just added. Now add a Code activity to the right branch of the IfElse activity (the previous Code activities were deleted to avoid confusion). Name this Code activity MissingPartNumber and generate the handlers for it. Add the following:

```
msgbox ("Part Number is required when entering a Purchase Order")
```

Based on the logic shown earlier in this section, you must place another IfElse statement inside the left branch. The reason for this is that if a part number is provided, then the next parameter (purchase date) must be examined. Move the AddPurchaseOrder Code activity that you created in Chapter 2 to the left branch of the IfElse activity. The workflow should look like Figure 3-8.

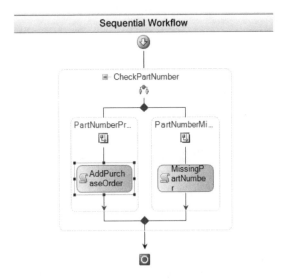

Figure 3-8. *CheckPartNumber IfElse Activity with branches*

Execute the workflow, and provide values for the parameters as prompted. You'll get the message box that the part number is required for a purchase order, but this time you won't get the message with the purchase order number in it. Instead of the purchase order number message box, you'll encounter an exception message. This is because the purchase order output parameter has no value. To account for this situation, open Module1.vb again and change OnWorkflowCompleted to the following:

```
Shared Sub OnWorkflowCompleted(ByVal sender As Object,
ByVal e As WorkflowCompletedEventArgs)
    If Not e.OutputParameters("PurchaseOrderNumber") Is Nothing Then
        MsgBox("Purchase Order Number is: " &
        e.OutputParameters("PurchaseOrderNumber").ToString)
    End If
    WaitHandle.Set()
End Sub
```

The new If statement within the OnWorkflowCompleted sub determines if there's a value for the output parameter PurchaseOrderNumber. If an error is encountered during validation of the parameters, the PurchaseOrderNumber output parameter won't have a value, and therefore will error out if you attempt to display it.

The next step is to add all the necessary condition subs. After you add the condition subs, then you can add the IfElse activities and name them, along with setting the Condition property. Follow the same pattern as was done for the part number, and your resulting code should look like the following:

```
Public Sub PartNumberPresentCondition(ByVal sender As Object,
ByVal e As ConditionalEventArgs)
    e.Result = StrPartNumber <> String.Empty
End Sub
Public Sub PartNumberMissingCondition(ByVal sender As Object,
ByVal e As ConditionalEventArgs)
    e.Result = StrPartNumber = String.Empty
End Sub
Public Sub PurchaseDatePresentCondition(ByVal sender As Object,
ByVal e As ConditionalEventArgs)
    e.Result = IsDate(DtePurchaseDate)
End Sub
Public Sub PurchaseDateMissingCondition(ByVal sender As Object,
ByVal e As ConditionalEventArgs)
    e.Result = Not IsDate(DtePurchaseDate)
End Sub
Public Sub ExpectedDatePresentCondition(ByVal sender As Object,
ByVal e As ConditionalEventArgs)
    e.Result = IsDate(DteExpectedDate)
End Sub
Public Sub ExpectedDateMissingCondition(ByVal sender As Object,
ByVal e As ConditionalEventArgs)
    e.Result = Not IsDate(DteExpectedDate)
End Sub
```

```
Public Sub BuyerLoginPresentCondition(ByVal sender As Object,
ByVal e As ConditionalEventArgs)
    e.Result = StrBuyerLogin <> String.Empty
End Sub
Public Sub BuyerLoginMissingCondition(ByVal sender As Object,
ByVal e As ConditionalEventArgs)
    e.Result = StrBuyerLogin = String.Empty
End Sub
Public Sub BuyerNamePresentCondition(ByVal sender As Object,
ByVal e As ConditionalEventArgs)
    e.Result = StrBuyerName <> String.Empty
End Sub
Public Sub BuyerNameMissingCondition(ByVal sender As Object,
ByVal e As ConditionalEventArgs)
    e.Result = StrBuyerName = String.Empty
End Sub
Public Sub FutureExpectedDateCondition(ByVal sender As Object,
ByVal e As ConditionalEventArgs)
    e.Result = DteExpectedDate >= Now
End Sub
Public Sub PastExpectedDateCondition(ByVal sender As Object,
ByVal e As ConditionalEventArgs)
    e.Result = DteExpectedDate < Now
End Sub
Public Sub QuantityOrderedGreater0Condition(ByVal sender As Object,
ByVal e As ConditionalEventArgs)
    e.Result = IntQuantityOrdered > 0
End Sub
Public Sub QuantityLessThan0Condition(ByVal sender As Object,
ByVal e As ConditionalEventArgs)
    e.Result = IntQuantityOrdered <= 0
End Sub
```

The logic that was provided earlier states that if the part number is present, test the purchase date to see if it's present. To do this, you need to add an IfElse activity to the left branch of the CheckPartNumber activity. Call this new IfElse activity CheckPurchaseDate, call the left branch PurchaseDatePresent, and call the right branch PurchaseDateMissing. Place the AddPurchaseOrder activity that was created in Chapter 2 within the PurchaseDatePresent branch of the CheckPurchaseDate activity. The PurchaseDateMissing branch needs a Code activity called MissingPurchaseDate that's similar to the MissingPartNumber activity. The resulting workflow will look like Figure 3-9.

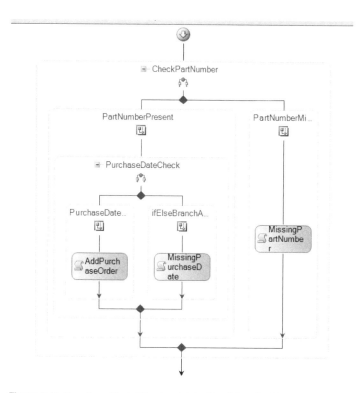

Figure 3-9. *PurchaseDateCheck within PartNumberPresent*

Continue this logic until you have a workflow with all the necessary activities. When all the activities are added, you should have the following ExecuteCode subs:

```
Private Sub MissingPartNumber_ExecuteCode(ByVal sender As System.Object,
ByVal e As System.EventArgs)
    MsgBox("Part Number is required when entering a Purchase Order")
End Sub
Private Sub MissingPurchaseDate_ExecuteCode(ByVal sender As System.Object,
ByVal e As System.EventArgs)
    MsgBox("Purchase Date is required when entering a Purchase Order")
End Sub
Private Sub MissingExpectedDate_ExecuteCode(ByVal sender As System.Object,
ByVal e As System.EventArgs)
    MsgBox("Expected Date is required when entering a Purchase Order")
End Sub
Private Sub MissingBuyerLogin_ExecuteCode(ByVal sender As System.Object,
ByVal e As System.EventArgs)
    MsgBox("Buyer Login is required when entering a Purchase Order")
End Sub
```

```
Private Sub MissingBuyerName_ExecuteCode(ByVal sender As System.Object,
ByVal e As System.EventArgs)
    MsgBox("Buyer Name is required when entering a Purchase Order")
End Sub
Private Sub ExpectedDateInPast_ExecuteCode(ByVal sender As System.Object,
ByVal e As System.EventArgs)
    MsgBox("When entering a Purchase Order expected date must be in the future")
End Sub
Private Sub OrderQuantityNotGreater0_ExecuteCode(ByVal sender As System.Object,
ByVal e As System.EventArgs)
    MsgBox("When entering a Purchase Order the quantity must be greater than 0")
End Sub
```

When the entire workflow is built, there will be many activities within the workflow, which might make it a little difficult to read and understand. Make sure your last two IfElse activities look as they do in Figure 3-10.

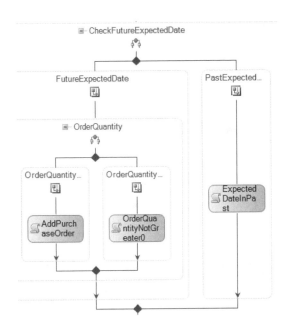

Figure 3-10. *Last two IfElse activities in workflow*

Notice that the last IfElse activity (FutureExpectedDate) has a Code activity within both branches. When this activity is encountered, that means all previous activities have executed the left branch of the IfElse activities (they have all been True), and if the order quantity is greater than zero, then the purchase order can be added. Otherwise, the purchase order can't be added because the order quantity is less than zero.

Conclusion

This chapter covered the various ways to branch within a workflow, and how to handle decisions. This chapter covered the IfElse activity for handling decisions, and the While activity to show how you can use conditions to execute activities until a condition is met. The next chapter will cover activities that facilitate flow within the workflow.

CHAPTER 4

■ ■ ■

Flow Activities

This chapter will cover activities that impact how a workflow flows. I've already introduced some of these activities briefly, such as the Delay and State activities. This chapter will expand on those activities more, and provide more code examples. We'll begin by looking at four activities that are specific to the State Machine workflow, and that aren't available in the Sequential workflow.

State Machine–Specific Control Activities

Four control activities are specific to the State Machine workflow and can't be used within a Sequential workflow. These are the State activity, the StateInitialization activity, the StateFinalization activity, and the SetState activity.

The State activity is the main activity used within a State Machine workflow. The State activity is the building block of a State Machine workflow, and represents a state that the State Machine workflow can be in. The State Machine workflow must have a state at all times. Most activities within a State Machine workflow take place within the State activity. In the preceding two chapters, I used the State activity to show how the State Machine workflows would work with the various activities that have been covered.

You can add the StateInitialization activity to a State activity to allow child activities to take place when the state is begun or transitioned into. This activity would be the same as a load event when talking about a Windows form or Web page. Any activities within the StateInitialization activity occur only when the state is first executed.

You can add the StateFinalization activity to a State activity to allow child activities to take place when the state is ended or transitioned out of. This activity would be the same as an exit event when talking about a Windows form or Web page. Any activities within the StateFinalization activity occur only when the state is about to be left.

Finally, the SetState activity allows the State Machine to transition from one state to the next. This would be the same as a hyperlink within a Web page taking control of the Web site from one page to the next. This is the only way to transition from one state to the next.

You must place all three of these activities (StateInitialization, StateFinalization, and SetState) within a State activity container; you can't just place them within the workflow. They're dependent on the State activity. This shows that, for the most part, the State activity is a container for other activities. This makes sense, because the State activity is considered the building block of the State Machine workflow, and the State Machine workflow requires State activities.

State-Related Activities

Create a new VB State Machine Workflow Console Application called
VBStateActivitiesConsoleApplication. In previous chapters you set the default state—the one
that was already created when the workflow was created—as the completed state. Instead, this
time drag and drop a StateInitialization activity from the toolbar onto the default State activity.
Remember, you must house the StateInitialization, StateFinalization, and SetState activities
inside a State activity. Click the State activity and open the properties. Set the name to be State1.
While on the Properties page, click the SetToInitialState link. This makes the State1 activity the
first activity to be fired when the workflow is entered. Every State Machine workflow must have
an initial state.

Next, click the StateInitialization activity within the State1 activity (called
stateInitializationActivity1) and click the properties page. Change the name to Initialization1.
Double-click the Initialization1 activity. This opens that activity within a new window that's
dedicated just to that activity. You can see the breadcrumb at the top left of the window
(Workflow1:State1). This shows you where you are within the workflow structure. This view
allows you to add activities to the StateInitialization activity (Initialization1) more easily.
Although the StateInitialization activity is a container for other activities, you don't need to add
activities. To show this, debug the workflow. You see a console application window pop up, but
nothing more happens. That's because there are no activities that perform work within the
workflow at the moment. The workflow would also never leave State1 because there's no
SetState activity to move the workflow execution to another state. Add a Code activity to the
Initialization1 called Code1. Generate Handlers for the Code activity, and within the
Code1_ExecuteCode sub add `Msgbox("code1")`. The code for this sub is as follows:

```
Private Sub Code1_ExecuteCode(ByVal sender As System.Object, ByVal e As
System.EventArgs)
    MsgBox("Code1")
End Sub
```

Add a StateFinalization activity from the Toolbox to the workflow. You'll notice you can't
drop the activity within the Initialization1 activity. Instead, you need to right-click the workflow
surface and choose Back to State Composition View. You were in a view that was dedicated to
the Initialization1 activity. Once you're back to the State Composition View, you can then drop
a StateFinalization activity called Finalization1 within the State1 activity. When you double-
click the Finalization1 activity, you'll be back to the previous view that's specific to the
Finalization1 activity. Drop a SetState activity from the Toolbox into the Finalization1 activity.
Again, you'll find you can't do this. At first, this doesn't seem to make sense. The StateFinalization
activity is performed when the workflow is exiting the state, and you should be able to use that
activity to set the next state. However, a StateFinalization activity is the last action to occur
before the state is exited. You must set the state first (more on this shortly). For now, add a Code
activity called Code2 to Finalization1. Generate the Handlers, but add `Msgbox("code2")`. The
code for this sub is as follows:

```
Private Sub code2_ExecuteCode(ByVal sender As System.Object, ByVal e As
System.EventArgs)
    MsgBox("Code2")
End Sub
```

Return to the State Composition View and a State activity called State2. Make this the completed state. Now, add a SetState activity called ToState2 to State1 (the original state). You'll find that you can't add the SetState activity to a State activity. The reason for this is the SetState activity must be included inside another activity that performs some type of action. For example, you can include it in the EventDriven activity, but you can't directly add the SetState activity to the StateFinalization or State activity. However, you can add it to the StateInitialization activity. Double-click Initialization1, and when the Initialization1 view appears, add the SetState activity called ToState2 and set the TargetStateName property to State2. Initialization1 should look like Figure 4-1.

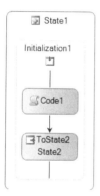

Figure 4-1. *Initialization1 activity*

Return to the State Composition View. Again, you can do this by right-clicking in the workflow area, or you can click the breadcrumb area in the top left of the Initialization1 view, as shown in Figure 4-2. If you click the Workflow crumb, you'll return to the workflow, and if you click the State crumb, you'll return to the highlighted state.

Figure 4-2. *Workflow and Activity breadcrumb*

The completed workflow looks like Figure 4-3.

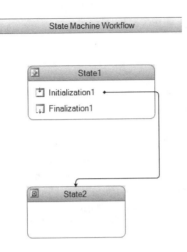

Figure 4-3. *Completed workflow*

To see how and when the StateInitialization and StateFinalization activities work, add a breakpoint to State1 and debug the workflow. When the application begins and the breakpoint is encountered, press F11. This takes you into the Initialization1 activity. Continue to step through the code with F11, and you go into the Code1 activity. The message box appears, then the code moves to the State2 activity, the SetState activity. After the SetState activity, execution of the workflow goes to the Finalization1 activity and the Code2 activity. This shows that State1 is about to be exited.

You can see with this example and the walkthrough that you can use the StateInitialization activity to perform setup or preparation tasks, such as setting variables that are to be used. You can also use it if you're using data—for example, to make a database connection. You can use the StateFinalization activity to perform cleanup tasks, such as closing a database connection just before the state is exited.

You can use these activities to initialize and clean up for a specific State activity. You can also use the New and Finalize subs for the workflow to do the same things. If you view the code for the workflow (not an activity, the actual workflow), you can choose the workflow name (mine is Workflow1) from the top left drop-down within the code editor. Then, choose New from the right. There's already code there for the Sub New, but add a new line, Msgbox("Workflow started"). The completed Sub New code is as follows:

```
Public Sub New()
    MyBase.New()
    InitializeComponent()
    Me.InitialStateName = "State1"
    MsgBox("Workflow started")
End Sub
```

Notice the Me.InitialStateName = "State1" line of code. This lets the State Machine workflow know which state is the initial state. Add a breakpoint to this line of code. Next, choose

Finalize from the top right drop-down to create the Finalize sub. Add `Msgbox("Workflow Closing")` here. The completed `Sub Finalize` code is as follows:

```
Protected Overrides Sub Finalize()
    MyBase.Finalize()
    MsgBox("Workflow Closing")
End Sub
```

Debug the workflow. You get an interesting result: you see the Workflow Started and Workflow Completed message boxes several times each before the breakpoint on the State1 activity is even activated. Due to this behavior, you should avoid using the New and Finalize methods of the workflow.

As with the previous chapters, I won't show the code for the State Machine workflow application in C#. The code is the same, with the exceptions that were mentioned in Chapter 2.

Delay, Suspend, and Terminate

The Delay activity has been used in the previous chapters. As a reminder, the Delay activity allows you to control the timing of the workflow by building delays into it. These delays can be hours or days. The workflow pauses a period of time, as specified in the Interval property, when the Delay activity is executed.

The Suspend activity suspends the workflow operation and logs an error. You can use this to intervene when an error condition is met, and you can also specify a message that gets logged with the error. This is similar to the Try . . . Catch block of code, along with writing to the event log. The Try and Catch interrupt the flow of your program and might stop the program, or might just require user intervention before moving on. The Suspend activity performs the same type of operation. When the Suspend activity is encountered, the workflow pauses as with the Delay activity, except the Suspend activity waits for the workflow to be started by some external action (usually by an administrator). That's unlike the Delay activity, which only waits a set period of time. When a Suspend activity is encountered, all state information is saved and associated with the current instance. The information can be recovered when the workflow execution resumes.

The Terminate activity immediately stops the workflow. You can use this in the event of some fatal error or other unusual situation. This would be the same as a Try . . . Catch that stopped your program rather than allowing the user to respond to the error (as in the Suspend activity). When a workflow is terminated, an error is logged, and a message can be provided for more information.

The Suspend and Terminate activities are used most often in exception handling. They provide a basis for exception handling with workflows by logging errors and either waiting for user intervention (Suspend activity) or just stopping the workflow altogether (Terminate activity).

Delay, Suspend, and Terminate in VB

This section will cover the Delay, Suspend, and Terminate activities using VB. First these activities will be included in a Sequential workflow and then in a State Machine workflow. The next sections will show these same activities using C#.

Sequential Workflow

This section will provide an example of a workflow that uses the Delay, Suspend, and Terminate activities. Create a new VB Sequential Workflow Console Application called VBDelaySuspendTerminateSequential. Add a Delay activity to the workflow called Delay1. While setting the name properties, also notice the TimeoutDuration property. Set the property to 00:00:30, for 30 seconds. This is in hours, minutes, and seconds, and sets the delay. When the workflow executes the Delay1 activity, this TimeoutDuration property will determine the amount of time to wait before moving to the next activity. You can use this if you have a Sequential workflow that needs to flow to a certain point and then wait. You might have a While activity with a delay in it that looks for the presence of a file or certain data. The While activity would include an activity to look for the file or data. If it isn't there, the workflow would wait (using a Delay activity) for a set period of time and then look again.

Drag an IfElse activity after the Delay activity. Leave the default name. View the code of the workflow to add the branch conditions. First, add a private variable to the workflow called IntCounter and define it as an integer with a value of 10:

```
Private IntCounter As Integer = 10
```

Next, create the two branch conditions, one to determine if the value of IntCounter is greater than 1 and the other to determine if the value of IntCounter is less than or equal to 1:

```
Public Sub CounterGreater1Condition(ByVal sender As Object, ByVal e As
ConditionalEventArgs)
    e.Result = IntCounter > 1
End Sub
Public Sub CounterLessEqual1Condition(ByVal sender As Object, ByVal e As
ConditionalEventArgs)
    e.Result = IntCounter <= 1
End Sub
```

Return to the designer and give the left branch of the IfElse activity the name CounterGreater1, and set the condition to CounterGreater1Condition. Give the right branch of the IfElse activity the name CounterLessEqual1, and set the condition to CounterLessEqual1Condition. If you don't remember how to use the IfElse activity, look back to Chapter 3. Now the IfElse activity is built, but there aren't child activities. Add a new Suspend activity as the first child of the left branch (CounterGreater1Condition) of the IfElse activity. Call this activity SuspendError, because this Suspend activity is being used to raise an error that something is unusual about the value of the counter. You can use the Suspend activity in this way to stop processing of an instance of a workflow if some condition is met that a user must interact with. For example, you might have a Suspend activity within a While activity that determines if an error counter is greater than some value. If the error counter is greater than some value (such as in this example), then suspend the workflow execution and warn the user. Your workflow should look like Figure 4-4.

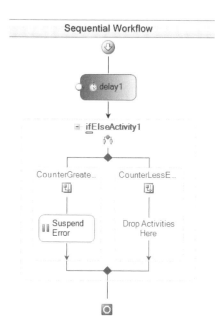

Figure 4-4. *Workflow with Delay and Suspend activities*

Add a breakpoint to the Delay1 activity and debug the workflow. You'll notice the Delay1 activity is executed, and the workflow pauses for 30 seconds. Then the left branch of the IfElse activity is executed, because that's the branch whose condition is True. Finally, the SuspendError activity is executed. However, notice that nothing happens. The console application remains open, and so does the workflow. The Suspend activity paused the workflow; however, the workflow doesn't know what to do when it's suspended. A little more coding is involved to make the Suspend activity work, so stop the debugging of the workflow.

Open the Module1.vb file to open the code for the console application. Find the line of code that creates a new instance of the WorkflowRuntime class:

```
Dim workflowRuntime As New WorkflowRuntime())
```

Right-click WorkflowRuntime() and choose Go To Definition to open the Object Browser. This takes you to the object model for the WorkflowRuntime class. If you scroll down the right side of the Object Browser, you'll see events such as WofkflowStarted, WorkflowSuspended, and WorkflowTerminated. These are all events that can be raised within the WorkflowRuntime class. Now you need to add code to Module1 to handle the WorkflowSuspended event, so when the event is raised the workflow runtime will know what actions to perform.

Add the following sub to handle the WorkflowSuspended event:

```
Shared Sub OnWorkflowSuspended(ByVal sender As Object, ByVal e As
WorkflowSuspendedEventArgs)
    Msgbox(e.Error)
    WaitHandle.Set()
End Sub
```

Notice the e.Error parameter to the message box. "Reason" is a property of the WorkflowSuspendedEventsArgs class, and can be used to provide a reason for the workflow being suspended. This sub displays to the user the reason the workflow was suspended. However, first the workflow runtime must know that this sub is going to handle the WorkflowSuspended event. To do this, add the following code within the Main sub after the other AddHandler statement:

```
AddHandler workflowRuntime.WorkflowSuspended, AddressOf OnWorkflowSuspended
```

This line of code tells the WorkflowRuntime class that there's a Handler called OnWorkflowSuspended, which should be executed when the WorkflowSuspended event of the WorkflowRuntime class is raised. The resulting Sub Main is as follows:

```
Shared Sub Main()
    Dim workflowRuntime As New WorkflowRuntime()
    AddHandler workflowRuntime.WorkflowCompleted, AddressOf OnWorkflowCompleted
    AddHandler workflowRuntime.WorkflowTerminated, AddressOf OnWorkflowTerminated
    AddHandler workflowRuntime.WorkflowSuspended, AddressOf OnWorkflowSuspended
    Dim workflowInstance As WorkflowInstance
    workflowInstance = workflowRuntime.CreateWorkflow(GetType(Workflow1))
    workflowInstance.Start()
    WaitHandle.WaitOne()
End Sub
```

Now that the Handler is in place, start debugging the workflow again. Again, you'll see the workflow move through the Delay1 activity, to the IfElse activity, and finally to the Suspend activity. The message box then appears but has no contents. This is because the Error property of the WorkflowSuspendedEventsArgs class must be set. To set this property, you have to provide a value to the Error property of the Suspend activity. Stop the debugging and return to the code of the workflow. Within the Sub New, add the following line:

```
SuspendError.Error = "counter>1"
```

This line sets the Error property of the SuspendError activity and lets the user know the reason the workflow is suspended is that counter is greater than 1. The resulting Sub New is as follows:

```
Public Sub New()
    MyBase.New()
    InitializeComponent()
    SuspendError.Error = "counter>1"
End Sub
```

Debug the workflow again and see that counter>1 appears in the message box.

The user is then told why the workflow has been suspended, but what can the user do about it? Right-click the WorkflowInstance in Module1.vb and choose Go To Definition to open the Object Browser. Notice this class has a method called Resume, as well as methods called Suspend and Terminate, which both accept parameters. The Resume method of the WorkflowInstance class restarts a suspended workflow. This takes a little bit of work to accomplish. Go back to the Module1 code and the OnWorkflowSuspended sub. Add Dim wfinstance As WorkflowInstance to create a variable called wfinstance that's an instance of the

WorkflowInstance class. Wfinstance can now hold a copy of the WorkflowInstance class that was suspended. Add another line:

```
wfinstance = e.WorkflowInstance
```

Notice that WorkflowInstance is a property of the WorkflowSuspendedEventsArgs class. It represents the workflow instance that was suspended, and everything about that workflow instance. Add one last line of code:

```
wfinstance.resume()
```

The resulting OnWorkflowSuspended is as follows:

```
Shared Sub OnWorkflowSuspended(ByVal sender As Object, ByVal e As
WorkflowSuspendedEventArgs)
    Dim wfinstance As WorkflowInstance
    wfinstance = e.WorkflowInstance
    wfinstance.Resume()
    WaitHandle.Set()
End Sub
```

The next step in this example is to add a Code activity to the left IfElse branch. Call this Code activity CodeResume, and add Handlers for ExecutionCode. Within the ExecutionCode sub for CodeResume, add `Msgbox("Workflow Resumed")`. The completed sub is as follows:

```
Private Sub CodeResume_ExecuteCode(ByVal sender As System.Object, ByVal e As
System.EventArgs)
    MsgBox("Workflow Resumed")
End Sub
```

When the workflow is resumed, this Code activity will be executed and the message box will appear. Debug the workflow; the first message box appears when the workflow is suspended and the second when the workflow resumes.

The final step in this example is to allow the user to determine what to do next. Add a message box that allows the user to determine if the workflow should be resumed or terminated. Use the following block of code within the OnWorkflowSuspended sub:

```
Shared Sub OnWorkflowSuspended(ByVal sender As Object, ByVal e As
 WorkflowSuspendedEventArgs)
    Dim wfinstance As WorkflowInstance
    wfinstance = e.WorkflowInstance
    If MsgBox(e.Error & " Do you want to continue?", MsgBoxStyle.YesNo, "Workflow
        Suspended") = MsgBoxResult.Yes Then
        wfinstance.Resume()
    Else
        wfinstance.Terminate("User Choice")
        WaitHandle.Set()
    End If
End Sub
```

Notice the Terminate method call. Again, in this example Terminate is a method of the WofkflowInstance class. This isn't the Terminate activity, but just a method. This method terminates the workflow, and is the same as the Terminate activity that you'll add later. Debug the workflow again, and when prompted say Yes to resume the workflow. You'll see the workflow resumed message box. If you execute the workflow again and choose No, the workflow will terminate. This ability to resume a workflow from the point it stopped can be important. If there's an error within a workflow and the user can make a choice and resume the workflow, this is better than having the workflow terminate.

However, you can choose to terminate a workflow if a condition is either met or not met. In this case, if IntCounter is less than or equal to 1, the workflow will terminate. Add a Terminate activity to the right branch of the IfElse condition and call this activity TerminateError. View the code for the workflow again and add `TerminateError.Error = "Counter<=1"` to the New sub just under the SuspendError.Error property assignment. This provides a reason for the workflow to be terminated. Also, set the default value of IntCounter to 1. The completed Sub New is as follows:

```
Public Sub New()
    MyBase.New()
    InitializeComponent()
    SuspendError.Error = "counter>1"
    TerminateError.Error = "Counter<=1"
End Sub
```

Open the Module.vb file and find the OnWorkflowTerminated sub, which should already be created by default. Replace the `console.writeline` with `MsgBox(e.Exception.Message)`. The completed OnWorkflowTerminated looks like the following:

```
Shared Sub OnWorkflowTerminated(ByVal sender As Object, ByVal e As
 WorkflowTerminatedEventArgs)
    MsgBox(e.Exception.Message)
    WaitHandle.Set()
End Sub
```

This displays the error message that's assigned to TerminateError.Error when the workflow is terminated. Execute the workflow, and the terminate message box appears just before the workflow is terminated.

One last little test of this workflow: go back to the workflow and view the code. Change the default value of IntCounter back to 10. Execute the workflow, and when prompted if you want to continue, choose No. You'll notice that when the workflow terminates, instead of the value provided to the Error property of TerminateError, the parameter provided to the Terminate method of the workflow instance is displayed:

```
wfinstance.Terminate("User Choice")
```

The reason for this is that the TerminateError activity wasn't executed to perform the termination. Instead, when the Terminate method of the workflow instance was called, the parameter provided was used as the error to be displayed. Remember this when you want to write out an event log or display a message when the workflow terminates.

State Machine Workflow

Create a new VB State Machine Workflow Console Application called VBDelaySuspendTerminateState, but don't close the Sequential workflow project yet. The good part about this example is you can use all the same code from the Sequential workflow. First, copy over the code in Module1.vb, including the AddHandler statement and the OnWorkflowTerminated and OnWorkflowSuspended subs:

```vb
Shared Sub Main()
    Dim workflowRuntime As New WorkflowRuntime()
    AddHandler workflowRuntime.WorkflowCompleted, AddressOf OnWorkflowCompleted
    AddHandler workflowRuntime.WorkflowTerminated, AddressOf OnWorkflowTerminated
    AddHandler workflowRuntime.WorkflowSuspended, AddressOf OnWorkflowSuspended
    Dim workflowInstance As WorkflowInstance
    workflowInstance = workflowRuntime.CreateWorkflow(GetType(Workflow1))
    workflowInstance.Start()
    WaitHandle.WaitOne()
End Sub
Shared Sub OnWorkflowCompleted(ByVal sender As Object, ByVal e As
WorkflowCompletedEventArgs)
    WaitHandle.Set()
End Sub

Shared Sub OnWorkflowTerminated(ByVal sender As Object, ByVal e As
WorkflowTerminatedEventArgs)
    MsgBox(e.Exception.Message)
    WaitHandle.Set()
End Sub
Shared Sub OnWorkflowSuspended(ByVal sender As Object, ByVal e As
WorkflowSuspendedEventArgs)
    Dim wfinstance As WorkflowInstance
    wfinstance = e.WorkflowInstance
    If MsgBox(e.Error & " Do you want to continue?", MsgBoxStyle.YesNo, "Workflow
        Suspended") = MsgBoxResult.Yes Then
        wfinstance.Resume()
    Else
        wfinstance.Terminate("User Choice")
        WaitHandle.Set()
    End If
End Sub
```

Next, open the Workflow Designer and name the default state InitialState. Set it as the initial state. Add another State activity called ResumeState. Drag a Delay activity to the workflow. You'll notice again that you can't drop a Delay activity to the workflow directly, or to the State activity. Instead, you need to add an EventDriven activity to the default state. Double-click the EventDriven activity and add a Delay activity to the EventDriven activity. Call this activity Delay1 and set the timeout duration property to ten seconds. After the delay, add an IfElse activity, using the same names as the Sequential workflow and the same conditions. You can copy the two condition subs from the Sequential workflow to the State Machine workflow. Make sure you set up the condition property of each IfElse branch to point to the appropriate condition. Add a Suspend activity called SuspendError to the left side of the IfElse activity. Add a Terminate activity called TerminateError to the right side of the IfElse activity. Finally, add a SetState activity called ToResume after the SuspendError activity, and set its TargetStateName to ResumeState. The completed EventDriven activity with the InitialState activity should look like Figure 4-5.

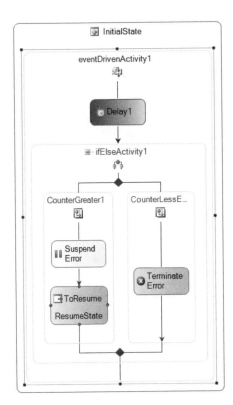

Figure 4-5. *EventDriven activity*

Next, view the code for the workflow and make sure to add the IntCounter declaration and the assignment to the Error property of SuspendError and TerminateError. Finally, return to the State Composition View and add an EventDriven activity to the ResumeState activity. Within this EventDriven activity, add a Delay activity called Delay2, and a Code activity called CodeResume. Generate the Handlers for the CodeResume activity, and add a message box stating the workflow is resuming:

```
Private IntCounter As Integer = 10
Public Sub New()
    MyBase.New()
    InitializeComponent()
    SuspendError.Error = "Counter>1"
    TerminateError.Error = "Counter<=1"
End Sub
Public Sub CounterGreater1Condition(ByVal sender As Object, ByVal e As
ConditionalEventArgs)
    e.Result = IntCounter > 1
End Sub
Public Sub CounterLessEqual1Condition(ByVal sender As Object, ByVal e As
ConditionalEventArgs)
    e.Result = IntCounter <= 1
End Sub
Private Sub CodeResume_ExecuteCode(ByVal sender As System.Object, ByVal e As
System.EventArgs)
    MsgBox("Workflow Resumed")
End Sub
```

Execute the workflow, and the first time, choose Yes you want to continue when prompted. You should then see the Workflow Resume message box. You'll then notice the workflow doesn't terminate. There's no complete state set, so the State Machine workflow doesn't terminate. Stop the workflow and execute the workflow again. This time, choose No when prompted. The workflow should then terminate with the Counter<=1 message.

Delay, Suspend, and Terminate in C#

The Sequential workflow using C# is mostly the same as using VB, but with some code changes. Create the workflow in the project, CDelaySuspendTerminateSequential, similar to what you did with the VB example. Add a Delay activity called Delay1 with a TimeoutDuration property of 00:00:30. Add an IfElse activity after the Delay activity. On the left side of the IfElse activity call the branch GreaterThan1 and on the right side of the IfElse activity call the branch LessThanEqual1. Finally, add a Suspend activity to the left branch of the IfElse activity, and call this Suspend activity SuspendError. Your workflow should look like Figure 4-6.

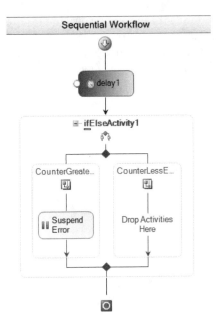

Figure 4-6. *New Sequential workflow in C#*

Add the following code to the workflow (right-click, then View Code):

```
public sealed partial class Workflow1: SequentialWorkflowActivity
{
    private int IntCounter = 10;
    public Workflow1()
    {
        InitializeComponent();
    }

    private void GreaterThan1Condition(object sender, ConditionalEventArgs e)
    {
        e.Result = IntCounter >1;
        IntCounter++;
    }

    private void LessThanEqual1Condition(object sender, ConditionalEventArgs e)
    {
        e.Result = IntCounter <=1;
        IntCounter++;
    }
}
```

Go back to the designer and set the Condition property of the two branches of the IfElse activity to point to the correct procedure that was just created. While within the designer, add a Terminate activity called TerminateError to the right side of the IfElse activity.

The workflow is now mostly set up. The `Main` sub within Program.cs now needs code added to handle the suspended and terminated actions. `Main` should look like the following code:

```
static void Main(string[] args)
{
    WorkflowRuntime workflowRuntime = new WorkflowRuntime();
    AutoResetEvent waitHandle = new AutoResetEvent(false);
    workflowRuntime.WorkflowCompleted += delegate(object sender,
      WorkflowCompletedEventArgs e) {waitHandle.Set();};
    workflowRuntime.WorkflowTerminated += OnWorkflowTerminated;
    workflowRuntime.WorkflowSuspended += OnWorkflowSuspended;
    WorkflowInstance instance = workflowRuntime.CreateWorkflow(typeof
    (CDelaySuspendTerminateSequential.Workflow1));
    instance.Start();
    waitHandle.WaitOne();
}
```

You also need to create two new procedures within Program.cs:

```
static void OnWorkflowTerminated(object sender, WorkflowTerminatedEventArgs e)
{
    Console.WriteLine("Terminated");
}
static void OnWorkflowSuspended(object sender, WorkflowSuspendedEventArgs e)
{
    Console.WriteLine("suspended");
}
```

Execute the workflow. There's a delay while the timeout of 30 seconds expires, then the console window displays Suspended. This shows that the workflow was suspended. As with the VB example, you can add prompts for the user to decide to continue or terminate.

There's no difference between the State Machine workflow in VB and C# except for the coding changes that were covered with the C# Sequential workflow, so I won't show the code and workflow for the State Machine in C#.

Sequence and Parallel Activities

The Sequence and Parallel activities allow you to set how child activities are executed. Both activities are containers for other activities. In fact, the Parallel activity contains two Sequence activities by default. A Sequence activity is the only type of activity that can be placed inside a Parallel activity. However, any type of activity can be placed inside a Sequence activity. The Sequence activity completes when the last child activity completes. With the Parallel activity, you can perform two or more activities independent of one another. The Parallel activity also waits for all activities to complete before completing.

The Sequential and State Machine workflow examples for the Sequence and Parallel activities are the same in VB and C#. Only minor code changes are necessary, so only the VB examples will be shown here.

Sequence Workflow

Create a new VB Sequential Workflow Console Application called
VBSequenceParallelSequentialConsole. The first part of the example will show the Sequence
activity alone, and the second part will show the Parallel activity made up of two Sequence
activities. Add a Sequence activity to the workflow, leaving the name the default. Next, add a
Code activity to the Sequence activity. Call the Code activity Sequence1. Generate Handlers for
this Code activity, and add a message box stating "Sequence 1." Add another Code activity
within the Sequence activity, and call the Code activity Sequence2. Generate Handlers for this Code
activity, and add a message box stating "Sequence 2." Following is the code for these two subs:

```
Private Sub Sequence1_ExecuteCode(ByVal sender As System.Object, ByVal e As
System.EventArgs)
    MsgBox("sequence 1")
End Sub
Private Sub Sequence2_ExecuteCode(ByVal sender As System.Object, ByVal e As
System.EventArgs)
    MsgBox("sequence 2")
End Sub
```

Finally, add a Delay activity called SequenceDelay with a TimeoutDuration property of ten
seconds. The Sequence activity portion of this workflow is shown in Figure 4-7.

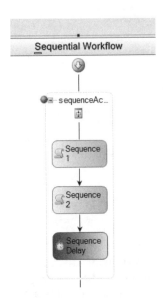

Figure 4-7. *Sequence activity*

After the Sequence activity, drag a Parallel activity onto the Workflow Designer. Notice the
Parallel activity is made up of two Sequence activities. Add a new Code activity to the left
Sequence activity within the Parallel activity; call this activity ParallelLeft. Generate Handlers for
this Code activity and add a message box stating "Parallel Left." Next, add a Code activity to the
Sequence activity on the right within the Parallel activity. Call this Code activity ParallelRight.

Generate Handlers for this Code activity, and add a message box stating "ParallelRight." The code for these subs is as follows:

```
Private Sub ParallelLeft_ExecuteCode(ByVal sender As System.Object, ByVal e As
System.EventArgs)
    MsgBox("parallel left")
End Sub
Private Sub ParallelRight_ExecuteCode(ByVal sender As System.Object, ByVal e As
System.EventArgs)
    MsgBox("parallel right")
End Sub
```

After the ParallelRight activity, add a Delay activity called ParallelDelay with a TimeoutDuration property of ten seconds. The completed Parallel activity is shown in Figure 4-8.

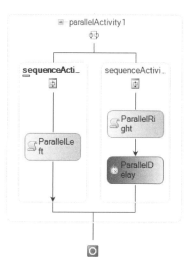

Figure 4-8. *Parallel activity*

In most cases, you wouldn't need a Sequence activity followed by a Parallel activity, but this example shows how each completes. To best see this, add a breakpoint to the Sequence activity at the beginning of the workflow. Execute the workflow, and you'll see that each activity within the Sequence activity is executed in order. When the Parallel activity is encountered, the left Sequence activity is executed first, and then the right. After all activities within the Parallel activity are completed, the Parallel activity completes, and so does the workflow.

State Machine Workflow

Close the Sequential workflow project and create a new VB State Machine Console Application called VBSequenceParallelStateMachineConsole. Rename the default State activity to InitialState and set the state to be the initial state. Add another State activity called LastState. Remember, the only activities with the State activity are EventDriven, StateInitialization, or StateFinalization. Add a StateInitialization activity to the InitialState activity. Within the StateInitialization activity add a Sequence activity, leaving the default name. Within the Sequence activity, add two Code activities, one called Sequence1 and one called Sequence2. Generate the Handlers for each, and add a message box with the name of the activity in it. The code for these two subs is as follows:

```
Private Sub Sequence1_ExecuteCode(ByVal sender As System.Object, ByVal e As
System.EventArgs)
     MsgBox("Sequence 1")
End Sub
Private Sub Sequence2_ExecuteCode(ByVal sender As System.Object, ByVal e As
System.EventArgs)
     MsgBox("Sequence 2")
End Sub
```

Finally, after the Sequence activity, but still within the StateInitialization activity, add a SetState activity called GoToLastState with a TargetStateName property of LastState. Your StateInitialization for the InitialState activity should look like Figure 4-9.

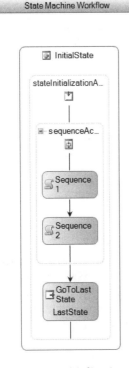

Figure 4-9. *StateInitialization activity*

Return to the State Composition View and add a StateInitialization activity to the LastState activity. Within this StateInitialization activity, add a Parallel activity. Add a Code activity called ParallelLeft to the left Sequence activity within the Parallel activity. Generate the Handlers for

this activity, and add a message box with "ParallelLeft" in it. Add two Code activities—
ParallelRight1 and ParallelRight2—to the right side of the Sequence activity within the Parallel
activity. Generate Handlers for these two Code activities, and add a message box with the
activity name in it. The code for these subs follows:

```
Private Sub ParallelRight1_ExecuteCode(ByVal sender As System.Object, ByVal e As
System.EventArgs)
    MsgBox("Parallel Right 1")
End Sub
Private Sub ParallelRight2_ExecuteCode(ByVal sender As System.Object, ByVal e As
System.EventArgs)
    MsgBox("Parallel Right 2")
End Sub
```

Your completed StateInitialization activity for the LastState activity is shown in Figure 4-10.

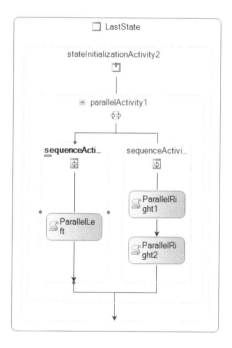

Figure 4-10. *Completed StateInitialization activity for the LastState activity*

Again, add a breakpoint to the InitialState activity and debug the workflow. You'll see
the workflow operations, much like you did with the Sequential workflow. The Sequence
activity is executed first because it's part of the InitialState activity. Then, the control is given
to the LastState activity, and the Parallel activity takes place. Notice how all activities within the
Sequence and Parallel activity complete before moving to the next activity.

EventDriven Activity

This activity, like several others in this chapter, has been covered previously. The EventDriven activity is a container for other activities. The EventDriven activity is triggered by an event, and the first activity must wait for some external event to occur. Within a Sequential workflow, you must use a Listen activity. The Listen activity is a composite activity made up of two EventDriven activities (this will be covered more in Chapter 7). You can use a Delay activity as the first activity within the EventDriven activity to pause workflow first. Then, when the delay has expired, the next activity within the EventDriven activity is executed. In this case, the Delay activity acts as an event to trigger the next activity within the EventDriven activity.

Real-World Example

This chapter will build on the purchase order console application that was begun in earlier chapters. Chapter 3 finished by adding IfElse activities to the Purchase Order workflow to determine if all the information necessary for a purchase order to be entered was present. If the data wasn't present, a Code activity was fired that displayed a message box. To extend the example with the activities from this chapter, we're going to change the Code activity to a Terminate activity. This Terminate activity terminates the workflow and displays a message to the user if one of the data requirements isn't met.

Open the VBPurchaseOrderConsoleApplication created in Chapter 2 and expanded in Chapter 3. View the code in the Workflow1.vb file. In the previous chapter, an ExecuteCode sub for each Code activity provided the user with a message box. To use the Terminate activity instead, each of these subs needs to become a public read-only property instead. This allows the Terminate activity to use the public property as a source for the error message. Create the following public properties:

```
Public ReadOnly Property MissingPartNumberError() As String
    Get
        Return "Part Number is required when entering a Purchase Order"
    End Get
End Property
Public ReadOnly Property MissingPurchaseDateError() As String
    Get
        Return "Purchase Date is required when entering a Purchase Order"
    End Get
End Property
Public ReadOnly Property MissingExpectedDateError() As String
    Get
        Return "Expected Date is required when entering a Purchase Order"
    End Get
End Property
Public ReadOnly Property MissingBuyerLoginError() As String
    Get
        Return "Buyer Login is required when entering a Purchase Order"
    End Get
End Property
```

```
Public ReadOnly Property MissingBuyerNameError() As String
    Get
        Return "Buyer Name is required when entering a Purchase Order"
    End Get
End Property
Public ReadOnly Property ExpectedDateInPastError() As String
    Get
        Return "When entering a Purchase Order expected date must be in the
        future"
    End Get
End Property
Public ReadOnly Property OrderQuantityNotGreater0Error() As String
    Get
        Return "When entering a Purchase Order the quantity must be greater than
        0"
    End Get
End Property
```

Next, delete all the ExecuteCode subs that provided the same messages. Go back to the workflow and delete the MissingPartNumber activity. Replace it with a Terminate activity with the name MissingPartNumber. While viewing the properties of the activity, click the ellipse next to the Error property. The "Bind 'Error' to an activity's property" box appears. Choose MissingPartNumberError and click OK, as shown in Figure 4-11.

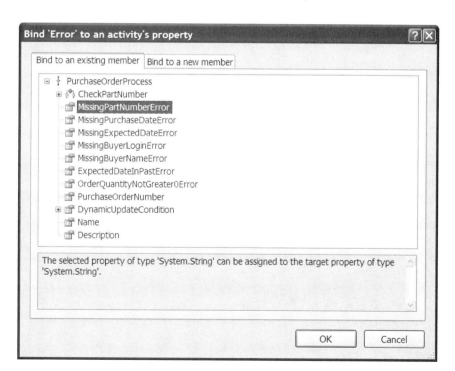

Figure 4-11. *Binding the error to the activity property*

Continue this pattern for the remaining Code activities, replacing each one with a Terminate activity.

The last step is to make sure the OnWorkflowTerminated sub within Module1.vb has a message box to display any exception that's thrown:

```
Shared Sub OnWorkflowTerminated(ByVal sender As Object, ByVal e As
 WorkflowTerminatedEventArgs)
    MsgBox(e.Exception.Message)
    WaitHandle.Set()
End Sub
```

Execute the application. When prompted for the expected date, enter a date that's in the past. You'll see a message box display the message that the expected date is in the past. This occurs because the ExpectedDateInPast Terminate activity was triggered because the False (right branch) condition was met.

Conclusion

This chapter has covered several of the activities that provide flow within a workflow. These activities move the execution of the workflow from one step or activity to another, or execute multiple activities. The real-world example in this chapter showed how to add a Terminate activity to the Purchase Order workflow instead of a Code activity when conditions aren't met. The next chapter will cover rules-based workflow. The real-world example in the next chapter will show how to replace all the IfElse activities in the Purchase Order workflow with rules-based activities instead.

CHAPTER 5

■■■

Rules-Based Workflow

A rules-based workflow is a workflow made up of activities that have rules associated with them. These rules are essentially If-Else statements with a condition and action. A rules-based workflow is a good way to model actual business processes, as business processes have business rules associated with them. You can use rules to define criteria that must be met for an activity to take place. This chapter will show you how to use the Policy activity to create a rules-based workflow.

Rules in WF

Most workflow applications model a business process. Business processes have business rules associated with them. For example, an order entry business process might require that for an order over $1,000 a special credit check must be done. The business rule would be as follows: if the order amount is greater than 1,000, then perform a special credit check. This logic can easily be created as an If-Else statement, or in the case of WF, an IfElse activity. However, you can also make this a rule within the workflow. One advantage of creating a rule instead of a hard-coded activity is that you can change the rule more easily. If the business begins to sell more expensive items and wants to change the order limit to $5,000, a rule can be changed easily, but an IfElse activity requires that activity to be changed.

WF provides several ways to model business process logic. You can use the workflow model itself by using activities, you can use rules, or you can use code. You're free to make that determination. There are no set standards for the best way to use each of the methods. The best approach is the one that best models the business process you're trying to replicate.

WF provides two ways to use rules, first as a condition on an activity, second as a forward-chaining RuleSet using the Policy activity. Forward chaining is the ability of actions of one rule to cause another dependent rule to be reevaluated.

WF has four activities to which conditions can be applied: IfElse, While, Replicator, and Conditional Activity Group (CAG). Conditions within one of these activities determine if the activity executes or not. Up to this point, you've used CodeConditions and configured Handlers in the code beside to determine if an activity should be executed. The other option is RuleConditionReference, which points to a RuleCondition definition in a .rules file associated with the workflow. Open the VBIfElseSequentialExample from Chapter 3. Click the Branch1 activity and open the Properties window. You'll see the property called Condition. In the example in Chapter 3, you selected CodeCondition, but if you click the drop-down box you'll see you can choose either Code Condition or Declarative Rule Condition, as shown in Figure 5-1.

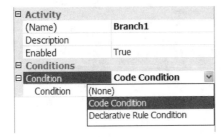

Figure 5-1. *Code Condition or Declarative Rule Condition for the Condition property*

Now, to see the Declarative Rule Condition in action, close the opened project and create a new VB Sequential Workflow Console Application project called VBConditionRulesSequentialConsole. Add a new IfElse activity to the workflow. Rename the left branch GreaterThan0 and the right branch LessThanEqual0. View code for the workflow and add `Private IntValue As Integer = 1` to the workflow class. This variable will be used to determine which branch to execute. View the designer again. Click the GreaterThan0 branch and view the properties. Choose Declarative Rule Condition from the Condition drop-down, as shown in Figure 5-2.

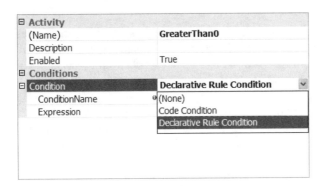

Figure 5-2. *Choose Declarative Rule Condition.*

Click the ellipse next to the ConditionName property when it appears. This brings up the Select Condition dialog box, shown in Figure 5-3.

Click the New Condition button and the Rule Condition Editor appears. This is where you can add your rules to the condition.

When adding rules to a workflow you can use the "this" keyword to access the workflow. Using the "this" keyword, you can access the IntValue variable that was just created within the workflow. Type **this**, followed by a period, to get the intellisense for the workflow. Choose IntValue, as shown in Figure 5-4.

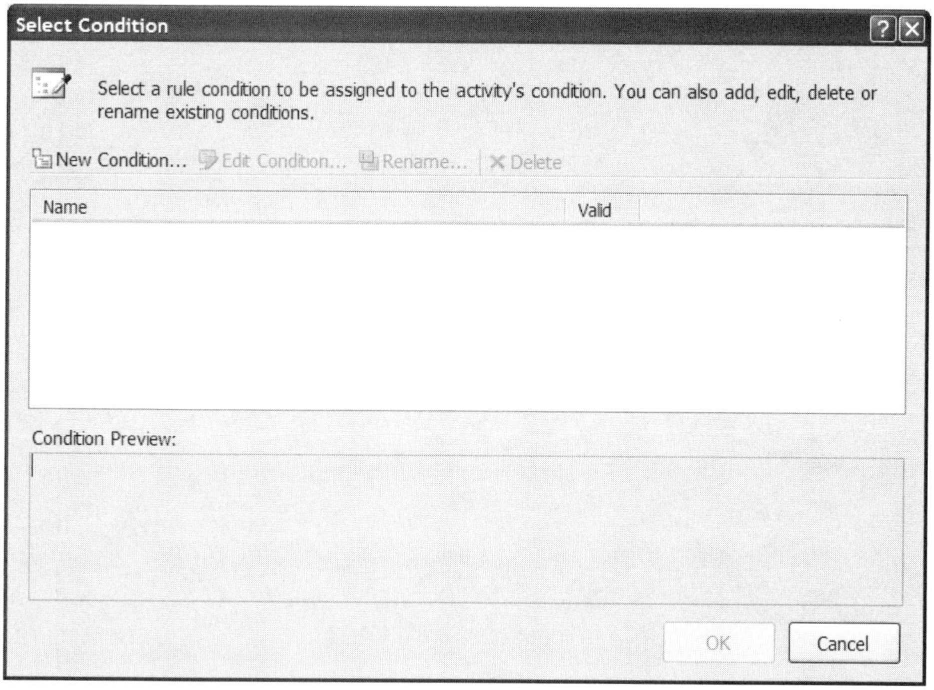

Figure 5-3. *Select Condition dialog box*

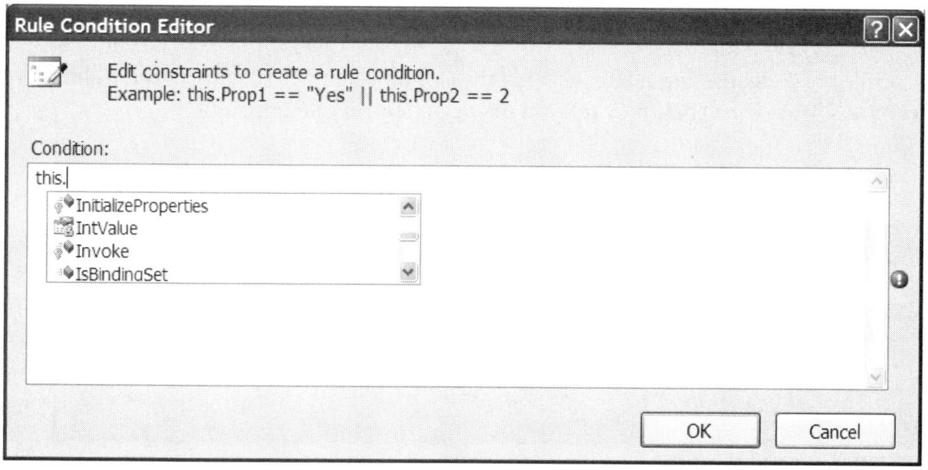

Figure 5-4. *Choose IntValue from the drop-down.*

After you choose IntValue, add >0 so the line reads as follows:

```
this.IntValue>0
```

Click OK to save the condition. You're back at the Select Condition dialog. The condition just created is displayed as Condition1, as shown in Figure 5-5.

Select Condition

Select a rule condition to be assigned to the activity's condition. You can also add, edit, delete or rename existing conditions.

New Condition... 　Edit Condition... 　Rename... 　✕ Delete

Name	Valid
Condition1	Yes

Condition Preview:
this.IntValue > 0

OK   Cancel

Figure 5-5. *Condition1 within the Select Condition dialog*

Notice the Valid column after the name of the condition. This shows whether the condition is valid or not, and whether it will be executed properly You can also preview the condition without entering the condition name by using the Condition Preview. The Condition Preview area is at the bottom of the Select Condition dialog, as shown in Figure 5-6.

Condition Preview:
this.IntValue > 0

OK   Cancel

Figure 5-6. *Condition Preview section of the Select Condition dialog*

Using the buttons at the top of the Select Condition dialog, you can create a new condition, edit an existing condition, rename a condition, or delete a condition. Click OK, and the Select Condition dialog box closes. Open the Properties window for the GreaterThan0 branch and notice the ConditionName and Expression properties. The ConditionName property gives the name of the condition that was just created, and the Expression property gives the statement entered as the rule. Figure 5-7 shows the GreaterThan0 property with the Condition expanded.

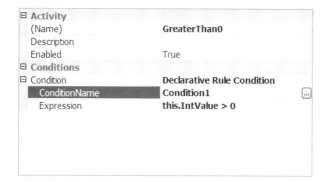

Figure 5-7. *GreaterThan0 property with the Condition property expanded*

Follow the same steps to add a condition to the LessThanEqual0 branch. Use
`this.IntValue <=0` as the condition. After you add the condition in the Rule Condition Editor,
you'll notice there are now two conditions within the Select Condition box. Figure 5-8 shows
the two conditions, and the Condition Preview shows the code for the LessThanEqual0 condition.

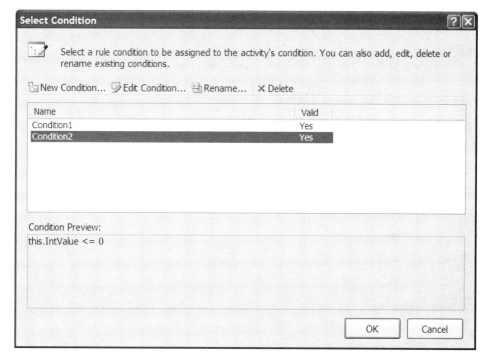

Figure 5-8. *Both conditions with the new condition in the Condition Preview area*

As you can see, the Select Condition dialog shows you all conditions defined for this workflow, not only for the activity you're currently working on. Click OK in the Select Condition
dialog box.

Now that both branches of the IfElse activity have a condition set, add a Code activity to the GreaterThan0 branch called GreaterThan0Code. Generate Handlers for this activity and add the following code:

```
msgbox ("Value greater than 0")
```

The completed code for the generated Handler is as follows:

```
Private Sub GreaterThan0Code_ExecuteCode(ByVal sender As System.Object,
    ByVal e As System.EventArgs)
    MsgBox("Value greater than 0")
End Sub
```

Add a Code activity to the LessThanEqual0 branch called LessThanEqualCode. Generate Handlers for this activity and add the following code:

```
msgbox("Value Less than or Equal 0")
```

Following is the completed code:

```
Private Sub LessThanEqual0Code_ExecuteCode(ByVal sender As System.Object, ByVal e As
    System.EventArgs)
    MsgBox("Value less than or equal 0")
End Sub
```

Now execute the workflow, and you'll see the GreaterThan0 branch was executed.

After the workflow has completed and debugging has stopped, open the Solution Explorer for this project. If you aren't already showing all files, click the second button from the left on the top of the Solution Explorer to view all files for the project. Once you do that, a plus sign appears next to the Workflow1.vb file name. Click it and you'll see two files below it, as shown in Figure 5-9.

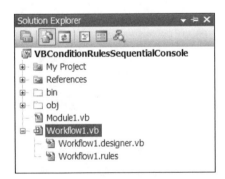

Figure 5-9. *All files within Solution Explorer for Workflow1*

Notice the file called Workflow1.rules. This is the rules file that contains any rules for this workflow. Double-click the file to open it. You'll see that the file is XML. You can find the conditions embedded in the XML file by looking for the RuleExpressionCondition tag:

```
<RuleExpressionCondition Name="Condition1">
```

The first part of the condition, the operator, is spelled out in the OperatorExpression tag. This tag, in this case, is called CodeBinaryOperatorExpression because of the type of operator used. The tag begins with `<ns0:CodeBinaryOperatorExpression Operator="GreaterThan":`

```
<ns0:CodeBinaryOperatorExpression Operator="GreaterThan" xmlns:ns0="clr-
namespace:System.CodeDom;Assembly=System, Version=2.0.0.0, Culture=neutral,
PublicKeyToken=b77a5c561934e089">
```

This shows the operator for this condition and goes on to provide specifics about its type to the .NET Framework. The next tag of interest is the CodeFieldReferenceExpression tag. This tag provides the name of the item being referenced by the condition, in this case IntValue:

```
<ns0:CodeFieldReferenceExpression FieldName="IntValue">
```

Finally, the CodePrimitiveExpression.Value tag provides the value the condition uses to compare against:

```
<ns0:CodePrimitiveExpression.Value>
<ns1:Int32 xmlns:ns1="clr-namespace:System;Assembly=mscorlib, Version=2.0.0.0,
Culture=neutral, PublicKeyToken=b77a5c561934e089">0</ns1:Int32>
<ns0:CodePrimitiveExpression.Value>
```

This rules file is the reason using rules for conditions of IfElse activities is a better way to set conditions. Going back to the original example, if the order-entry business rules change so that special credit checks are done for orders over $5,000 instead of $1,000, you could open this file and change the CodePrimitiveExpression.Value tag to accomplish this rule change. You could perform this change on the fly while the workflow is being executed. Any workflow instance that hadn't yet executed the IfElse activity would use the new condition value. If you used the CodeCondition condition type, the workflow would need to be stopped, the CodeCondition criteria within the IfElse activity changed, and the workflow started again.

Before leaving this topic, I'll provide a list of the operators that can be used within a Rules condition (see Table 5-1).

Table 5-1. *Valid Rules Condition Operators*

Operator	Symbol
Equal	(== or =)
Greater than	>
Greater than or equal	>=
Less than	<
Less than or equal	<=
Addition	+
Subtraction	–
Multiply	*
Divide	/

Table 5-1. *Valid Rules Condition Operators (Continued)*

Operator	Symbol
Modulus	MOD
And add	&&
Or or	||
Not not	!
Bitwise and	&
Bitwise or	|

Creating a rule using this method and using the Condition property works the same for both Sequential workflows and State Machine workflows. The steps are the same for C# and VB as well.

Rules and the Policy Activity

Within WF a Policy activity contains the definition and execution of a RuleSet, which is a collection of rules with a set of execution steps. When you create a RuleSet for a Policy activity, the same types of actions occur as when you create a rule for an activity condition, as previously shown. A rules file is created for the workflow, and all rules are captured in this file. The steps to create the RuleSet are only a little different.

Create a new VB Sequential Workflow Console Application called VBPolicySequentialConsole. Drag a Policy activity onto the Sequential workflow, leaving the default name. View code for the workflow and add the following declaration to the class:

```
Private IntValue As Integer = 1
```

Click the Policy activity and view the properties. Find the RuleSetReference property, as shown in Figure 5-10.

This property points to the RuleSet this Policy activity will use. This is similar to the example earlier, with the IfElse activity pointing to a Rule. In this case, a RuleSet is made up of one or more rules. Click the ellipse next to the RuleSetReference property, and the Select Rule Set dialog box appears.

To create a RuleSet for this Policy activity, click the New RuleSet button, which opens the Rule Set Editor, as shown in Figure 5-11. This editor allows you to add multiple rules to the RuleSet.

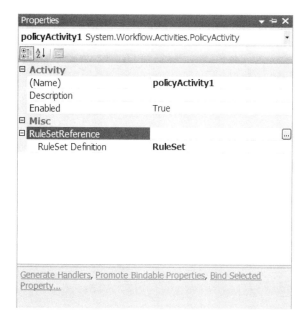

Figure 5-10. *RuleSetReference property*

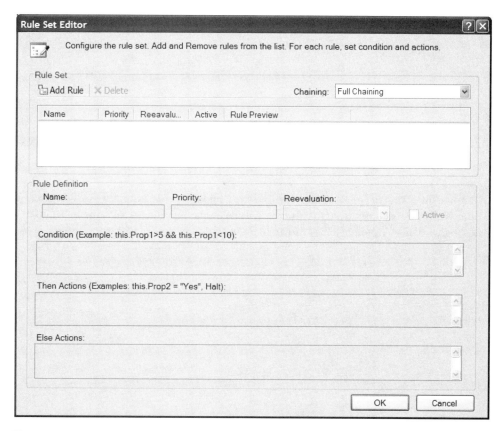

Figure 5-11. *Rule Set Editor*

Click the Add Rule button. A new rule called Rule1 is added to the list, and you can begin to edit the rule. The Rule Set Editor looks like Figure 5-12.

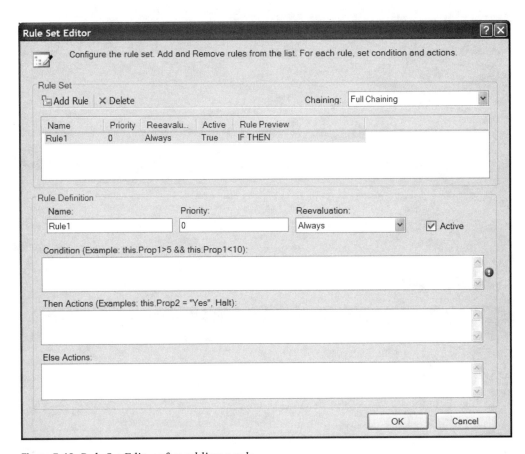

Figure 5-12. *Rule Set Editor after adding a rule*

Change the Name to GreaterThan0. Within the Condition area, enter **this.IntValue>0**. In the Then Actions area, enter **this.IntValue=0**. This rule sets the value of IntValue to 0 if it's greater than 0. The completed rule is shown in Figure 5-13.

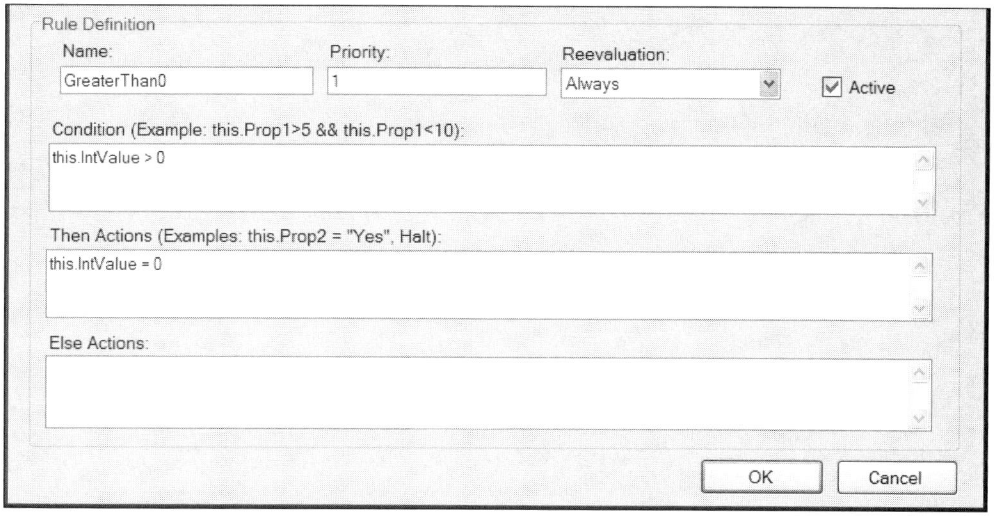

Figure 5-13. *GreaterThan0 rule definition*

Click OK in the Rule Set Editor and on the Select Rule Set dialog boxes. Add a Code activity before the Policy activity called BeforePolicyCode. Generate Handlers for the Code activity and add `msgbox("Before Policy: " & IntValue)` to the code generated. Here's the code:

```
Private Sub BeforePolicyCode_ExecuteCode(ByVal sender As System.Object,
    ByVal e As System.EventArgs)
    MsgBox("Before Policy: " & IntValue)
End Sub
```

Add a Code activity after the Policy activity called AfterPolicyCode. Generate Handlers for the Code activity and add `msgbox("After Policy: " & IntValue)` to the code generated. The code for this sub is as follows:

```
Private Sub AfterPolicyCode_ExecuteCode(ByVal sender As System.Object,
    ByVal e As System.EventArgs)
    MsgBox("After Policy: " & IntValue)
End Sub
```

This simple example shows the value in IntValue before and after the Policy activity is executed. Execute the workflow. The first message box will have the value of 1 and the second the value of 0. This is because the condition was met, and the value was changed as a result of the execution of the Then Actions box. View the code of the workflow and set the default for IntValue to be 0. Execute the workflow again. This time both message boxes show 0. That's because the first rule didn't execute the Then Action because the condition wasn't met.

Open the RuleSet for the Policy activity again. Add a new rule called Equal0. Add `this.IntValue==0` (be sure to use two equal signs) to the condition box and `this.IntValue=-1` to the Then Actions area. Figure 5-14 shows the completed Equal0 rule definition.

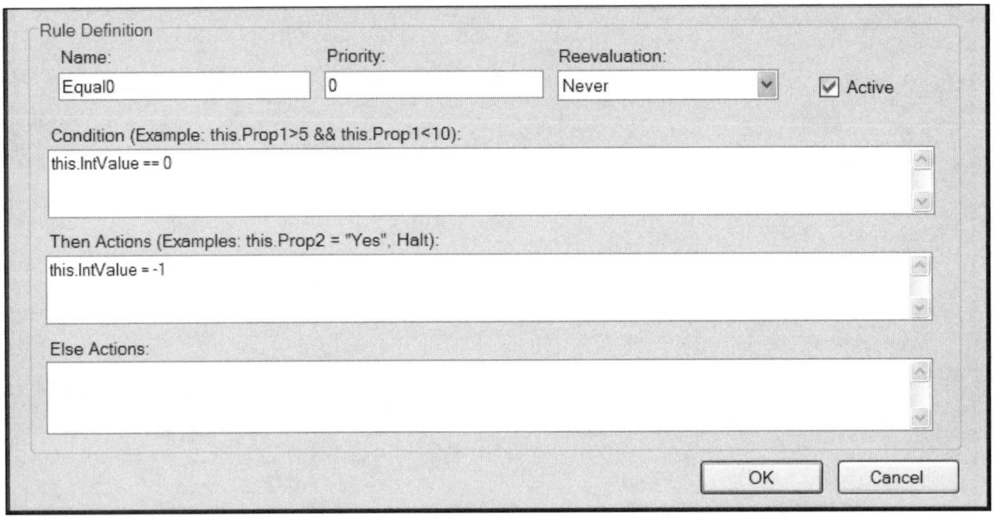

Figure 5-14. *Equal0 rule definition*

Execute the workflow. You'll see the value is 0 before the Policy activity but -1 afterward. The Equal0 rule within the RuleSet is the one that was executed.

Each rule in the RuleSet has a priority value (next to the name), with a default of 0. The rules within a RuleSet are a list of rules sorted by priority. The rule with the highest priority value is evaluated first. Next, the Then or Else action is executed. If the condition evaluates to Else and there's no Else action, then the next rule is evaluated. Also, if an action of a rule updates a field or property used by a previous rule (one with a higher priority), the previous rule is reevaluated and actions are taken as necessary. This continues until all rules within the RuleSet are evaluated.

Sequential Chaining

There's also a Chaining property for a RuleSet. You'll find this as a drop-down at the top right of the Rule Set Editor. Chaining sets the dependencies between rules. The simplest chaining is Sequential. With this option selected, each rule is evaluated in order based on the priority. To see this in action, view the code and change the default value of IntValue to 1. Then change the Then Action of the Equal0 rule to set IntValue to 1. Execute the workflow. You'll see the value is 1 before the Policy activity, but 0 after the Policy activity. This isn't what you would expect. The GreaterThan0 rule sets the value to 0, and the Equal0 rule sets the value to 1. The rules within the RuleSet are to be executed in order. The problem is that the priority of both rules is 0. So only the first rule in that priority is executed when using Sequential chaining. Open the Rule Set Editor again. Change the priority of the GreaterThan0 rule to 1 and set the Chaining to Sequential chaining. With this change, the GreaterThan0 rule, with a priority of 1, is executed first and sets the value to 0. Then, the Equal0 rule, with a priority of 0, is executed and changes the value to 1. Execute the workflow, and you'll see that the value is 1 both before and after the Policy activity.

Within the Then Actions and Else Actions areas of a rule, you can use the Halt command. This can be the only command within the box or included with others. The Halt command prevents further execution of rules within the RuleSet. To see this, open the Rule Set Editor and edit the GreaterThan0 rule. After the `this.IntValue=0` statements within the Then Actions box, add **Halt**. The rule definition now looks like Figure 5-15.

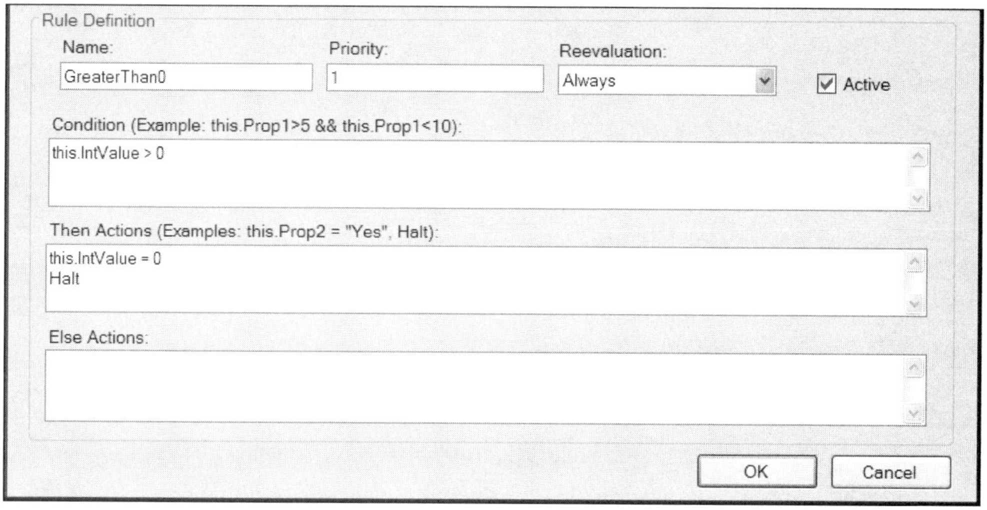

Figure 5-15. *Rule definition with Halt in the Then Actions*

Execute the workflow, and you'll see before the Policy activity the value is 1, and after the Policy activity the value is 0. That's different from the last execution of the workflow. Besides simply setting values, you can also call methods defined within the workflow from the Then Actions and Else Actions of a rule. View the code and add the following lines of code:

```
Private Sub GreaterThan0()
    MsgBox("Greater than 0")
End Sub
```

Open the Rule Set Editor and edit the GreaterThan0 rule. Remove the Halt statement from the Then Actions area and replace it with `this.GreaterThan0()`. Figure 5-16 shows the updated Then Actions area.

Make sure you have the parenthesis at the end; otherwise, you'll get an error message when you attempt to click OK on the Rule Set Editor. The Rule Set Editor is case sensitive with regard to properties and methods. This means you must use the exact same case for properties, and you must add the parenthesis after a method call. Execute the workflow. You'll get the "before Policy activity" message, the "Greater than 0" message, and the "after Policy activity" message. Of course, you can use the ability to call a method to do more than just display a message box. You can also call a method to set values or retrieve data.

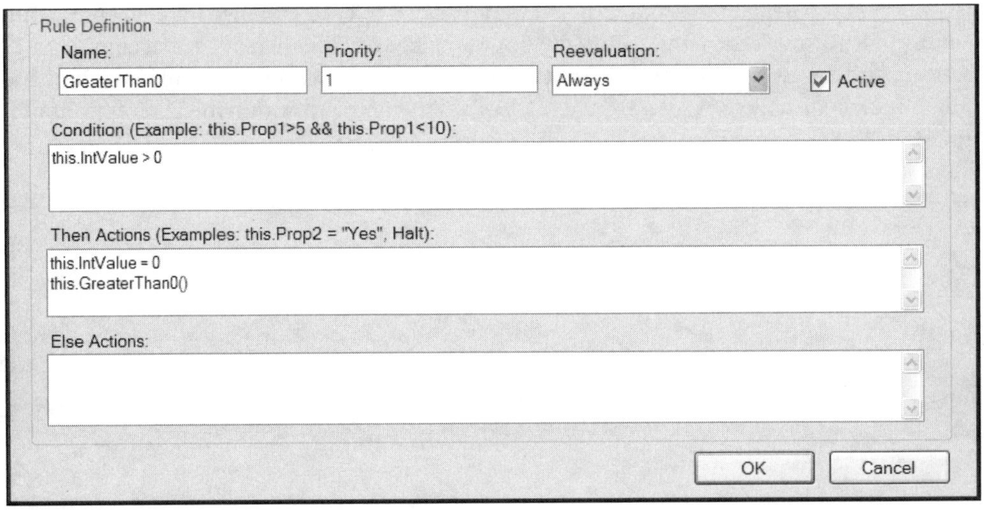

Figure 5-16. *Revised Then Actions with GreaterThan0*

Full Chaining

The preceding set of examples used the Sequential chaining property. Another option for chaining is Full. This means all dependencies might be evaluated multiple times. Open the Rule Set Editor and edit the GreaterThan0 rule. Notice there's an option for Reevaluate. Your options are Always or Never. If you choose Always, each rule that executes after this rule will cause this rule to reevaluate. You need to be careful with this option. If you don't use this option correctly, you'll end up in an infinite loop. Remove the `this.IntValue=0` statement from the Then Actions area of the GreaterThan0 rule, but leave the method call to GreaterThan0. Change the Chaining property to Full chaining. Close the Rule Set Editor and view the code for the workflow. Change the statement within the GreaterThan0 sub to be `IntValue=0`:

```
Private Sub GreaterThan0()
    IntValue=0
End Sub
```

Execute the workflow. You'll see the "before Policy" message box appear, but that will be all. The other message box won't appear. This is because the rules are in an infinite loop. Because both the rules within the RuleSet have their reevaluate property set to Always and the chaining is Full, each time a rule executes the other rule is reevaluated. The GreaterThan0 rule, which executes first, sets the value to 0, and the Equal0 rule, which executes second, sets the value to 1. When the Equal0 rule sets the value to 1, the GreaterThan0 rule is reevaluated because of the Always Reevaluate property.

Open the Rule Set Editor again and change the Reevaluate property of the Equal0 rule to Never. When the rules are executed this time, the GreaterThan0 rule will set the value to 1, the Equal0 rule will set the value to 0, and the GreaterThan0 rule will be reevaluated and set the value to 1. The Equal0 rule won't be reevaluated, and won't change the value. Execute the workflow to see this happen. Before the Policy activity, the value is 1, and after the Policy activity, the value is 0.

Real-World Example

In this chapter, to make the IfElse activities easier to change, you're going to remove the CodeConditions from all the IfElse activities within the Purchase Order application and replace them with Declarative Rule Conditions. By doing this, if the workflow was in production, the rules could be changed on the fly without needing to redistribute the application or even rebuild the application. Instead, the rules file could be changed.

To begin, open the VBPurchaseOrderConsole application. Open the PurchaseOrderProcess workflow and click each of the left and right branches of the various IfElse activities. Change the Condition property to None for now. After you change the CodeCondition to None, you'll see a red exclamation point appear near that branch of the IfElse activity, as shown in Figure 5-17.

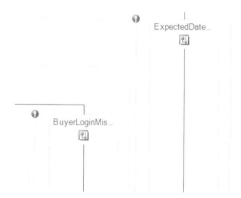

Figure 5-17. *Red exclamation points after changing CodeCondition to None*

The next step is to go to each IfElse activity branch and add the necessary condition. To do this, you need the code that defines the condition within the workflow code. For example, view the code for the workflow and find the sub PartNumberPresentCondition. This sub has the following condition, which needs to be evaluated for this branch:

```
e.Result = StrPartNumber <> String.Empty
```

You don't need the e.Result portion, only the part after the equal sign. Copy this condition and then view the workflow again. Click the PurchaseDatePresent branch of the CheckPurchaseDate IfElse activity. Change the Condition to Declarative Rule Condition and expand the Condition property, as shown in Figure 5-18.

Click the ellipse next to the ConditionName property to open the Select Condition dialog. Click New Condition to get to the Rule Condition Editor. Paste the condition that you copied from the code (StrPartNumber <> String.Empty) into the Rule Condition Editor, as shown in Figure 5-19. Click OK.

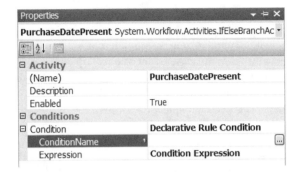

Figure 5-18. *PurchaseDatePresent branch with Declarative Rule Condition property*

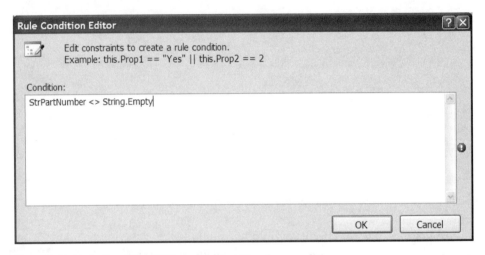

Figure 5-19. *Rule Condition Editor with Part Number condition*

When the Rule Condition Editor closes and you're looking at the Select Condition dialog, notice the Condition Preview shows the condition as `this.StrPartNumber!=String.Empty`. The Rule Condition Editor took care of cleaning up the code. While you're in the Select Condition dialog, click the Rename button. When the Rename Condition dialog appears, enter PartNumberPresent as the "New name for condition," as shown in Figure 5-20. This gives the condition a more meaningful name than Condition1. Click OK after entering the name. The new name appears in the Select Condition dialog.

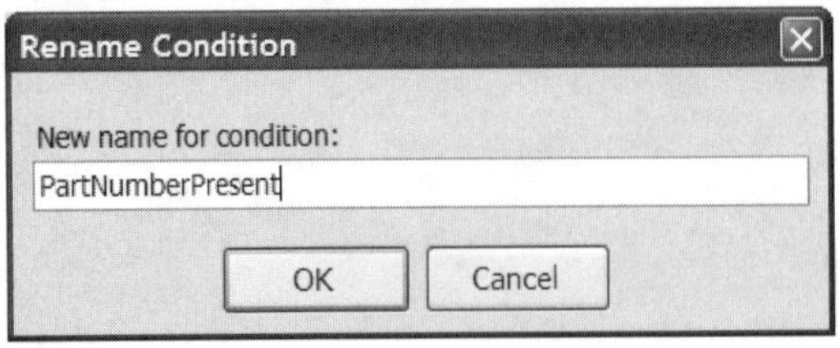

Figure 5-20. *Rename the condition to PartNumberPresent*

Click OK in the Select Condition dialog, then click the PartNumberPresent branch again and view the properties. The properties now include a reference to the condition name PartNumberPresent, and include the expression, as shown in Figure 5-21.

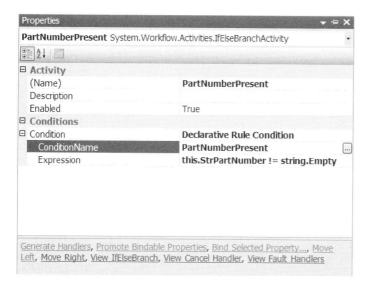

Figure 5-21. *PartNumberPresent properties*

Finally, view the code for the workflow and find the PartNumberPresentCondition sub. Delete this sub, as it's no longer needed. The new Declarative Rule Condition replaced this condition. Continue the following steps for the remaining branches of the IfElse activities:

1. Change the Condition property to Declarative Rule Condition from Code Condition.

2. Click the ellipse next to the ConditionName property to get the Select Condition dialog.

3. Click the New Condition button.

4. Enter the condition that was used in the Condition sub previously.

5. Click OK in the Rule Condition Editor.

6. Click the newly created rule and click the Rename button to rename the rule.

7. Enter the new name of the rule in the Rename Condition dialog.

8. Click OK in the Rename Condition dialog and in the Select Condition dialog.

9. Remove the Condition sub from the workflow code.

When all the conditions have been set, the Select Condition dialog will look like Figure 5-22.

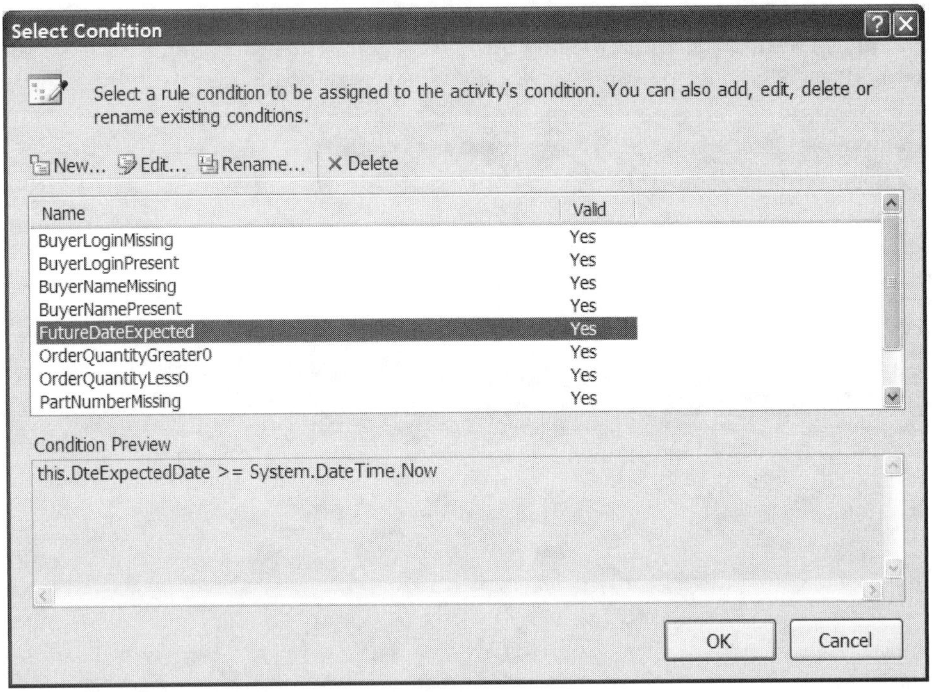

Figure 5-22. *Completed Select Condition dialog*

When you view the code of the PurchaseOrderProcess workflow, the Condition subs are no longer needed. The PurchaseOrderProcess workflow code should only include the read-only properties:

```
Public ReadOnly Property MissingPartNumberError() As String
     Get
          Return "Part Number is required when entering a Purchase Order"
     End Get
End Property
Public ReadOnly Property MissingPurchaseDateError() As String
     Get
          Return "Purchase Date is required when entering a Purchase Order"
     End Get
End Property
Public ReadOnly Property MissingExpectedDateError() As String
     Get
          Return "Expected Date is required when entering a Purchase Order"
     End Get
End Property
Public ReadOnly Property MissingBuyerLoginError() As String
     Get
          Return "Buyer Login is required when entering a Purchase Order"
     End Get
End Property
```

```
Public ReadOnly Property MissingBuyerNameError() As String
    Get
        Return "Buyer Name is required when entering a Purchase Order"
    End Get
End Property
Public ReadOnly Property ExpectedDateInPastError() As String
    Get
        Return "When entering a Purchase Order expected date must be in the future"
    End Get
End Property
Public ReadOnly Property OrderQuantityNotGreater0Error() As String
    Get
        Return "When entering a Purchase Order the quantity must be greater than 0"
    End Get
End Property
```

The write-only properties should also be included:

```
Public WriteOnly Property PartNumber() As String
    Set(ByVal value As String)
        StrPartNumber = value
    End Set
End Property
Public WriteOnly Property PurchaseDate() As Date
    Set(ByVal value As Date)
        DtePurchaseDate = value
    End Set
End Property
Public WriteOnly Property ExpectedDate() As Date
    Set(ByVal value As Date)
        DteExpectedDate = value
    End Set
End Property
Public WriteOnly Property BuyerLogin() As String
    Set(ByVal value As String)
        StrBuyerLogin = value
    End Set
End Property
Public WriteOnly Property BuyerName() As String
    Set(ByVal value As String)
        StrBuyerName = value
    End Set
End Property
Public WriteOnly Property QuantityOrdered() As Integer

    Set(ByVal value As Integer)
        IntQuantityOrdered = value
    End Set
End Property
```

```
Public ReadOnly Property PurchaseOrderNumber() As String
    Get
        Return StrPurchaseOrderNumber
    End Get
End Property
```

Finally, execute the workflow and enter an expected date that's in the past. You should get the error message "When entering a Purchase Order expected date must be in the future." This shows that the rules were evaluated and the ExpectedDateInPast Terminate activity was executed.

Conclusion

This chapter introduced the concept of rules-based workflows and how they can be accommodated in WF. First, this chapter looked at using rules within conditions of an IfElse activity and then looked at the Policy activity. This chapter explained how to use the Rule Set Editor to define rules that can be used within a Policy activity. The real-world example in this chapter showed how to change the Purchase Order application built in previous chapters to use Declarative Rule Condition instead of Code Condition. The next chapter will cover workflow and Web services.

CHAPTER 6

■■■

Workflow and Web Services

Windows Workflow Foundation provides an activity to work with Web services, as well as several activities that allow your workflow to become a Web service. Web services are slowly becoming more prevalent in applications, especially with the usage of Service-Oriented Architecture (SOA). This chapter will introduce the InvokeWebService activity, which allows you to work with an existing Web service. I'll also introduce three other activities—WebServiceInput, WebServiceOutput, and WebServiceFault—that allow you to create your workflow as a Web service.

InvokeWebService Activity

In this chapter, I'm not going to argue the pros and cons of using Web services. Web services are an architectural component that many developers use in their applications, although many other developers don't. Plenty of books and articles are available about Web services and the use of them. This chapter will concentrate on using a Web service from within workflow using the InvokeWebService activity.

You can use the InvokeWebService activity in both the Sequential and State Machine workflows. It's similar to using a Web service in any other .NET application. First, you must reference the Web service, then you can access it. This section of the chapter will demonstrate a simple Web service that simply returns a value of True. Although this is impractical in the real world, it gives a good example of how the interaction works. At the end of this chapter, I'll show a more practical use of this activity.

The first step in this example is to create a simple Web service. The completed Web service, SimpleWebService, is included with the code download. However, if you wish to build the Web service, here are the steps to do it. If you aren't familiar with Web services, you can find an introduction to Web services in Chapter 10 of my book *Beginning Object-Oriented ASP.NET 2.0 with VB.NET* (Apress, 2005).

Create a new Web site, choose ASP.NET Web Service, and call the service SimpleWebService. When the Web service is created, open the Service.vb file if it isn't already open. Replace the HelloWorld default Web method with the following:

```
Public Function IsUser(ByVal UserName As String) As Boolean
    If UserName = "Brian" Then
        Return True
    Else
        Return False
    End If
End Function
```

Build the Web service, then close the project. To test the Web service, enter **http://localhost/ SimpleWebService/Service.asmx** in your Web browser. The Service Web Service default page appears, listing the Web methods (IsUser). Click the IsUser link, enter **Brian** as the UserName parameter, and click Invoke. An XML document appears in a new browser window; it says True. Close the XML document window, enter **Me** as the UserName parameter, and click Invoke. This time the XML document contains False. This shows the Web service is working correctly.

Create a new VB Sequential Workflow Console Application called VBWebServiceSequentialConsole. Drag an InvokeWebService activity onto the Workflow Designer. As soon as the activity is added to the workflow, the Add Web Reference window appears. Click the Web Services on the Local Machine link. A list of the Web services on the local machine is listed here. Find the link with the URL listed as http://localhost/SimpleWebService/Service.asmx. The Services column lists Service. Click the URL. The Service default page appears as it did in the browser previously. Change the Web Reference Name to SimpleWebService and click the Add Reference button. This is the same as adding a Web Reference to a VB or C# application.

After the Add Web Reference window closes, click the InvokeWebService activity and view the properties. Change the name to InvokeSimpleWebService. Click the MethodName property and choose IsUser from the drop-down. Each InvokeWebService activity allows you to interact with one Web method exposed by the Web service. Once you choose IsUser, the (ReturnValue) and UserName properties appear under Parameters, as shown in Figure 6-1. These two properties allow you to provide values or variable names that contain the values to send to the Web method when it's called.

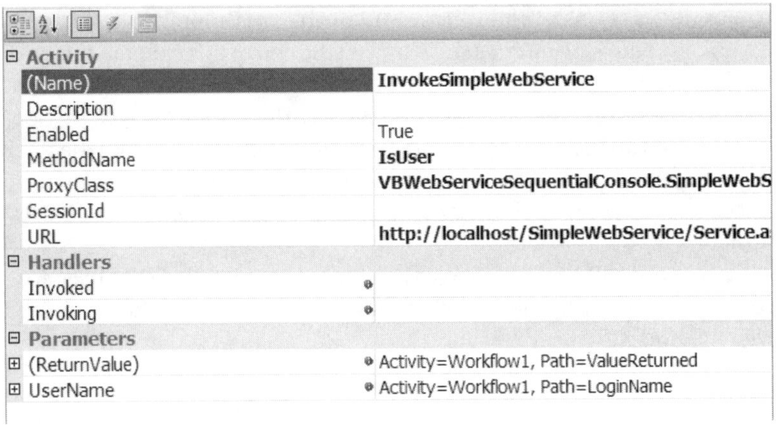

Figure 6-1. *InvokeSimpleWebService properties*

View the code for the workflow to add the necessary variables. Add the following code within the workflow class declaration:

```
Public LoginName As String = "Brian"
Public ValueReturned As Boolean = False
```

Return to the Workflow Designer, click the InvokeSimpleWebService activity, and view the properties. Click the ellipse next to the UserName property. This opens the Bind to Property window. Choose LoginName from the tree under Workflow1, as shown in Figure 6-2.

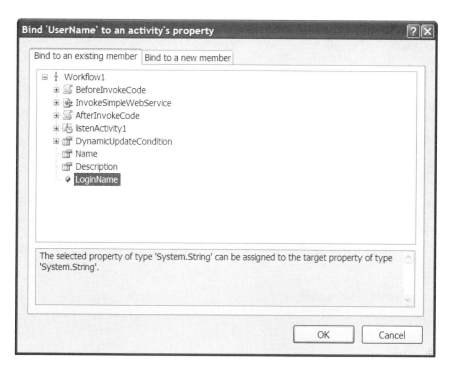

Figure 6-2. *Choose LoginName as an existing member to bind to.*

Right-click the (ReturnValue) property name and choose Commands if it's not already selected. You should now see a Promote Bindable Properties link at the bottom of the Properties window. Click the Promote Bindable Properties link. A default value is placed in the Return Value property. Click the ellipse next to the Return Value property; this brings up the Bind Property window again. Choose ValueReturned from the list under Workflow1, as shown in Figure 6-3.

The Parameters properties for InvokeSimpleWebService look like Figure 6-4.

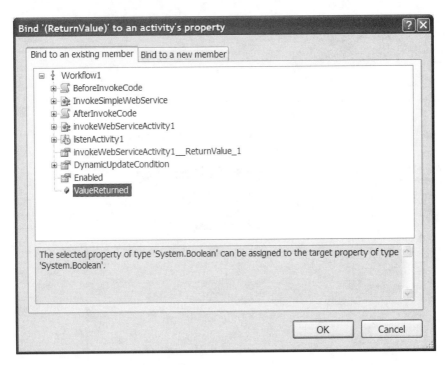

Figure 6-3. *Select the ValueReturned property.*

(Name)	**InvokeSimpleWebService**
Description	
Enabled	True
MethodName	**IsUser**
ProxyClass	**VBWebServiceSequentialConsole.Sim**
SessionId	
URL	**http://localhost/SimpleWebService/S**
⊟ Handlers	
Invoked	◉
Invoking	◉
⊟ Parameters	
⊟ (ReturnValue)	◉ Activity=Workflow1, Path=ValueReturned
Name	**Workflow1**
Path	**ValueReturned**
⊟ UserName	Activity=Workflow1, Path=LoginName [...]
Name	**Workflow1**
Path	**LoginName**

Figure 6-4. *Parameters properties with ReturnValue and UserName set*

Drag a Code activity onto the Workflow Designer before the InvokeSimpleWebService activity. Call this Code activity BeforeInvokeCode, generate Handlers for the activity, and add the following code to the sub generated:

```
MsgBox("Before Invoke: " & ValueReturned)
```

This displays a message box with the value of blnReturn prior to the Web service being called. Next, drag a Code activity onto the Workflow Designer after the InvokeSimpleWebService. Call this Code activity AfterInvokeCode, generate Handlers for the activity, and add the following code to the sub generated:

```
MsgBox("After Invoke: " & ValueReturned)
```

Execute the workflow, and you'll see the Before box appear with False and the After box appear with True. This shows that the workflow called out to the Web service providing the variable LoginName as a parameter, and received the parameter ValueReturned back.

As with many of the other examples so far, there's little change between the Sequential workflow and the State Machine workflow. The only difference is that the InvokeWebService activity must be placed inside an EventDriven activity, like any other activity within a State Machine workflow. Also, the logic behind the code is the same between VB and C#.

Workflow As Web Service

Using the WebServiceInput, WebServiceOutput, and WebServiceFault activities, you can expose your workflow as a Web service. This has some advantages, especially within an SOA environment, and when deploying a Windows-based application instead of a Web-based application. This section will show an example of a simple workflow that's exposed as a Web service.

First, create a VB Sequential Workflow Library called VBAsWebServiceSequentialLibrary. This is the first library application built in this book; make sure you select Sequential Workflow Library. Change the name of the Workflow1.vb file to WorkflowAsService.vb. Open the workflow file (WorkflowAsService.vb) and view the code. Add `Public ValueEntered As Integer` to the workflow class declaration. This variable holds the inputted value and allows manipulation of it. Next, you must define the interface that will be exposed. An interface is what other applications wanting to use this Web service will see. It defines any methods or properties that other applications can use to interact with the Web service, and is a core OOP concept. To define the interface, add the following:

```
Public Interface IWorkflowAsWebService
    Function AcceptValue(ByVal InputValue As Integer) As Integer
End Interface
```

Any application wanting to use this Web service will see only the AcceptValue method, and will see that this method expects a parameter that is of type Integer. Next, view the designer and add a WebServiceInput activity to the workflow. Leave the default name, but click the ellipse next to Interface Type. This displays a window that allows you to pick a .NET Type. You want to select the interface that was just defined. You can do this by clicking the Current Project folder on the left and selecting the defined interface, as shown in Figure 6-5.

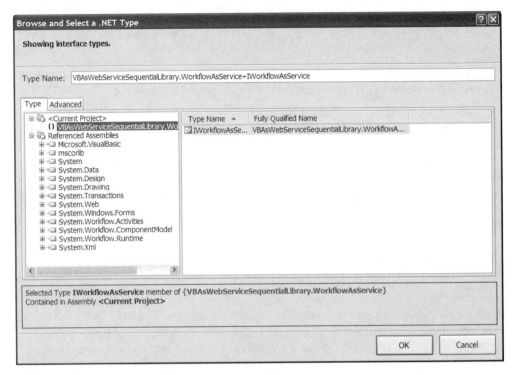

Figure 6-5. *Select the newly defined IWorkflowAsService interface.*

Set IsActivating to True, because the first WebServiceInput activity within a workflow must have the IsActivating property set to True. From the drop-down list next to the Method Name property, choose AcceptValue. This links the call to the WebServiceInput activity to the interface. When an application using this Web service makes a call to this Web service and executes AcceptValue, the workflow engine will know to call this WebServiceInput activity. Finally, from the drop-down next to InputValue under the parameters, select IntInputValue. Click the Promote Bindable Properties link at the bottom of the Properties window. Click the ellipse next to the InputValue property and choose ValueEntered from the Bind Properties dialog box. This ties the value passed in as a parameter to AcceptValue to the ValueEntered variable defined within the workflow. The properties of the WebServiceInput activity look like Figure 6-6.

Add a WebServiceOutput activity to the workflow. Leave the name as the default. Use the drop-down next to InputActivityName to select WebServiceInputActivity1. This property ties the two activities together, so the input activity is receiving information, the output is sending the information, and it's the same information. Click the Promote Bindable Properties link at the bottom of the Properties window. Click the ellipse next to the Return Value property and choose ValueEntered from the Bind Properties dialog box. Again, this ties the value returning to the application that calls this Web service to the variable declared within this class.

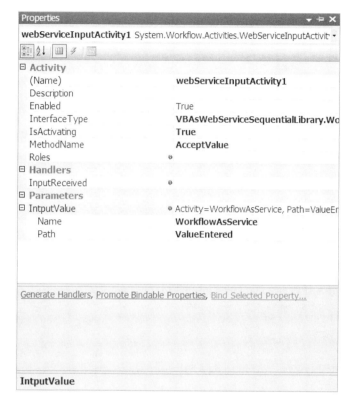

Figure 6-6. *Properties for the WebServiceInput activity*

Next, click GenerateHandlers at the bottom of the Properties window. This generates code to be executed when the activity is executed. When the sub is created, add `IntInputValue = IntInputValue + 10`. This simply adds 10 to the value provided by the calling application. Now the workflow is complete. The workflow will accept a value, add 10 to that value, and return it to the calling application. This simple example shows how you can use a workflow as a Web service.

The final step to make a workflow into a Web service is to publish the workflow as a Web service. To do this, right-click the project name within the Solution Explorer and choose Publish as Web Service. A solution is created within the Solution Explorer, and all the necessary files are also created. To view the created Web service, right-click the file with the ASMX extension (VBAsWebServiceSequentialLibrary.WorkflowAsService_WebService.asmx) and choose View In Browser. This opens the ASMX file in the browser. Click the AcceptValue link to test the AcceptValue method. Enter **10** as the InputValue and click the Invoke button. The result of 20 appears in the XML file. This shows the workflow working as a Web service.

Conclusion

This chapter covered how to interact with a Web service and how to create a workflow to be used as a Web service. The next chapter will discuss how to interact with a workflow from a Windows application.

CHAPTER 7

■ ■ ■

Interacting with Workflow

This chapter will cover how to interact with a workflow from a Windows or ASP.NET application. The previous chapters have explained the various types of workflow and all the activities that can be used within a workflow. The previous chapters have also shown a simple example of how to use each type of activity and workflow. Beginning with this chapter, you'll start to build more complex workflows and learn to create a real-world application from a workflow. Besides showing you how to interact with a workflow, this chapter will also cover how to handle faults within workflows, and how to roll back work already performed by a workflow if a fault occurs.

Workflow Messaging

WF implements a messaging event system between workflows and the runtime host. The communication is defined by an interface, and is implemented in a service class that's added to the runtime. WF uses two ways to handle events. The first is DoSomething/SomethingDone using a local service. Using this means of interaction requires a method invoked on a local service and an event raised back to provide feedback on the success or failure of the workflow. Using this scenario, the local service begins a thread that performs the necessary work. That thread raises the event to indicate completion. The second means of interaction is a generic inbound event scenario. This scenario can be used most often with State Machine workflows. The reason is that this type of scenario is best for cases where you don't know the length of time needed to do the work. For example, if a supervisor receives an employee performance review to examine and approve, the review might wait with the supervisor for an extended period of time before the supervisor acts on the review.

CallExternalMethod Activity in VB

Create a new VB Sequential Workflow Console Application called VBCommunicationSequentialConsoleApplication. Open Module1.vb and add the following lines to the top of the code page:

```
Imports System.Threading
Imports System.Workflow.Runtime
Imports System.Workflow.Activities
```

Add a new, empty class to the project called ReviewService.vb. This is the local service that will act as the intermediary between the workflow and a Windows form. The first step is to define the interface and to add the ExternalDataExchange attribute to the interface. That way, the workflow knows this interface defines the communication between the class and the workflow. To do this, add the following code above the Public Class declaration (at the top of the code page):

```
<ExternalDataExchange()> _
Public Interface IReview
Function CreateReview(ByVal Reviewer As String, ByVal Reviewee As String) As Boolean
End Interface
```

This code defines the interface called IReview with a function called CreateReview. The workflow uses this interface to create an initial performance review, and accepts two parameters: Reviewer and Reviewee. The interface is now defined, but there's no code associated with the interface. To do this, change the public class declaration for ReviewService to the following:

```
Public Class ReviewService: Implements IReview
```

When you do this, a function definition for CreateReview will automatically be created. If the definition isn't automatically created, use the following code to define the sub:

```
Public Function CreateReview(ByVal Reviewer As String, ByVal Reviewee As String)
As Boolean Implements IReview.CreateReview
```

Within this definition, notice the parameters are listed as they were in the interface and at the end of the definition line as Implements IReview.CreateReview. This code shows that this function is going to implement the function CreateReview that was defined within the interface. For a simple example, add the following code to the CreateReview function:

```
Msgbox("Reviewer: " & Reviewer)
Return True
```

The ReviewService.vb file should now contain the following code:

```
<ExternalDataExchange()> _
Public Interface IReview
Function CreateReview(ByVal Reviewer As String, ByVal Reviewee As String) As Boolean
    Event ReviewApproved()
    Event ReviewNotApproved()
End Interface
Public Class ReviewService : Implements IReview

Public Function CreateReview(ByVal Reviewer As String, ByVal Reviewee As String) As
    Boolean Implements IReview.CreateReview
    MsgBox("Reviewer: " & StrReviewer)
    Return True
End Function
End Class
```

Now that the you've defined the service class, you can define the workflow. The activity that calls methods outside the workflow is the CallExternalMethod activity. This activity is used to call methods defined within an interface of type ExternalDataExchange. This is the reason for the first line of the IReview interface declaration <ExternalDataExchange>. This is an attribute that defines the interface as being of type ExternalDataExchange. Add a CallExternalMethod activity to Workflow1 using the designer. Change the name to CallCreateReview. The properties for the CallExternalMethod are shown in Figure 7-1.

Figure 7-1. *CallCreateReview properties*

Click the ellipse next to the InterfaceType property for this activity. The type selection dialog box appears, as shown in Figure 7-2.

Notice the statement "Showing interfaces marked with an ExternalDataExchangeAttribute." Only the interfaces that were defined with the ExternalDataExchange attribute are shown in this list. If you didn't add the attribute to the beginning of the interface declaration, you won't see a type listed. If you did add the attribute, you'll see IReview as the only interface defined within the current project in this list. Select IReview, as shown in Figure 7-3, and click OK.

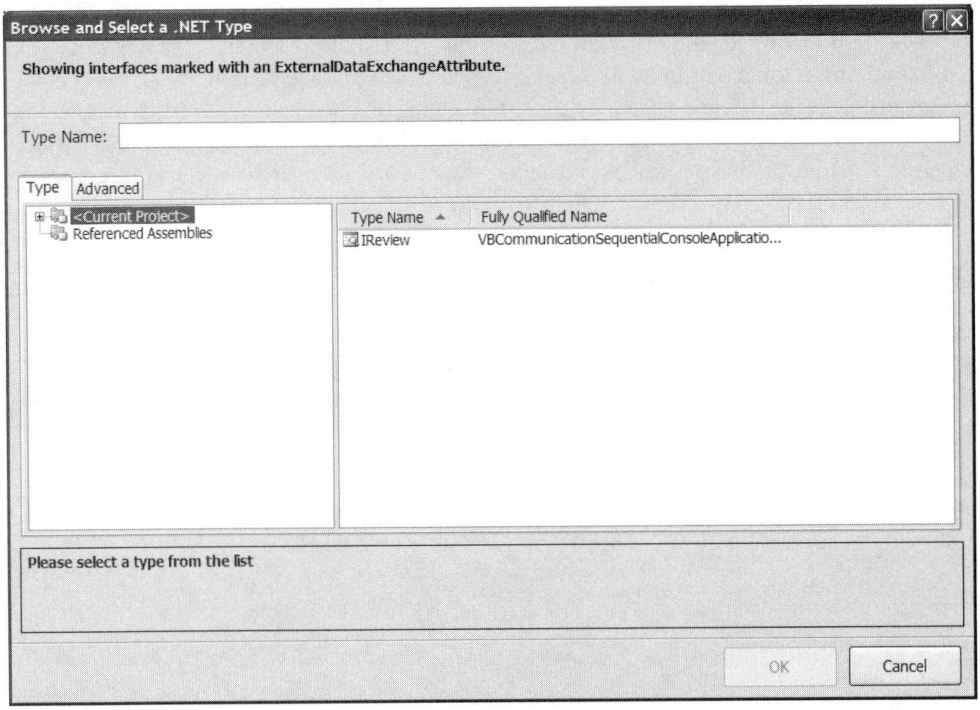

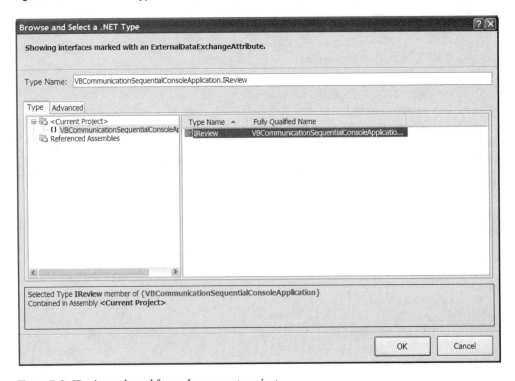

Figure 7-2. *Select a .NET type.*

Figure 7-3. *IReview selected from the current project*

From the MethodName property, choose CreateReview. The Parameters properties appear, as shown in Figure 7-4.

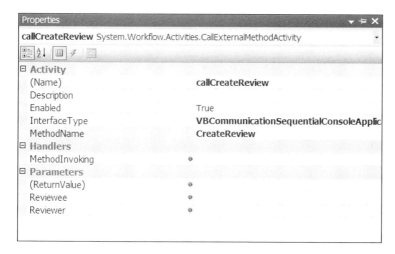

Figure 7-4. *Select MethodName and note Parameters are available.*

Enter **You** for the Reviewee property and **Me** for the Reviewer property. For now, don't be concerned with the return value.

Finally, the workflow runtime must know the ReviewService class. To do this, you must add the service class as a service to the runtime. Open Module1.vb again and add the following two lines within Sub Main after the Using statement:

```
Dim LocalService As New ReviewService
workflowRuntime.AddService(LocalService)
```

This code creates a new instance of the ReviewService, which defines an interface and the class to handle that interface. The second line adds the instance of that service to the workflow runtime. Following is the entire Sub Main code:

```
Shared Sub Main()
    Using workflowRuntime As New WorkflowRuntime()
    Dim LocalService As New ReviewService
    workflowRuntime.AddService(LocalService)
    AddHandler workflowRuntime.WorkflowCompleted, AddressOf OnWorkflowCompleted
    AddHandler workflowRuntime.WorkflowTerminated, AddressOf OnWorkflowTerminated
    Dim workflowInstance As WorkflowInstance
    workflowInstance = workflowRuntime.CreateWorkflow(GetType(Workflow1))
    workflowInstance.Start()
    WaitHandle.WaitOne()
    End Using
End Sub
```

After adding this code, the workflow runtime will recognize the ReviewService class as a service class that defines a communication channel with the workflow. Add a breakpoint to the fourth line of code just added:

```
workflowRuntime.AddService(LocalService)
```

Also, open ReviewService.vb and add a breakpoint to the message box line. Execute the workflow, and when the first breakpoint is encountered, the workflow runtime will add a copy of the ReviewService class to the runtime as a service. The workflow runtime then creates an instance of the workflow. The CallExternalMethod activity is encountered, then the message box within the CreateReview function is encountered. The message box appears with "Reviewer: Me" in it.

This example shows only a one-way communication between the workflow and the service class. The next section will show this same code in C#, and the following section will show the communication back from the service class to the workflow.

CallExternalMethod Activity in C#

The previous section showed how to use the CallExternalMethod activity and a service class written in VB. This section will show the same example, but written in C#. Create a new C# Sequential Workflow Console Application called CCommunicationSequentialConsoleApplication.

Add a new, empty class to the project called ReviewService.cs. Add a project reference to System.Windows.Forms. Within the using declarations at the top of the code page, add the following using declarations: using System.Workflow.Activities; and System.Windows.Forms. The using declarations at the top of the ReviewService.cs file look like the following:

```
using System;
using System.Collections.Generic;
using System.Text;
using System.Workflow.Activities;
using System.Workflow.ComponentModel;
using System.Workflow.Runtime;
using System.Windows.Forms;
```

The first step is to define the interface and to add the ExternalDataExchange attribute to the interface so the workflow knows this interface defines the communication between the class and the workflow. To do this, add the following code above the Class declaration (at the top of the code page):

```
[ExternalDataExchange]
internal interface IReview
{
    Boolean CreateReview(String Reviewer, String Reviewee);
}
```

This code defines the interface called IReview with a function called `CreateReview`. The workflow uses this interface to create an initial performance review and accepts two parameters: Reviewer and Reviewee. The interface is now defined, but there's no code associated with the interface. If the `CreateReview` function isn't automatically defined, add the following code to the class:

```
public Boolean CreateReview(String Reviewer, String Reviewee)
```

To do this, change the class declaration for ReviewService to the following:

```
class ReviewService: IReview
```

For a simple example, add the following code to the `CreateReview` function:

```
MessageBox.Show("Reviewer: " + Reviewer);
return true;
```

The `CreateReview` function should have the following code:

```
public Boolean CreateReview(String Reviewer, String Reviewee)
{
    MessageBox.Show("Reviewer: " + Reviewer);
    return true;
}
```

Now that you've defined the service class, you can define the workflow. Add a CallExternalMethod activity to Workflow1 using the designer. Change the name to CallCreateReview. As with the VB example, open the Properties window and click the ellipse next to the Interface Type property for this activity. The type selection box will appear again. As with the VB example, only the interfaces that were defined with the ExternalDataExchange attribute are shown in this list. If you didn't add the attribute to the beginning of the interface declaration, you won't see a type listed. If you did add the attribute, you'll see IReview as the only interface defined within the current project in this list. Select IReview and click OK. From the MethodName property, choose CreateReview. The Parameters properties appear. Enter **You** for the Reviewee property and **Me** for the Reviewer property. For now, don't be concerned with the return value.

Finally, the ReviewService class must be known by the workflow runtime. To do this, you must add the service class as a service to the runtime. Immediately after the class definition, add the following:

```
static ReviewService LocalService;
```

Within `Sub Main`, add the following two lines after the bracket ({) following the `using Workflow` statement:

```
LocalService = new ReviewService() ;
workflowRuntime .AddService (LocalService);
```

This code creates a new instance of the ReviewService, which defines an interface and the class to handle that interface. The second line adds the instance of that service to the workflow runtime. `Sub Main` should look like the following:

```
static ReviewService LocalService;
static void Main(string[] args)
{
using(WorkflowRuntime workflowRuntime = new WorkflowRuntime())
{
    LocalService = new ReviewService() ;
    workflowRuntime .AddService (LocalService);
    AutoResetEvent waitHandle = new AutoResetEvent(false);
    workflowRuntime.WorkflowCompleted += delegate(object sender,
    WorkflowCompletedEventArgs e) {waitHandle.Set();};
    workflowRuntime.WorkflowTerminated += delegate(object sender,
    WorkflowTerminatedEventArgs e)
{
    Console.WriteLine(e.Exception.Message);
    waitHandle.Set();
};
WorkflowInstance instance = workflowRuntime.CreateWorkflow(typeof
(CCommunicationSequentialConsoleApplication.Workflow1));
instance.Start();
waitHandle.WaitOne();
}
}
```

After adding this code, the workflow runtime will recognize the ReviewService class as a service class that defines a communication channel with the workflow. Add a breakpoint to the second line of code just added. Also, open ReviewService.vb and add a breakpoint to the message box line. Execute the workflow. The first breakpoint is encountered, and the workflow runtime adds a copy of the ReviewService class to the runtime as a service. The workflow runtime then creates an instance of the workflow. The CallExternalMethod activity is encountered; then the message box within the CreateReview function is encountered. The message box appears with "Reviewer: Me" in it.

Events in VB

This section will cover the Listen and HandleExternalEvent activities. These two activities wait for an event to be raised (Listen activity) and then handle that event (HandleExternalEvent activity). Open the VBCommunicationSequentialConsoleApplication again. The first step is to define an event or events within the interface for the service class. Open the ReviewService.vb class file and add the following two lines to the Interface declaration:

```
Event ReviewApproved As EventHandler(Of ExternalDataEventArgs)
Event ReviewNotApproved As EventHandler(Of ExternalDataEventArgs)
```

The completed Interface declaration is as follows:

```
Public Interface IReview
Function CreateReview(ByVal Reviewer As String, ByVal Reviewee As String) As Boolean
    Event ReviewApproved As EventHandler(Of ExternalDataEventArgs)
    Event ReviewNotApproved As EventHandler(Of ExternalDataEventArgs)
End Interface
```

Next, you must define the events within the ReviewService class. After the `CreateReview` function add the following four lines:

```
Public Event ReviewApproved(ByVal sender As Object,
ByVal e As ExternalDataEventArgs) Implements IReview.ReviewApproved
Public Event ReviewNotApproved(ByVal sender As Object,
ByVal e As ExternalDataEventArgs) Implements IReview.ReviewNotApproved
```

These lines define an event within the class, and define which event within the interface each class-defined event will implement. The ReviewService class should now look like the following code:

```
Public Function CreateReview(ByVal Reviewer As String, ByVal Reviewee As String)
As Boolean Implements IReview.CreateReview
MsgBox("Reviewer: " & StrReviewer)
Return True
End Function
Public Event ReviewApproved(ByVal sender As Object,
ByVal e As ExternalDataEventArgs) Implements IReview.ReviewApproved
Public Event ReviewNotApproved(ByVal sender As Object,
ByVal e As ExternalDataEventArgs) Implements IReview.ReviewNotApproved
```

Next, you must add two subs to the class to handle the events:

```
Private Sub ApproveReview(ByVal sender As Object,
ByVal e As ExternalDataEventArgs) Handles Me.ReviewApproved
MsgBox("Reviewer: " & StrReviewer & " has approved the review for " &
StrReviewee)
End Sub
Private Sub DoNotApproveReview(ByVal sender As Object,
    ByVal e As ExternalDataEventArgs) Handles Me.ReviewNotApproved
    MsgBox("Reviewer: " & StrReviewer & " has not approved the review for " &
    StrReviewee)
End Sub
```

Notice the Handles keyword at the end of each line. This keyword ties this sub to an event defined within the class. When the event is raised, the sub will be called. After you've defined the subs, you need to change the `CreateReview` function. First, add two declarations at the beginning of the class, one for StrReviewer and one for StrReviewee. Define both as a string. Next, you need to add a sub to ask the users if they approve or not, and to raise the correct event (either ReviewApproved or ReviewNotApproved). To do this, add the following code:

```
Private Sub AskForApproval(ByVal o As Object)
    If MsgBox("Do you approve the review for: " & StrReviewee & " ?",
    MsgBoxStyle.YesNo, "Approve review?") = MsgBoxResult.Yes Then
    RaiseEvent ReviewApproved(Nothing, Nothing)
    Else
    RaiseEvent ReviewNotApproved(Nothing, Nothing)
    End If
 End Sub
```

The RaiseEvent keyword causes the execution of the event following. If the user approves the review, then the ReviewApproved event is raised. Otherwise, the ReviewNotApproved event is raised. Finally, make changes to the CreateReview sub that call the newly created AskForApproval sub, but on a different thread:

```
StrReviewer = Reviewer
StrReviewee = Reviewee
MsgBox("Reviewer: " & StrReviewer)

ThreadPool.QueueUserWorkItem(New System.Threading.WaitCallback
(AddressOf AskForApproval))

Return True
```

The QueueUserWorkItem method of the ThreadPool creates a new thread and waits for the user to do something. That something is defined within the AskForApproval sub. The thread waits for the user to perform the action before continuing. The ReviewService.vb file should have the following code:

```
<ExternalDataExchange()> _
Public Interface IReview
    Function CreateReview(ByVal Reviewer As String,
    ByVal Reviewee As String) As Boolean
    Event ReviewApproved As EventHandler(Of ExternalDataEventArgs)
    Event ReviewNotApproved As EventHandler(Of ExternalDataEventArgs)
End Interface
Public Class ReviewService : Implements IReview
    Private StrReviewer As String
    Private StrReviewee As String
    Public Function CreateReview(ByVal Reviewer As String,
    ByVal Reviewee As String) As Boolean Implements IReview.CreateReview
    StrReviewer = Reviewer
    StrReviewee = Reviewee
    MsgBox("Reviewer: " & StrReviewer)
    ThreadPool.QueueUserWorkItem(New System.Threading.WaitCallback
    (AddressOf AskForApproval))
    Return True
    End Function
    Public Event ReviewApproved(ByVal sender As Object,
    ByVal e As ExternalDataEventArgs) Implements IReview.ReviewApproved
    Public Event ReviewNotApproved(ByVal sender As Object,
    ByVal e As ExternalDataEventArgs) Implements IReview.ReviewNotApproved
    Private Sub AskForApproval(ByVal o As Object)
    If MsgBox("Do you approve the review for: " & StrReviewee & " ?",
    MsgBoxStyle.YesNo, "Approve review?") = MsgBoxResult.Yes Then
    RaiseEvent ReviewApproved(Nothing, Nothing)
    Else
    RaiseEvent ReviewNotApproved(Nothing, Nothing)
```

```
        End If
    End Sub
    Private Sub ApproveReview(ByVal sender As Object,
    ByVal e As ExternalDataEventArgs) Handles Me.ReviewApproved
    MsgBox("Reviewer: " & StrReviewer & " has approved the review for "
    & StrReviewee)
    End Sub
    Private Sub DoNotApproveReview(ByVal sender As Object, ByVal e As
    ExternalDataEventArgs) Handles Me.ReviewNotApproved
    MsgBox("Reviewer: " & StrReviewer & " has not approved the review for "
    & StrReviewee)
    End Sub
End Class
```

Add a breakpoint to the MsgBox line in the preceding code (within the CreateReview function). Execute the workflow. When the breakpoint is encountered, press F11 through the message box. Press F11 again and the threadpool code executes. Press F11 again, and instead of entering the AskForApproval sub, the Return True code is executed and control goes out of the CreateReview function. If you continue instead of pressing F11, the message box asking for approval appears for a brief second, if at all. The reason is the workflow has executed the activity and has moved on. There's no next activity within the workflow, so the workflow terminates. This is the reason for adding a Listen activity.

Return to the Workflow Designer. Add a Listen activity from the Toolbox to the designer, after the callCreateReview activity. The Listen activity waits for an external event to occur. The Listen activity, like some other activities, is a composite activity. It's made up of at least one HandleExternalEvent activity. Change the name of the Listen activity to ReviewResponse. Add a HandleExternalEvent activity to the left side of the Listen activity. Change the Name property to HandleReviewApproval. Click the ellipse next to the InterfaceType property and choose IReview from the type selection window. Then, choose ReviewApproved from the EventName property drop-down. Figure 7-5 shows the completed HandleReviewApproval property page.

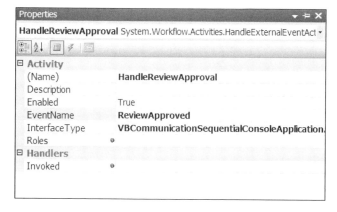

Figure 7-5. *HandleReviewApproval properties*

Add another HandleExternalEvent activity and change the Name property to HandleReviewNotApproved. Click the ellipse next to the InterfaceType property and choose IReview from the type selection window. Choose ReviewNotApproved from the EventName property.

Now view the code for the workflow and add two new subs to be called when each event is triggered:

```
Private Sub OnApproved(ByVal sender As Object,
    ByVal e As ExternalDataEventArgs)
    MsgBox("Approved")
End Sub
Private Sub OnNotApproved(ByVal sender As Object,
    ByVal e As ExternalDataEventArgs)
    MsgBox("Not Approved")
End Sub
```

View the Workflow Designer again and the properties for the HandleReviewApproved activity. Add OnApproved to the Invoked property. When this event is invoked, the OnApproved sub will be called. Do the same with the HandleReviewNotApproved activity and the OnNotApproved sub. Execute the workflow, and when prompted, say Yes, you want to approve. You'll then get a message box of Approved.

Events in C#

The previous section explained how to accommodate events by listening and then handling them in VB. This section will show how to accomplish the same work in C#. Be sure the following using statements are present in ReviewService.cs:

```
using System.Workflow.Runtime;
using System.Windows.Forms;
using System.Threading;
```

The first step is to define an event or events within the interface for the service class. Open the ReviewService.cs class file and add the following two lines to the Interface declaration:

```
event EventHandler<ExternalDataEventArgs> ReviewApproved;
event EventHandler<ExternalDataEventArgs> ReviewNotApproved;
```

These two lines define two event handlers that use a parameter of type ExternalDataEventArgs. The completed interface code follows:

```
[ExternalDataExchange]
interface IReview
{
    Boolean CreateReview(String Reviewer, String Reviewee);
    event EventHandler<ExternalDataEventArgs > ReviewApproved;
    event EventHandler<ExternalDataEventArgs > ReviewNotApproved;
}
```

Next, you must define the events within the ReviewService class. Before the CreateReview sub, add the following two lines:

```
public event EventHandler<ExternalDataEventArgs> ReviewApproved;
public event EventHandler<ExternalDataEventArgs> ReviewNotApproved;
```

These two lines define an event within the class, and define which event within the interface each class-defined event will implement. Instead of two subs created to handle the events, a new class is defined that's passed back in the event handle. It's of type ExternalDataEventArgs. Add the following code to the beginning of the class file, after the namespace declaration:

```
[Serializable]
internal class ReviewEventArgs : ExternalDataEventArgs
{
    private string alias;
    public ReviewEventArgs(Guid InstanceID, string alias)
    : base(InstanceID)
{
    this.alias = alias;
 }
public string Alias
{
    get { return this.alias; }
    set { this.alias = value; }
}
}
```

After you've defined the events, you must declare the two variables. Add two declarations at the beginning of the class, one (before the event declaration) for StrReviewer and one for StrReviewee. Define both as a string. Next, assign the correct parameter to each value within the CreateReview function. The beginning of the class is as follows:

```
class ReviewService:IReview
{
    static String StrReviewer;
    static String StrReviewee;
    public event EventHandler<ExternalDataEventArgs > ReviewApproved;
    public event EventHandler<ExternalDataEventArgs > ReviewNotApproved;
    public Boolean CreateReview(String Reviewer, String Reviewee)
{
    StrReviewer = Reviewer;
    StrReviewee = Reviewee;
    MessageBox.Show("Reviewer: " + Reviewer);
    return true;
}
```

Next, you need to add a sub to ask the user if he or she approves or not, and you need to raise the correct event (either ReviewApproved or ReviewNotApproved). To do this, add the following code:

```
public void AskForApproval(Object O)
{
    DialogResult Result;
    ReviewEventArgs  revieweargs = O as ReviewEventArgs ;
    Guid instanceId = revieweargs.InstanceId;
    string alias = revieweargs.Alias;
    Result = MessageBox.Show("Do you approve the review for " + StrReviewee + " ?",
    "Approval", MessageBoxButtons.YesNo);
    if (Result == DialogResult.Yes)
    {
    ReviewApproved(null, revieweargs);
    }
    else
    {
    ReviewNotApproved(null, revieweargs);
    }
}
```

If the user approves the review, then the ReviewApproved event is raised. Otherwise, the ReviewNotApproved event is raised. Finally, make changes to the CreateReview sub that call the newly created AskForApproval sub, but on a different thread:

```
ThreadPool.QueueUserWorkItem (AskForApproval ,new
ReviewEventArgs(WorkflowEnvironment.WorkflowInstanceId,Reviewer ));
```

The QueueUserWorkItem method of the ThreadPool creates a new thread and waits for the user to do something. That something is defined within the AskForApproval sub. The thread waits for the user to perform the action before continuing. Following is all the code for the ReviewService.cs file:

```
namespace CCommunicationSequentialConsoleApplication
{
[Serializable]
internal class ReviewEventArgs : ExternalDataEventArgs
{
private string alias;
public ReviewEventArgs(Guid InstanceID, string alias)
: base(InstanceID)
{
    this.alias = alias;
}
public string Alias
{
    get { return this.alias; }
    set { this.alias = value; }
}
}
[FxternalDataExchange]
interface IReview
```

```
{
    Boolean CreateReview(String Reviewer, String Reviewee);
    event EventHandler<ExternalDataEventArgs  > ReviewApproved;
    event EventHandler<ExternalDataEventArgs  > ReviewNotApproved;
}
class ReviewService:IReview
{
    static String StrReviewer;
    static String StrReviewee;
    public event EventHandler<ExternalDataEventArgs > ReviewApproved;
    public event EventHandler<ExternalDataEventArgs > ReviewNotApproved;
    public Boolean CreateReview(String Reviewer, String Reviewee)
{
    StrReviewer = Reviewer;
    StrReviewee = Reviewee;
    MessageBox.Show("Reviewer: " + Reviewer);
    ThreadPool.QueueUserWorkItem (AskForApproval ,new
    ReviewEventArgs(WorkflowEnvironment.WorkflowInstanceId,Reviewer ));
    return true;
}
public void AskForApproval(Object O)
{
    DialogResult Result;
    ReviewEventArgs  revieweargs = O as ReviewEventArgs ;
    Guid instanceId = revieweargs.InstanceId;
    string alias = revieweargs.Alias;
    Result = MessageBox.Show("Do you approve the review for " + StrReviewee + " ?",
      "Approval", MessageBoxButtons.YesNo);
    if (Result == DialogResult.Yes)
    {
    ReviewApproved(null, revieweargs);
    }
    else
    {
    ReviewNotApproved(null, revieweargs);
    }
    }
}
}
```

Add a breakpoint to the MessageBox line in the preceding code (within the CreateReview sub). Execute the workflow. When the breakpoint is encountered, press F11 through the message box. Press F11 again, and the threadpool code executes. Press F11 again, and instead of entering the AskForApproval sub, the Return True code is executed and control goes out of the CreateReview sub. If you continue, instead of pressing F11, the message box asking for approval will appear for a brief second, if at all. That's because the workflow has executed the activity and has moved on. There's no next activity within the workflow, so the workflow terminates. This is the reason for adding a Listen activity.

Return to the Workflow Designer. Add a Listen activity from the Toolbox to the designer. The Listen activity waits for an external event to occur. The Listen activity, like some other activities, is a composite activity. It's made up of at least one HandleExternalEvent activity. Change the name of the Listen activity to ReviewResponse. Add a HandleExternalEvent activity to the left side of the Listen activity. Change the Name property to HandleReviewApproval. Click the ellipse next to the InterfaceType property, and choose IReview from the type selection window. Choose ReviewApproved from the EventName property drop-down. Add another HandleExternalEvent activity. Change the Name property to HandleReviewNotApproved. Click the ellipse next to the InterfaceType property and choose IReview from the type selection window. Choose ReviewNotApproved from the EventName property.

Now view the code for the workflow and add two new subs to be called when each event is triggered:

```
private void OnApproved(object sender, ExternalDataEventArgs e)
{
    MessageBox.Show("Approved");
}
private void OnNotApproved(object sender, ExternalDataEventArgs e)
{
    MessageBox.Show("Not Approved");
}
```

View the Workflow Designer again and the properties for the HandleReviewApproval activity. Add OnApproved to the Invoked property. When this event is invoked, the OnApproved sub will be called. Do the same with the HandleReviewNotApproved activity and the OnNotApproved sub. Execute the workflow, and when prompted say Yes, you want to approve. You'll then get a message box of Approved.

Workflow Fault Handling

When dealing with workflows from other applications, it's important to add fault handling to the workflows to handle any exceptions or faults that might occur. Workflows can have default Fault Handlers defined for various types of exceptions. These Handlers are called any time a specified exception occurs within the workflow. Create a new VB Sequential Workflow Console Application called VBFaultHandlerSequentialConsoleApplication. By default, a FaultHandlersActivity is already created for a new workflow. The FaultHandlersActivity contains only Fault Handler activities. The Fault Handler activity is a composite activity—that is, it's made up of other activities. To view and change the FaultHandlersActivity, find the three tabs at the bottom left of the Workflow Designer. The first of the three tabs (from the left) is the View Workflow tab, which allows you to view the workflow model. The second (middle) tab is the Cancel Handler tab. The third tab is the View Faults tab. Click this tab to get to the Faults area to be able to add activities to a FaultHandlersActivity.

First, add a Fault Handler activity from the Toolbox to the FaultHandlersActivity that's already within the designer. Open the properties and change the name of this Fault Handler to GeneralFault. Click the ellipse next to the Fault Type property. This opens a window of all types derived from System.Exception, as shown in Figure 7-6.

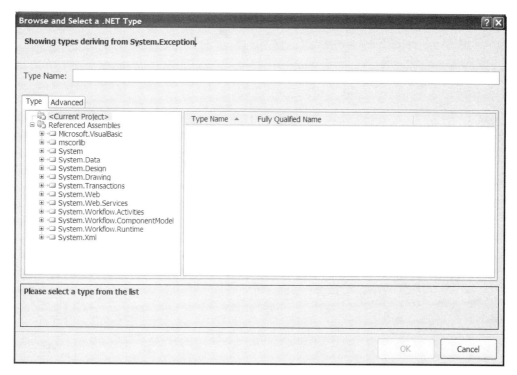

Figure 7-6. *Select an exception type.*

From this list, select the exception that will trigger this Fault Handler. For a general, catch-all exception, select `System.Exception` from within the `mscorlib` namespace, as shown in Figure 7-7. Add a Code activity to the GeneralFault Fault Handler activity called GeneralFaultCode. Generate Handlers for this Code activity, and within the ExecuteCode sub add `MsgBox("General Fault Error")`.

Add another Fault Handler activity to the FaultHandersActivity. Call this activity WorkflowTerminatedFault and set the FaultType property to WorkflowTerminatedException from within the `System.Workflow.ComponentModel` namespace. Add a Code activity to this Fault Handler called TerminatedFault. Generate the Handlers for this Code activity and add `MsgBox("Terminated Fault")`.

Click the first tab on the left at the bottom of the designer to View Workflow. Add a Code activity called FirstActivity and generate Handlers. Within the Handler code add `MsgBox("First Activity")`:

```
Private Sub FirstActivity_ExecuteCode(ByVal sender As System.Object,
ByVal e As System.EventArgs)
MsgBox("First Activity")
end Sub
```

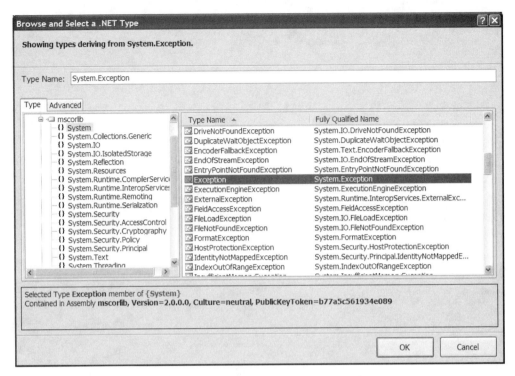

Figure 7-7. *Choose System.Exception from the mscorlib namespace.*

A Throw activity is an activity that throws an exception. You must define the exception the activity will throw, but you don't need to define a Fault Handler for that exception if you don't want to. Using this activity is the same as using the Throw part of a Try . . . Catch . . . Throw code block. This can be useful if you're checking for a specific item. If that item isn't there, you'll want to throw an exception. In this case, the activity also shows how the Fault Handler activity is executed. Leave the name of the Throw activity as the default name, and for the FaultType choose DriveNotFound from `mscorlib.System.IO`. This is just a random exception to see how the Fault Handler works. Execute the workflow.

You'll receive a "build failed" message. The message states that the WorkflowTerminatedException must be added before the Handler for Exception. The reason for this is the Exception type is the default or catch-all type. When a FaultHandlersActivity is triggered, each Fault Handler is evaluated from left to right. The first Fault Handler activity that matches the exception is the one that's executed. Therefore, if you use the Exception type, which is the catch-all, it must be the last in the list of Fault Handler activities. To fix this problem, view the Faults of the workflow again, and move the WorkflowTerminatedFault activity to the leftmost area within the FaultHandlersActivity, as shown in Figure 7-8.

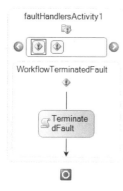

Figure 7-8. *Workflow exceptions for the Sequential workflow*

Execute the workflow again. The First Activity message appears, then the General Fault Error message appears. When the Throw activity is encountered, the Fault Handler is triggered. The first Fault Handler is for Workflow Terminated, but the workflow was not terminated by the Throw activity, so the next Fault Handler is triggered. The next Fault Handler is the Exception Fault Handler, which is the catch-all. Therefore, it's triggered, and the message box appears.

If you choose to, you can create your own exception class that defines an exception within your application and use that exception as the Fault Type for a Fault Handler. When you view the list of exceptions from which to choose, the common thread is that they're all of type Exception. So, you can create a class that inherits from System.Exception and that you want to use to define an exception.

Add a new, empty class to the project called MyException. When the code window appears, add Inherits System.Exception. The code is simply as follows:

```
Public Class MyException
Inherits System.Exception

End Class
```

Return to the Workflow Designer and view the properties for the Throw activity. Click the ellipse next to the FaultType property. Notice under Current Project that there's now a namespace for this project. When you click that namespace, MyException appears on the right, as shown in Figure 7-9.

Choose MyException as the FaultType. View the workflow Faults again by clicking the third tab on the bottom left of the Workflow Designer. Change the FaultType property of the WorkflowTerminated Fault Handler to MyException. Now this Fault Handler will be triggered when the Throw activity is triggered. Finally, change the TerminatedFault Code activity to display a message box of "My Exception was thrown." Execute the workflow.

As with some of the other chapters, I'm not going to show the C# example for the Throw and Fault Handler activities. There's only a limited difference in the code between VB and C#.

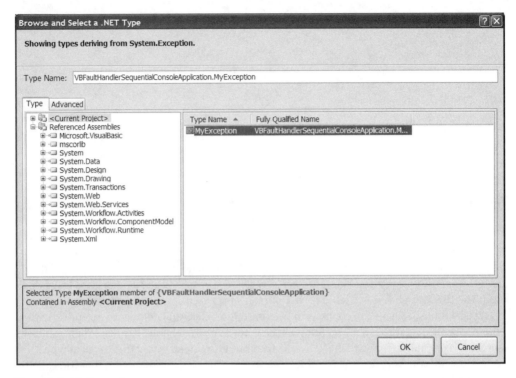

Figure 7-9. *MyException*

Transaction Scope and Compensate

The Transaction Scope activity is a composite activity—it contains other activities and defines a transaction. You can use this activity to make sure a set of activities completes or is rolled back like a transaction. The Compensate activity allows you to call code that undoes, or compensates for, operations already performed by a workflow when an error occurs. This usually is within the context of a transaction scope. The Transaction Scope activity contains other activities. If those activities don't complete, you can use the Compensate activity to undo what was done.

Create a new VB Sequential Workflow Console Application called VBTransactionScopeCompensateSequentialConsole. A common scenario for using a Transaction Scope activity would be if you want to insert a record in two different tables, but if either one fails the transaction is rolled back. This simple example works in both VB and C#. In the next chapter, I'll give another example that inserts data into a database.

Add a Transaction Scope activity to the workflow. Add a Code activity to the Transaction Scope activity. Change the name of the Code activity to Insert1 and generate Handlers for it. Within the Handlers, add msgbox("Insert1"). Add a second Code activity with a name of Insert2 and generate Handlers for it. Within the Handlers, add msgbox("Insert2"). Next, add a Throw activity to the Transaction Scope activity. Leave the name the default. View the code of the workflow. Add a private sub that's triggered when the exception is thrown:

```
Private Sub OnException(ByVal sender As System.Object, ByVal e As System.EventArgs)
MsgBox("Exception encountered, rolling back")
End Sub
```

Return to the Workflow Designer and view the properties of the Throw activity. Set the FaultType property to `System.Exception`. View the workflow Faults and add a new Fault Handler to the Fault Handler activity. Call this Fault Handler GeneralFault and set the FaultType to `System.Exception`. Finally, add a Code activity to this Fault Handler called GeneralFaultCode. Instead of generating Handlers for this Code activity, click the drop-down list next to the ExecuteCode property and select OnException. When any exception is encountered, this code will be executed and will trigger the OnException sub code. Execute the workflow. The exception code is triggered because there's a Throw activity within the transaction scope.

The only difference between the Sequential workflows shown here and the State Machine workflows is that you must include the Transaction Scope activity within an EventDriven activity for a State Machine workflow.

Conclusion

This chapter began by explaining how communication between workflow and other applications can be accomplished. I provided an example of how to create a service class and an interface along with the use of the CallExternalMethod, Listen, and HandleExternalEvent activities. This chapter concluded with a discussion of fault or exception handling within workflows. The next chapter will discuss how to create your own custom activities to use and reuse within your workflows, just like creating a class library.

CHAPTER 8

■ ■ ■

Custom Activities

All the chapters to this point have provided details about—and showed examples of—the out-of-the-box activities provided with WF. However, you might need to use the existing activities to create new activities specifically for your problem domain. WF has provided extensibility so you can expand the set of activities available from which to build workflows. This chapter will explain the steps involved in creating a custom activity for both a Sequential workflow and a State Machine workflow.

Basics of a Custom Activity

You can derive a custom activity from either an out-of-the-box activity or another custom activity. To build a simple custom activity, create a new VB Workflow Activity Library called SimpleActivity. When the new project opens, you'll see the designer has an activity in it to which you can add other activities. You use this to create a composite activity made up of either multiple out-of-the-box activities or your custom activities. Change the name of Activity1.vb in the Solution Explorer to SimpleActivity.

Remember that an activity is simply a class, so you can work with it in that way. SimpleActivity inherits from the Sequence activity by default. View the properties of the SimpleActivity activity and you'll see the Base Class property, which has already been set to System.Work➥ flow.Activities.SequenceActivity. You can also add a description that will be shown when the activity is in the Toolbox. Add **"This is a simple activity"** as the description.

Add a Code activity to the activity called SimpleCode. Generate the Handler for the Code activity and add msgbox("Simple") to the resulting sub. Add another Code activity called ActivityCode. Generate the Handler for the Code activity and add msgbox("Activity") to the resulting sub.

Add a new VB Sequential Workflow Console Application to the solution called VBCustomActivitySequentialConsole. As soon as the solution is opened, build the solution. Once the solution is built, view the Toolbox and you'll see there's a new activity called SimpleActivity, as shown in Figure 8-1.

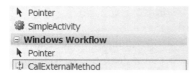

Figure 8-1. *New SimpleActivity in the Toolbox*

Drag the SimpleActivity from the Toolbox to the Sequential workflow. Click your mouse on the SimpleActivity. The result should look like Figure 8-2.

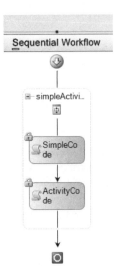

Figure 8-2. *SimpleActivity within a Sequential workflow*

Notice the description for the SimpleActivity is the description entered when creating the activity. Also notice there's a lock in the upper-left corner of each Code activity within the SimpleActivity. This lets you know you cannot make changes to these activities. If you click one of the Code activities inside the SimpleActivity and view the properties, you'll see the properties are all disabled. Execute the workflow, and you'll see the Simple message box appear and then the Activity message box appear. This example shows a simple composite activity made up of existing activities. You can also create activities from scratch by inheriting from the Activity class. The next section will show creating a new activity from the Activity class.

Creating a new activity in this manner is the same in VB or C#. Also, you can change the base class activity from Sequential activity to State activity to create an activity that can be used in a State Machine workflow. The same steps are involved in both, so I won't show creating a State activity.

This example has shown how to use a custom activity if the activity project and workflow project are in the same solution. In most cases, this won't happen. Instead, you'll create a new workflow project and you'll want to add an existing custom activity to the workflow. To show how this works, close the solution and create a new VB Sequential Workflow Console application called VBCustomActivityToolBoxSequential. View the Toolbox and notice you no longer see the SimpleActivity within the Toolbox. Right-click the Toolbox and select Choose Items. The Choose Toolbox Items dialog box appears with several tabs. Click the Activities tab, and you'll see all the out-of-the-box activities listed. Also notice the directory column for these activities is Global Assembly Cache. You can add your activity to the Global Assembly Cache if you'd like. However, if you do this, you'll need to do it on every workstation that might have a workflow application running on it and that uses that activity. The upside to adding a custom activity to the Global Assembly Cache is that you don't need to add it to every project you create. So if you have an activity—for example, a logging activity—that you want to add to every workflow project, then it's a good idea to add that activity to the Global Assembly Cache. You can also add the activity as a project reference like any other component.

Click the Browse button on the Choose Toolbox Items box. Navigate to the C:\workflows folder that you created and have been putting your projects in. Find the SimpleActivity folder that contains the SimpleActivity project that was just created. Navigate to the bin folder, select the SimpleActivity.dll file, and click Open. You'll now see the SimpleActivity added to the bottom of the Choose Toolbox Items Activities tab. Click OK and you'll see the SimpleActivity at the bottom of the Toolbox, as shown in Figure 8-3.

Figure 8-3. *SimpleActivity in the Toolbox*

Drag and drop the SimpleActivity from the Toolbox to the workflow. You'll see the same behavior as last time: there's a lock in the upper-left corner of each Code activity within the SimpleActivity. Execute the workflow, and you'll see the message boxes appear as they did with the last example.

Creating a New Activity from the Activity Class

This section will show how you can inherit from the Activity class to create new activities. These activities will have the same base characteristics of the out-of-the-box activities.

Example in VB

If you want to create a new activity that isn't a composite, you can either inherit from the Activity class or you can inherit from another activity if you only want to modify an existing activity. You can also add functionality to the custom activity by using related classes called activity components, which each provide a specific piece of functionality. Five activity components are available:

- *Validator*: Provides custom validation logic

- *Designer*: Provides custom behavior within the VS environment

- *Toolbox Item*: Provides custom behavior within the Toolbox of VS

- *Serializer*: Provides any custom serialization required

- *Code Generator*: Allows compile-time code generation

You can inherit these activity components into new classes, and you only need to change what you want to change—the remaining functionality will stay the same. A new activity specifies its activity components by adding custom attributes, allowing the client to find the activity's capabilities.

Create a new VB Workflow Activity Library project called SendEmailVB. Rename Activity1.vb to SendEmailVB.vb. Again, the composite Activity1 will be within the workflow.

Click the ellipse next to the BaseClass property. This opens the .NET Type dialog box. Click the System.Workflow.ComponentModel assembly under the Referenced Assemblies selection. Click the Activity type so the type name at the top of the box is System.Workflow.Component➥ Model.Activity. Click OK. This changes the class the activity inherits from to the Activity class instead of the SequentialActivity class that was used in the previous example. You'll also notice that the design of the activity within the designer has changed. Change the Description property to **"Use to send email via SMTP, uses VB."**

You define properties for a new activity using the DependencyProperty. To create a DependencyProperty, first you need to declare the property using the following format:

```
Public Shared [Property Name] as DependencyProperty =
DependencyProperty.Register([Name others will see],
GetType([data type],GetType[activity class name])
```

Add these properties at the beginning of the class declaration. The properties for this activity (and the beginning of the class) would be defined as follows:

```
Public Class SendEmailVB
    Inherits System.Workflow.ComponentModel.Activity
    Public Shared FromProperty As DependencyProperty =
        DependencyProperty.Register("From", GetType(String),
        GetType(SendEmailVB), New PropertyMetadata("someone@example.com"))
    Public Shared ToProperty As DependencyProperty =
        DependencyProperty.Register("To", GetType(String),
        GetType(SendEmailVB), New PropertyMetadata("someone@example.com"))
    Public Shared BodyProperty As DependencyProperty =
        DependencyProperty.Register("Body", GetType(String),
        GetType(SendEmailVB))
    Public Shared SubjectProperty As DependencyProperty =
        DependencyProperty.Register("Subject", GetType(String),
        GetType(SendEmailVB))
    Public Shared SmtpHostProperty As DependencyProperty =
        DependencyProperty.Register("SmtpHost", GetType(String),
        GetType(SendEmailVB), New PropertyMetadata("localhost"))
```

Notice the FromProperty, ToProperty, and SmtpHostProperty all have a New PropertyMetadata parameter. The reason for this is these properties are required. The PropertyMetadata provides both an example to the user of what is valid data and also provides a default. Without this parameter, when you compile the code later, the required properties would generate an error stating no value was provided. Next, you must define the property's Get and Set statements, and you can add attributes as well. One attribute is ValidationOption. This attribute defines whether the property should be validated at compile time. You can use the DescriptionAttribute to provide a description when the user puts the mouse over the property's name within the property window. The structure for a property is as follows:

```
<DesignerSerializationVisibilityAttribute _
(DesignerSerializationVisibility.Visible)> _
<ValidationOption(ValidationOption.Required)> _
<BrowsableAttribute(True)> _
```

```vb
<DescriptionAttribute("The ToAddress property is used to specify the
    receipient's email address.")> _
Public Property ToAddress() As String
    Get
        Return CType(MyBase.GetValue(SendEmailVB.ToProperty), String)
    End Get
    Set(ByVal value As String)
        MyBase.SetValue(SendEmailVB.ToProperty, value)
    End Set
End Property
```

Use this structure to define the remaining properties, following the Public Shared declarations shown earlier, as follows:

```vb
<DesignerSerializationVisibilityAttribute(DesignerSerializationVisibility.
    Visible)> _
<ValidationOption(ValidationOption.Required)> _
<BrowsableAttribute(True)> _
<DescriptionAttribute("The ToAddress property is used to specify the
receipient's email address.")> _
Public Property ToAddress() As String
    Get
        Return CType(MyBase.GetValue(SendEmailVB.ToProperty), String)
    End Get
    Set(ByVal value As String)
        MyBase.SetValue(SendEmailVB.ToProperty, value)
    End Set
End Property
<DesignerSerializationVisibilityAttribute(DesignerSerializationVisibility
.Visible)> _
<ValidationOption(ValidationOption.Optional)> _
<BrowsableAttribute(True)> _
<DescriptionAttribute("The Subject property is used to specify the
subject of the Email message.")> _
Public Property Subject() As String
    Get
        Return CType(MyBase.GetValue(SendEmailVB.SubjectProperty), String)
    End Get
    Set(ByVal value As String)
        MyBase.SetValue(SendEmailVB.SubjectProperty, value)
    End Set
End Property
<DesignerSerializationVisibilityAttribute(DesignerSerializationVisibility
.Visible)> _
<ValidationOption(ValidationOption.Required)> _
<BrowsableAttribute(True)> _
<DescriptionAttribute("The From property is used to specify the From
(Sender's) address for the email message.")> _
```

```vb
Public Property From() As String
    Get
        Return CType(MyBase.GetValue(SendEmailVB.FromProperty), String)
    End Get
    Set(ByVal value As String)
        MyBase.SetValue(SendEmailVB.FromProperty, value)
    End Set
End Property
<DesignerSerializationVisibilityAttribute(DesignerSerializationVisibility
.Visible)> _
<ValidationOption(ValidationOption.Optional)> _
<BrowsableAttribute(True)> _
<DescriptionAttribute("The Body property is used to specify the
Body of the email message.")> _
Public Property Body() As String
    Get
        Return CType(MyBase.GetValue(SendEmailVB.BodyProperty), String)
    End Get
    Set(ByVal value As String)
        MyBase.SetValue(SendEmailVB.BodyProperty, value)
    End Set
End Property
<DesignerSerializationVisibility(DesignerSerializationVisibility
.Visible)> _
<ValidationOption(ValidationOption.Required)> _
<Description("The SMTP host is the machine running SMTP that will
send the email.  The default is 'localhost'")> _
<Browsable(True)> _
Public Property SmtpHost() As String
    Get
        Return CType(MyBase.GetValue(SendEmailVB.SmtpHostProperty), String)
    End Get
    Set(ByVal value As String)
        MyBase.SetValue(SendEmailVB.SmtpHostProperty, value)
    End Set
End Property
```

Add a new VB Sequential Workflow Console Application project to the solution called VBSendEmailTest. Build the solution so the activity will be built. Open the VBSendEmailTest project and the Workflow1.vb file in the Workflow Designer. Open the Toolbox and notice the new activity called SendEmailVB. Drag and drop this activity onto the Workflow Designer. Click the SendEmailVB activity that you just added to the workflow and view the properties. You'll see the description is the same as you added to the activity. Notice the properties that were just added, as shown in Figure 8-4.

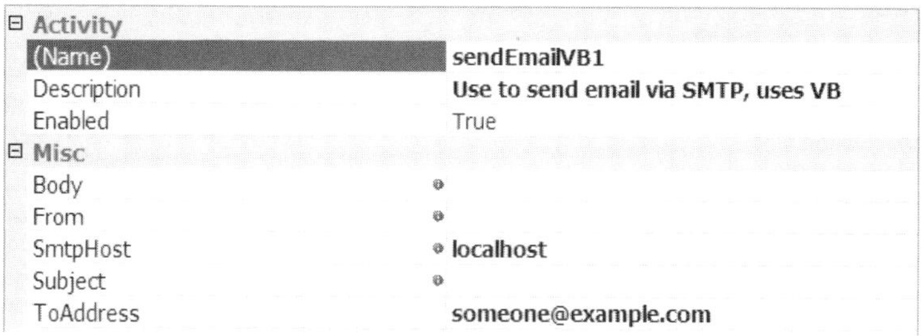

Activity	
(Name)	sendEmailVB1
Description	Use to send email via SMTP, uses VB
Enabled	True
Misc	
Body	⊘
From	⊘
SmtpHost	⊘ localhost
Subject	⊘
ToAddress	someone@example.com

Figure 8-4. *Properties of the SendEmailVB activity*

Notice the default values already provided for the required properties. These allow the user to know the type of information, and also allow the validation to take place. The properties have been defined, but you still need to define what will happen when the activity is executed. To do this, open the SendEmailVB project again and view the code for the activity. At the bottom of the code page, add the following function declaration:

```
Protected Overrides Function Execute
(ByVal context As ActivityExecutionContext) As ActivityExecutionStatus
```

This function will override the Execute built-in function of the Activity class. This function is called when the activity is to execute. Return to the top of the code page and add the following Imports statement:

```
Imports System.Net.Mail
```

This statement imports the Mail class and allows you to create and send e-mail. Return to the Execute function and add the following declarations:

```
Dim clsMail As New SmtpClient
Dim Message As New MailMessage
```

Add the following code to assign the necessary information and send the e-mail:

```
Message.From = New MailAddress(Me.FromAddress)
Message.To.Add(Me.ToAddress)
If Not String.IsNullOrEmpty(Me.Subject) Then
     Message.Subject = Me.Subject
End If
If Not String.IsNullOrEmpty(Me.Message) Then
     Message.Body = Me.Message
End If

clsMail.Host = Me.SMTPAddress
clsMail.Send(Message)
```

The completed Execute function looks like the following:

```
Protected Overrides Function Execute(ByVal context As ActivityExecutionContext) As
ActivityExecutionStatus
Dim clsMail As New SmtpClient
Dim Message As New MailMessage
Try
     Message.From = New MailAddress(Me.From)
     Message.To.Add(Me.ToAddress)
     If Not String.IsNullOrEmpty(Me.Subject) Then
          Message.Subject = Me.Subject
     End If
     If Not String.IsNullOrEmpty(Me.Body) Then
          Message.Body = Me.Body
     End If
     clsMail.Host = Me.SmtpHost
     clsMail.Send(Message)
     Catch ex As Exception
          MsgBox(ex.Message)
     End Try
     Return ActivityExecutionStatus.Closed
End Function
```

Return to the VBSendEmailTest project and the Workflow1.vb file. Set the properties for
the SendEmailVB activity accordingly and test the workflow. The address provided in the
ToAddress property should receive an e-mail.

As mentioned earlier in this section, you can add a Validator class to your activity. Add a
new class to the SendEmailVB project called SendEmailVBValidator. This class inherits from
the System.Workflow.ComponentModel.Compiler.ActivityValidator class and overrides the
ValidateProperties function of this class. To add inheritance, add the following lines of code:

```
Inherits System.Workflow.ComponentModel.Compiler.ActivityValidator
Public Overrides Function ValidateProperties(ByVal manager As ValidationManager,
ByVal obj As Object) As ValidationErrorCollection
```

The ValidateProperties function returns a ValidationErrorCollection, so you must define
one within this function to return. Also define an instance of the activity that you want to
validate:

```
Dim Errors As New ValidationErrorCollection
Dim activity As SendEmailVB = TryCast(obj, SendEmailVB)
```

Next, add code to validate the ToAddress and FromAddress properties of the activity, and
add errors to the collection if necessary:

```
If String.IsNullOrEmpty(activity.ToAddress) Then
     Errors.Add(New ValidationError("No To email address", 1))
     ElseIf Not activity.ToAddress.Contains("@") Then
     Errors.Add(New ValidationError("Invalid To email address", 2))
End If
```

```
If String.IsNullOrEmpty(activity.FromAddress) Then
    Errors.Add(New ValidationError("No from email address", 1))
    ElseIf Not activity.ToAddress.Contains("@") Then
    Errors.Add(New ValidationError("Invalid from email address", 2))
End If
```

Finally, add code to compile the list of errors, throw an exception if there are errors, and either way return the collection:

```
If Errors.HasErrors Then
    Dim ErrorsMessage As String = String.Empty
    For Each validationError As ValidationError In Errors
        ErrorsMessage = ErrorsMessage + String.Format("Validation error:
        Number{0}-'{1} ",
validationError.ErrorNumber,
        validationError.ErrorText)
    Next
    Throw New InvalidOperationException(ErrorsMessage)
End If
Return Errors
```

The completed class code looks like this:

```
Public Class SendEmailVBValidator
Inherits System.Workflow.ComponentModel.Compiler.ActivityValidator
Public Overrides Function ValidateProperties(ByVal manager As ValidationManager,
ByVal obj As Object) As ValidationErrorCollection
Dim Errors As New ValidationErrorCollection
Dim activity As SendEmailVB = TryCast(obj, SendEmailVB)
If activity IsNot Nothing Then
    If String.IsNullOrEmpty(activity.ToAddress) Then
        Errors.Add(New ValidationError("No To email address", 1))
    ElseIf Not activity.ToAddress.Contains("@") Then
        Errors.Add(New ValidationError("Invalid To email address", 2))
    End If
    If String.IsNullOrEmpty(activity.From) Then
        Errors.Add(New ValidationError("No from email address", 1))
    ElseIf Not activity.ToAddress.Contains("@") Then
        Errors.Add(New ValidationError("Invalid from email address", 2))
    End If
    If Errors.HasErrors Then
        Dim ErrorsMessage As String = String.Empty
        For Each validationError As ValidationError In Errors
            ErrorsMessage = ErrorsMessage + String.Format("Validation error:
            Number{0}-'{1} ",validationError.ErrorNumber,
            validationError.ErrorText)
        Next
```

```
        Throw New InvalidOperationException(ErrorsMessage)
    End If
End If
Return Errors
End Function
```

Open the SendEmailVB project and the SendEmailVB.vb file. You now must add an attribute to the class to tie the class with the Validator class. Make sure you have the underscore (_) at the end of the line:

```
<ActivityValidator(GetType(SendEmailVBValidator))> _
Public Class SendEmailVB
Inherits System.Workflow.ComponentModel.Activity
```

To test the validator, open the VBSendEmailTest project and click the properties of the SendEmailVB activity. Blank out the From property. Build the solution, and the build will fail with an error message that the From e-mail address hasn't been provided.

Example in C#

Create a new C# Workflow Activity Library project called SendEmailC. Rename Activity1.vb to SendEmailVB.vb. Again, the composite Activity1 will be within the workflow. Open the properties for this activity and change the Name property to SendEmailVB. Click the ellipse next to the BaseClass property. This opens the .NET type window. Click the System.Workflow.ComponentModel assembly under the Referenced Assemblies selection. Click the Activity type so the type name at the top of the box is System.Workflow.ComponentModel.Activity. Click OK. This changes the class the activity inherits from to the Activity class, instead of the SequentialActivity class that was used in the previous example. You'll also notice that the design of the activity within the designer has changed. Change the Description property to "**Use to send email via SMTP, uses C#.**"

You define properties for a new activity using the DependencyProperty. To create a DependencyProperty, first you need to declare the property using the following format:

```
Public static [Property Name] as DependencyProperty =
DependencyProperty.Register([Name others will see],
typeof([data type],typeof[activity class name]));
```

The properties for this activity would be defined as follows:

```
namespace SendEmailC
{
public partial class SendEmailC : System.Workflow.ComponentModel.Activity
{
   public static DependencyProperty FromProperty =
     DependencyProperty.Register("From", typeof(string),
          typeof(SendEmailActivity), new PropertyMetadata("someone@example.com"));
     public static DependencyProperty ToProperty =
         DependencyProperty.Register("To", typeof(string),
         typeof(SendEmailActivity), new PropertyMetadata("someone@example.com"));
```

```
public static DependencyProperty BodyProperty =
    DependencyProperty.Register("Body", typeof(string),
    typeof(SendEmailActivity));
public static DependencyProperty SubjectProperty =
    DependencyProperty.Register("Subject", typeof(string),
    typeof(SendEmailActivity));
public static DependencyProperty SmtpHostProperty =
    DependencyProperty.Register("SmtpHost", typeof(string),
    typeof(SendEmailActivity), new PropertyMetadata("localhost"));
```

Notice the FromProperty, ToProperty, and SmtpHostProperty all have a New
PropertyMetadata parameter. The reason for this is these properties are required.
The PropertyMetadata provides both an example to the user of what is valid data and also
provides a default. Without this parameter, when you compile the code later, the required
properties would generate an error stating no value was provided. Next, you must define the
property's Get and Set statements, and you can add attributes as well. One attribute is
ValidationOption. This attribute defines if the property should be validated at compile time.
You can use the DescriptionAttribute to provide a description when the user puts the mouse
over the property's name within the property window. The structure for a property is as follows:

```
[DesignerSerializationVisibilityAttribute(DesignerSerializationVisibility.Visible)]
[ValidationOption(ValidationOption.Required)]
[BrowsableAttribute(true)]
[DescriptionAttribute("The To property is used to specify the receipient's
email address.")]
public string To
{
    get
    {
        return ((string)(base.GetValue(SendEmailActivity.ToProperty)));
    }
    set
    {
        base.SetValue(SendEmailActivity.ToProperty, value);
    }
}
```

Use this structure to define the remaining properties as follows:

```
[DesignerSerializationVisibilityAttribute(DesignerSerializationVisibility.Visible)]
[ValidationOption(ValidationOption.Required)]
[BrowsableAttribute(true)]
[DescriptionAttribute("The To property is used to specify the receipient's
email address.")]
```

```csharp
public string To
{
    get
    {
        return ((string)(base.GetValue(SendEmailC.ToProperty)));
    }
    set
    {
        base.SetValue(SendEmailC.ToProperty, value);
    }
}
[DesignerSerializationVisibilityAttribute(DesignerSerializationVisibility.Visible)]
[ValidationOption(ValidationOption.Optional)]
[BrowsableAttribute(true)]
[DescriptionAttribute("The Subject property is used to specify the subject of
the Email message.")]
public string Subject
{
    get
    {
        return ((string)(base.GetValue(SendEmailC.SubjectProperty)));
    }
    set
    {
        base.SetValue(SendEmailC.SubjectProperty, value);
    }
}
[DesignerSerializationVisibilityAttribute(DesignerSerializationVisibility.Visible)]
[ValidationOption(ValidationOption.Required)]
[BrowsableAttribute(true)]
[DescriptionAttribute("The From property is used to specify the From
(Sender's) address for the email message.")]
public string From
{
    get
    {
        return ((string)(base.GetValue(SendEmailC.FromProperty)));
    }
    set
    {
        base.SetValue(SendEmailC.FromProperty, value);
    }
}
[DesignerSerializationVisibilityAttribute(DesignerSerializationVisibility.Visible)]
[ValidationOption(ValidationOption.Optional)]
[BrowsableAttribute(true)]
```

```
[DescriptionAttribute("The Body property is used to specify the Body
of the email message.")]
public string Body
{
    get
    {
        return (string)base.GetValue(SendEmailC.BodyProperty);
    }
    set
    {
        base.SetValue(SendEmailC.BodyProperty, value);
    }
}
[DesignerSerializationVisibility(DesignerSerializationVisibility.Visible)]
[ValidationOption(ValidationOption.Required)]
[Description("The SMTP host is the machine running SMTP that will
send the email.The default is 'localhost'")]
[Browsable(true)]
public string SmtpHost
    {
    get
    {
        return ((string)(base.GetValue(SendEmailC.SmtpHostProperty)));
    }
    set
    {
        base.SetValue(SendEmailC.SmtpHostProperty, value);
    }
}
```

Add a new C# Sequential Workflow Console Application project to the solution called CSendEmailTest. Build the solution so the activity will be built. Open the CSendEmailTest project and the Workflow1.cs file in the Workflow Designer. Open the Toolbox and notice the new activity called SendEmailC. Drag and drop this activity onto the Workflow Designer. Click the SendEmailC activity that you just added to the workflow and view the properties. You'll see the description is the same as you added to the activity, and notice the properties that were just added.

Notice the default values already provided for the required properties. These allow the user to know the type of information and also allow the validation to take place. The properties have been defined, but you still need to define what will happen when the activity is executed. To do this, open the SendEmailC project again and view the code for the activity. At the bottom of the code page, within the Partial Class, add the following function declaration:

```
protected override ActivityExecutionStatus Execute
(ActivityExecutionContext context):
```

This function will override the `Execute` built-in function of the Activity class. This function is called when the activity is to execute. Return to the top of the code page and add the following using statement:

```
using System.Net.Mail
```

This statement imports the Mail class and allows you to create and send e-mail. Return to the `Execute` function and add the following declarations:

```
SmtpClient clsmail = new SmtpClient();
MailMessage message = new MailMessage();
```

Add the following code to assign the necessary information and send the e-mail:

```
message.From = new MailAddress(this.From);
message.To.Add(this.To);
if (!String.IsNullOrEmpty(this.Subject))
{
    message.Subject = this.Subject;
}
if (!String.IsNullOrEmpty(this.Body))
{
    message.Body = this.Body;
}
clsmail.Host = this.SmtpHost;
clsmail.Send(message);
return ActivityExecutionStatus.Closed;
```

The completed `Execute` function looks like the following:

```
protected override ActivityExecutionStatus Execute(ActivityExecutionContext context)
{
    try
    {
        SmtpClient clsmail = new SmtpClient();
        MailMessage message = new MailMessage();
        message.From = new MailAddress(this.From);
        message.To.Add(this.To);
        if (!String.IsNullOrEmpty(this.Subject))
        {
            message.Subject = this.Subject;
        }
        if (!String.IsNullOrEmpty(this.Body))
        {
            message.Body = this.Body;
        }
        clsmail.Host = this.SmtpHost;
        clsmail.Send(message);
        return ActivityExecutionStatus.Closed;
    }
```

```
    catch
    {
        throw;
    }
}
```

Return to the CSendEmailTest project and the Workflow1.vb file. Set the properties for the SendEmailC activity accordingly and test the workflow. The address provided in the To property should receive an e-mail.

As mentioned earlier in this section, you can add a Validator class to your activity. Add a new class to the SendEmailC project called SendEmailCValidator. Add the following to the using statements:

```
using System.Workflow.ComponentModel.Compiler
```

This class will inherit from the System.Workflow.ComponentModel.Compiler.ActivityValidator class and override the ValidateProperties function of this class. To do this, add the following lines of code:

```
class SendEmailCValidator:ActivityValidator
{
public override ValidationErrorCollection ValidateProperties
(ValidationManager manager,object obj)
{
}
}
```

The ValidateProperties function returns a ValidationErrorCollection, so you must define one within this function to return. Also define an instance of the activity that you want to validate:

```
ValidationErrorCollection Errors = new
ValidationErrorCollection(base.ValidateProperties(manager, obj));
SendEmailC sendMailActivityToBeValidated = obj as SendEmailC;
```

Next, add code to validate the To and From properties of the activity, and add errors to the collection if necessary:

```
if (string.IsNullOrEmpty(sendMailActivityToBeValidated.To))
{
ValidationError CustomActivityValidationError =
new ValidationError("To Address Not Provided", 1);
Errors.Add(CustomActivityValidationError);
}
if (string.IsNullOrEmpty (sendMailActivityToBeValidated.From))
{
ValidationError CustomActivityValidationError =
new ValidationError("From Address Not Provided", 1);
Errors.Add(CustomActivityValidationError);
}
```

Finally, add code to compile the list of errors, throw an exception if there are errors, and either way return the collection:

```
if (Errors.HasErrors)
{
throw new InvalidOperationException();
}
return Errors;
```

The completed code for the Validator class is as follows:

```
class SendEmailCValidator:ActivityValidator
{
public override ValidationErrorCollection ValidateProperties(
ValidationManager manager,object obj)
{
    ValidationErrorCollection Errors = new
        ValidationErrorCollection(base.ValidateProperties(manager, obj));
    SendEmailC sendMailActivityToBeValidated = obj as SendEmailC;
    if (string.IsNullOrEmpty(sendMailActivityToBeValidated.To))
        {
        ValidationError CustomActivityValidationError =
            new ValidationError("To Address Not Provided", 1);
         Errors.Add(CustomActivityValidationError);
        }
    if (string.IsNullOrEmpty (sendMailActivityToBeValidated.From))
        {
        ValidationError CustomActivityValidationError =
            new ValidationError("From Address Not Provided", 1);
        Errors.Add(CustomActivityValidationError);
        }
        if (Errors.HasErrors)
        {
            throw new InvalidOperationException();
        }
        return Errors;
}
}
```

Open the SendEmailC project and the SendEmailC.cs file. You now must add an attribute to the class to tie the class with the Validator class. Make sure you have the underscore (_) at the end of the line:

```
[ActivityValidator(typeof(SendEmailCValidator))] _
```

To test the validator, open the CSendEmailTest project and click the properties of the SendEmailC activity. Blank out the From property. Build the solution, and the build will fail with an error message that the From e-mail address hasn't been provided.

Real-World Example

The previous sections of this chapter showed you how to create a custom activity, and had you create a custom activity that sends e-mail. You'll use this activity in Chapter 10 as part of the Employee Performance Review application. The existing purchase order application uses a Code activity to execute a SQL statement. This functionality could also be useful in many other workflow applications. For this reason, you're going to create a new activity called ExecuteSQL. You can use this activity to execute a SQL statement that inserts, updates, or deletes data.

Create a new VB Sequential Workflow Activity Library project called ExecuteSQL. Set the name of the activity to ExecuteSQL and the description to "Use for Insert, Update, Delete." Click the ellipse next to the Base Class property and change the base class to System.Work➥ flow.ComponentModel.Activity, as shown in Figure 8-5.

⊟ **Activity**	
(Name)	**ExecuteSQL**
Base Class	**System.Workflow.ComponentModel.Activity**
Description	**Use for Insert,Update, Delete**
Enabled	True

Figure 8-5. *Name and Description properties of the new activity*

This activity needs to accept two parameters. The first is the connection string to use, and the second is the SQL statement to execute. This activity also needs to return two parameters. The first is for success or failure, and the other is a number. You can use this number when inserting a record to show the ID of the newly inserted record. If this doesn't apply, just add a 0.

The next step is to define the properties. To do this, view the code of the ExecuteSQL activity, and you'll see the class structure. Add the property code so the class looks like the following:

```
Public Class ExecuteSQL
    Inherits System.Workflow.ComponentModel.Activity
    Public Shared ConnectionStringProperty As DependencyProperty =
        DependencyProperty.Register("ConnectionString", GetType(String),
        GetType(ExecuteSQL) , New PropertyMetadata("ConnectionString"))
    Public Shared SQLStatementProperty As DependencyProperty =
        DependencyProperty.Register("SQLStatement", GetType(String),
        GetType(ExecuteSQL), New PropertyMetadata("SQL Statement"))
    Public Shared StatusProperty As DependencyProperty =
        DependencyProperty.Register("Status", GetType(Boolean),
        GetType(ExecuteSQL))
    Public Shared NewIDProperty As DependencyProperty =
        DependencyProperty.Register("NewID", GetType(Integer),
        GetType(ExecuteSQL))
End Class
```

The Status and NewID properties should be read-only because they're return parameters. Create the necessary property statements as follows:

```vbnet
Public Class ExecuteSQL
    Inherits System.Workflow.ComponentModel.Activity
    Public Shared ConnectionStringProperty As DependencyProperty =
        DependencyProperty.Register("ConnectionString", GetType(String),
        GetType(ExecuteSQL))
    Public Shared SQLStatementProperty As DependencyProperty =
        DependencyProperty.Register("SQLStatement", GetType(String),
        GetType(ExecuteSQL))
    Public Shared StatusProperty As DependencyProperty =
        DependencyProperty.Register("Status", GetType(Boolean),
        GetType(ExecuteSQL))
    Public Shared NewIDProperty As DependencyProperty =
        DependencyProperty.Register("NewID", GetType(Integer),
        GetType(ExecuteSQL))
    <DesignerSerializationVisibilityAttribute(DesignerSerializationVisibility.
        Visible)> _
    <ValidationOption(ValidationOption.Required)> _
    <BrowsableAttribute(True)> _
    <DescriptionAttribute("The ConnectionString property is used to specify
    the connection string to use.")> _
    Public Property ConnectionString() As String
        Get
            Return CType(MyBase.GetValue(ExecuteSQL.ConnectionStringProperty),
            String)
        End Get
        Set(ByVal value As String)
            MyBase.SetValue(ExecuteSQL.ConnectionStringProperty, value)
        End Set
    End Property
    <DesignerSerializationVisibilityAttribute(DesignerSerializationVisibility.
    Visible)> _
    <ValidationOption(ValidationOption.Required)> _
    <BrowsableAttribute(True)> _
    <DescriptionAttribute("The SQL Statement property is used to specify
        the SQL Statement to execute.")> _
    Public Property SQLStatement() As String
        Get
            Return CType(MyBase.GetValue
            (ExecuteSQL.SQLStatementProperty), String)
        End Get
        Set(ByVal value As String)
            MyBase.SetValue(ExecuteSQL.SQLStatementProperty, value)
        End Set
    End Property
    <DesignerSerializationVisibilityAttribute(DesignerSerializationVisibility.
    Visible)> _
    <ValidationOption(ValidationOption.None)> _
```

```
      <BrowsableAttribute(True)> _
      <DescriptionAttribute("The Status property will provide the status of
            the execution")> _
      Public ReadOnly Property Status() As Boolean
          Get
              Return CType(MyBase.GetValue(ExecuteSQL.StatusProperty), Boolean)
          End Get
      End Property
      <DesignerSerializationVisibilityAttribute(DesignerSerializationVisibility.
            Visible)> _
      <ValidationOption(ValidationOption.None)> _
      <BrowsableAttribute(True)> _
      <DescriptionAttribute("The NewID property will provide the ID of the record
            inserted for an Insert statement")> _
      Public ReadOnly Property NewID() As Integer
          Get
              Return CType(MyBase.GetValue(ExecuteSQL.NewIDProperty), Integer)
          End Get
      End Property
```

Notice the first two properties have required a validation option and the last two don't. That's because the connection string and SQL statement are required, but the other two (Status and NewID) are output parameters and aren't required. The next step is to add a validation class, as was used in the earlier sections, to make sure the connection string and SQL Statement properties are provided. Add a new blank class to the project called ExecuteSQLValidator.

The new class needs to inherit from System.Workflow.ComponentModel.Compiler.Activity➥ Validator and override the ValidateProperties function as follows:

```
Public Class ExecuteSQLValidator
    Inherits System.Workflow.ComponentModel.Compiler.ActivityValidator
    Public Overrides Function ValidateProperties(ByVal manager As
        ValidationManager, ByVal obj As Object) As ValidationErrorCollection
        Dim Errors As New ValidationErrorCollection
        Dim activity As ExecuteSQL = TryCast(obj, ExecuteSQL)
    End Function
End Class
```

Add code to validate that the connection string and SQL statement properties have been provided, as follows:

```
Public Class ExecuteSQLValidator
    Inherits System.Workflow.ComponentModel.Compiler.ActivityValidator
    Public Overrides Function ValidateProperties
    (ByVal manager As ValidationManager,
        ByVal obj As Object) As ValidationErrorCollection
        Dim Errors As New ValidationErrorCollection
        Dim activity As ExecuteSQL = TryCast(obj, ExecuteSQL)
```

```
        If activity IsNot Nothing Then
            If String.IsNullOrEmpty(activity.ConnectionString) Then
                Errors.Add(New ValidationError("No connection string provided",1))
            End If
            If String.IsNullOrEmpty(activity.SQLStatement) Then
                Errors.Add(New ValidationError("No SQL Statment provided", 1))
            End If
            If Errors.HasErrors Then
                Dim ErrorsMessage As String = String.Empty
                For Each validationError As ValidationError In Errors
                    ErrorsMessage = ErrorsMessage +
                    String.Format("Validation error: Number{0}-'{1} ", _
                    validationError.ErrorNumber, validationError.ErrorText)
                Next
                Throw New InvalidOperationException(ErrorsMessage)
            End If
        End If
        Return Errors
    End Function
End Class
```

Add `<ActivityValidator(GetType(ExecuteSQLValidator))> _` above the class declaration for ExecuteSQL:

```
<ActivityValidator(GetType(ExecuteSQLValidator))> _
Public Class ExecuteSQL
    Inherits System.Workflow.ComponentModel.Activity
```

Finally, you must override the Execute function within the ExecuteSQL activity. Add this line to the end of the ExecuteSQL code page:

```
Protected Overrides Function Execute(ByVal context As ActivityExecutionContext)
As ActivityExecutionStatus
```

Because this activity deals with data, you need to import the Data namespace. Add the import line (Imports System.Data.SqlClient) above the ActivityValidator line added earlier:

```
Imports System.Data.SqlClient
<ActivityValidator(GetType(ExecuteSQLValidator))> _
Public Class ExecuteSQL
    Inherits System.Workflow.ComponentModel.Activity
```

Now add code to the Execute overridden function to execute the SQL Statement property:

```
Protected Overrides Function Execute(ByVal context As ActivityExecutionContext) As
    ActivityExecutionStatus
    Dim Local_Conn As New SqlConnection
    Dim Local_Comm As New SqlCommand
    Dim Local_NumberReturned As Long
    Try
```

```
    If Not Local_Conn.State = ConnectionState.Open Then
        Local_Conn.ConnectionString =
            MyBase.GetValue(ExecuteSQL.ConnectionStringProperty).ToString
        Local_Conn.Open()
        Local_Comm.CommandText = Me.SQLStatement
        Local_Comm.CommandType = CommandType.Text
        Local_Comm.Connection = Local_Conn
        Local_NumberReturned = CInt(Local_Comm.ExecuteScalar)
        MyBase.SetReadOnlyPropertyValue(ExecuteSQL.NewIDProperty,
            Local_NumberReturned)
        If Not IsDBNull(Local_NumberReturned) Then
            MyBase.SetReadOnlyPropertyValue(ExecuteSQL.StatusProperty, True)
        Else
            MyBase.SetReadOnlyPropertyValue(ExecuteSQL.StatusProperty, False)
        End If
        Local_Comm.Dispose()
    End If
    Catch newexception As SqlException
        Throw newexception
    Finally
        Dispose()
    End Try
End Function
```

Now build the ExecuteSQL project so the activity can be used in other workflows.

You'll now add the ExecuteSQL activity to the existing Purchase Order application that you've worked on in the past several chapters. Open the VBPurchaseOrderConsole project and open the PurchaseOrderProcess workflow. View the Toolbox, right-click the Toolbox, and click Choose Items. When the Choose Toolbox Items form appears, click the Activities tab and then the Browse button. Browse to the bin folder of the ExecuteSQL project, click the ExecuteSQL.dll file, then click Open. The ExecuteSQL activity now appears in the list, as shown in Figure 8-6.

Drag an ExecuteSQL task from the Toolbox to the workflow just after the AddPurchaseOrder activity. View the code for the workflow and add a new public property called ConnString. This property references the connection string setting for the workflow:

```
Public ReadOnly Property ConnString() As String
    Get
        Return My.Settings.ConnString.ToString
    End Get
End Property
```

Return to the Workflow Designer view and click the newly added ExecuteSQL activity. Change the name of the activity to InsertPurchaseOrder. Click the ellipse next to the ConnectionString property for the activity and choose the ConnString property from the "Bind 'ConnectionString' to an activity's property" form, as shown in Figure 8-7.

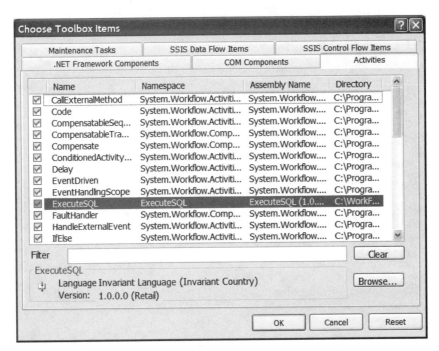

Figure 8-6. *ExecuteSQL is now available to be added to the Toolbox.*

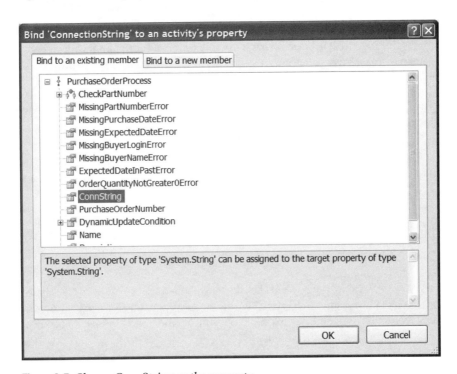

Figure 8-7. *Choose ConnString as the property.*

The existing Code activity sets the SQLStatement property. Click the AddPurchaseOrder Code activity and change the name to PrepareInsert. Leave the ExecuteCode property as it is. View the code for the workflow and find the AddPurchaseOrder_ExecuteCode sub. Move the Select statement from the SQLInsertUpdate sub to the AddPurchaseOrder_ExecuteCode sub, and assign the Select statement to the SQLStatement property of the InsertPurchaseOrder activity with the following code:

```
Private Sub AddPurchaseOrder_ExecuteCode(ByVal sender As System.Object,
    ByVal e As System.EventArgs)
    InsertPurchaseOrder.SQLStatement = "Insert into tblPurchaseOrders " & _
        (StrPartNumber,DtePurchaseDate,DteExpectedDate," & _
        "StrBuyerLogin,StrBuyerName,IntQuantityOrdered) " & _
        "values('" & StrPartNumber  & "','" & DtePurchaseDate & "'," & _
        "'" & DteExpectedDate & "','" & StrBuyerLogin & "'," & _
        "'" & StrBuyerName & "'," & IntQuantityOrdered & ") Select @@Identity"
End Sub
```

This activity won't prepare the InsertPurchaseOrder activity to insert the necessary information. After the InsertPurchaseOrder activity is executed, another Code activity needs to be added to set up the purchase order number and update the purchase order number. The SQLInsertUpdate sub is doing all this work.

View the Workflow Designer again, add a Code activity called GetPurchaseOrderNumber, and generate the Handlers for this activity. After the GetPurchaseOrderNumber activity, add another ExecuteSQL activity. Change the name to UpdatePurchaseOrderNumber and set the ConnectionString property, the same as was done with the previous ExecuteSQL activity. Your workflow should look like Figure 8-8.

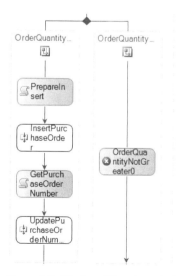

Figure 8-8. *Updated PurchaseOrderProcess workflow*

Within the GetPurchaseOrderNumber generated sub, add the code that's used to determine the purchase order number, using the return value from the InsertPurchaseOrder activity:

```
Private Sub GetPurchaseOrderNumber_ExecuteCode
    (ByVal sender As System.Object, ByVal e As System.EventArgs)
    Dim IntPurchaseOrderID As Integer
    IntPurchaseOrderID = InsertPurchaseOrder.NewID
    Select Case IntPurchaseOrderID
        Case Is < 10
            StrPurchaseOrderNumber = "00000" & IntPurchaseOrderID
        Case Is < 100
            StrPurchaseOrderNumber = "0000" & IntPurchaseOrderID
        Case Is < 1000
            StrPurchaseOrderNumber = "000" & IntPurchaseOrderID
        Case Is < 10000
            StrPurchaseOrderNumber = "00" & IntPurchaseOrderID
        Case Is < 100000
            StrPurchaseOrderNumber = "0" & IntPurchaseOrderID
        Case Else
            StrPurchaseOrderNumber = CStr(IntPurchaseOrderID)
    End Select
    UpdatePurchaseOrderNumber.SQLStatement = "Update tblpurchaseorders " & _
    "set StrPurchaseOrderNumber='" & StrPurchaseOrderNumber & "' " & _
    "where intpurchaseorderid = " & IntPurchaseOrderID
End Sub
```

You can now delete the SQLInsertUpdate sub. The additional activities will perform the Insert and the Update statements that were included in the code previously. The advantage of doing this is the activity that performs all the Execute commands and makes the connection to the database can be reused over and over again. You don't need to keep adding code to a Code activity to perform the command execution.

Execute the workflow and provide all the requested information. The purchase order is added just as it was before, except now you're using the new custom activity ExecuteSQL instead of the code within the workflow.

Conclusion

This chapter has covered the concept of custom activities, and also showed how to create two custom activities. You can add these custom activities to the Toolbox and use them for any new workflows you might want to create. This chapter concluded by adding the new ExecuteSQL custom activity to the Purchase Order Console application, and removing the code within the workflow that performed the work previously. The next chapter will show you how to deploy workflow applications.

CHAPTER 9

■■■

Deploying Workflow Applications

So far this book has covered the basics of workflow, all the out-of-the-box activities, and discussed designing workflows. Once a workflow application is constructed, it must be deployed. This chapter will cover how best to deploy a workflow application. This chapter will also cover how to persist workflow data so multiple users can use the same workflow.

Deployment Options

There are several options for deploying a workflow application. The deployment option you choose depends on the application and its process. If only one person will use the workflow application, which probably will be rare, or if the workflow application can stand alone, you can install the application on the client. If the workflow is to be used by the same application in various places and cannot stand alone, there are two options. You can install the workflow on a server and use .NET remoting to the workflow, or you can create the workflow as a Web service. If you're using an ASP.NET application, the workflow will be installed on the Web server.

All the installations mentioned in the previous section require at least one prerequisite. The basic prerequisite is that the .NET Framework 3.0 must be installed on the workstation or server from which the workflow application is to be run. If you plan to create your workflow application as a Web service or use an ASP.NET application and workflow, the Framework must be installed on the Web server. If you plan to have the workflow on the client, then the Framework must be installed on the client. As with previous .NET Framework versions, installing .NET Framework 3.0 requires administrator rights.

The simplest installation is just to take the executable file and load it on a client or server. Within the workflow folder that was created back in Chapter 2, add a folder called Chapter 9. Create a new VB Sequential Workflow Console Application called VBSimpleDeployment in the Chapter 9 folder. Add a single Code activity to the workflow and leave the name the default. Click "Generate Handlers" for the Code activity, and within the code Handler add `msgbox("I'm here")`. Build the solution and execute the workflow from within VS. You'll see a simple application that opens a console window, and the message box will appear.

The most simple installation is just to copy the executable file. You can find the executable file within a folder in the bin folder of the project. The bin folder contains either a debug folder or a release folder, depending on how you built the solution. By default, when you build a solution a debug folder is created and the executable file is put in there. However, you can change the project properties to build the final release of the application, and then the folder name would be release, not debug. You should find the file VBSimpleDeployment.exe in the folder chapter9\vbsimpledeployment\bin. Double-click the file. The console window appears, and the message box appears. Now copy the VBSimpleDeployment.exe file to the C drive root. Double-click the file and the console window and message box appear again. This type of installation and simple workflow would work best for a workflow that facilitates an automated process. For example, you could use this setup to build a workflow that reads a file or data, and sends e-mails or performs actions based on that data. This could be run from a scheduled task.

■**Note** To use the following example, and all examples in this chapter, you must have created the SQL Server database called Purchasing in Chapter 2.

Real-World Example

This example will use the simple installation method to deploy a simple workflow. This workflow will be a console application, but will be run from a scheduled task. The workflow simply reads data from the purchase order database, and if the expected date is in the past and the purchase order hasn't been received, the buyer will receive an e-mail notification.

Create a new VB Sequential Workflow Console Application called PurchaseOrderReceivedCheck. Add the ExecuteSQL activity created in Chapter 8. Set the SQL statement to the following:

```
Select StrPurchaseOrderNumber,dteExpectedDate,StrBuyerLogin,
IntQuantityOrdered from tblPurchaseOrders where dteExpectedDate <=getdate() and
blnReceived=0
```

This finds any purchase orders that haven't been received, and for which the expected date has passed. Next, for each line in the result set, send an e-mail to the buyer providing the purchase order number, expected date, and quantity ordered, and state that the purchase order hasn't been received.

Build the solution and copy the file PurchaseOrderReceivedCheck.exe to a new folder called PurchaseOrderReceivedCheck on the C drive root. Execute the file. You need to move all files from within the bin folder to the PurchaseOrderReceivedCheck folder. This is because the workflow needs the custom activities, which are DLL files. Execute the file, and an e-mail notification should be sent for the purchase order.

ClickOnce Deployment

The previous example showed a simple installation that can be done easily. However, if you want to change the application in any way, you must move the application to each workstation if it's installed on multiple workstations. Also, you must include the DLL files that represent the custom activities created in Chapter 8. In the past, this has been the issue with most Windows-based applications. Windows-based applications can have a rich user interface, but have been difficult to deploy. To correct this, Microsoft created the ClickOnce deployment technology and included it with VS2005.

ClickOnce deployment allows you to create a package that can be installed from a Web site that installs the application on the client. This could also be done in earlier versions of VS. What makes ClickOnce special is it allows you, as the developer, to set the package to look for updates. Using the update option on a ClickOnce package as a developer, you can make an update to the application and publish it. When the user of the application executes the application the next time, the package will recognize there's an update and ask the user to install it. This installation doesn't require administrator permissions on the workstation. The only exception to this is if the application has a prerequisite that isn't installed on the workstation. For example, the PurchaseOrderReceivedCheck application has a prerequisite of the .NET Framework 3. If a workstation doesn't have the .NET Framework 3 installed, an administrator must install it first. This architecture allows users to install an application to their desktop from a Web site, and when updates are available, the updates are delivered to their desktop automatically. For more information about ClickOnce deployment, see an article I've written entitled "ClickOnce Deployment with VS 2005" for the Web site ASPToday (http://www.ASPToday.com).

Deploying a project with ClickOnce is easy. You can create the application as you normally would. Changes need to be made when the application is ready to be installed. Open the Solution Explorer and double-click My Project. This opens the project properties window. Click the Publish tab on the left side. The Publish screen looks like Figure 9-1.

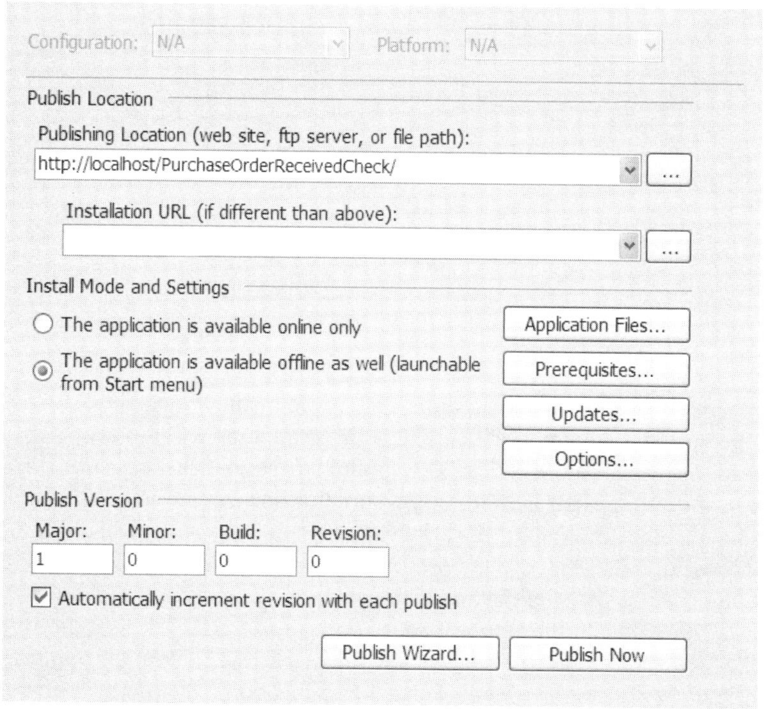

Figure 9-1. *Publish window from project properties*

The publishing location is where you want the users to access the application to install it. Any updates also will be installed to this location. This doesn't need to be a Web site, but that's the easiest for users to access. You can see mine is my local Web server, and a folder called

PurchaseOrderReceivedCheck. You have two choices of how the user will access the application: either online only or offline. If the application is available offline, it will be installed to the workstation, and a shortcut will be provided in the Start menu. You can also control the version of the publication. Each version must be unique for the update to be installed. You can configure how updates are received by clicking the Updates button. The Application Updates dialog appears, as in Figure 9-2.

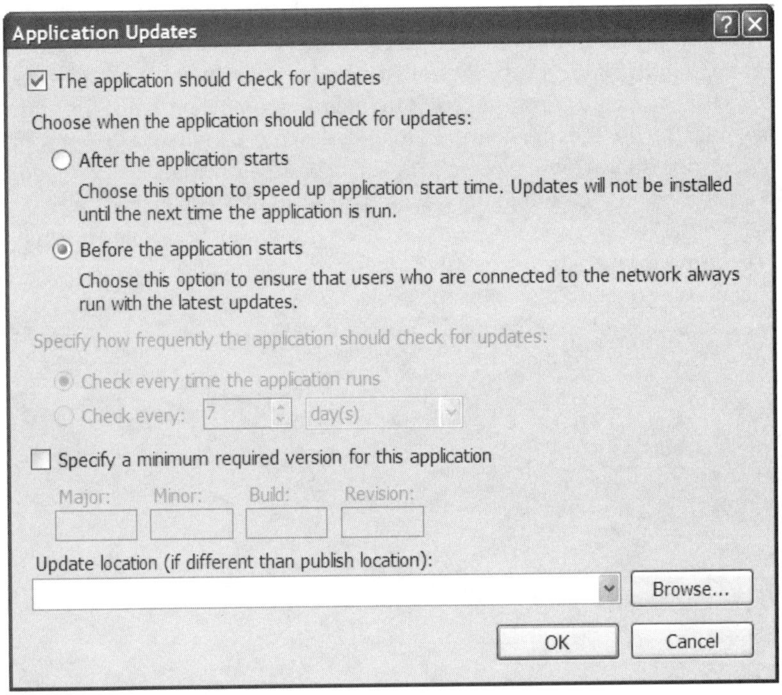

Figure 9-2. *Application Updates window*

The first choice you must make is whether updates are even to be made available. You can use ClickOnce installation as an easier method of application installation without even using the update features by unchecking the check box "The application should check for updates." Obviously, to allow the application to get updates, make sure this box is checked.

Once you've decided to allow updates for the application, you must choose when the application checks for those updates. You can choose "After the application starts" or "Before the application starts." If you choose "After the application starts," the checking and downloading of the update is done in the background while the application works. The next time the user executes the application, the update will be available. If you choose "Before the application starts," the checking occurs when the user executes the application. The update is then installed prior to the application executing, and the latest version is shown to the user. You can also specify that all instances of this application must use a specific version of the application. This is a way to force the updates to be installed. For this application, leave the default, "Before the application starts" and click OK.

After choosing the updates, click the Publish Now button. This begins the process of publishing the application to the location identified. You can follow the progress of the publishing by looking at the status in the bottom-left corner of the project properties window. When the publishing is completed, the status will be Publish Succeeded. Also, when the publishing is completed, a Web browser will appear with the deployment page. The deployment page has the application name, the version, and an Install button, as shown in Figure 9-3. Click the Install button and install the application. Immediately after installing the application, the application will be executed.

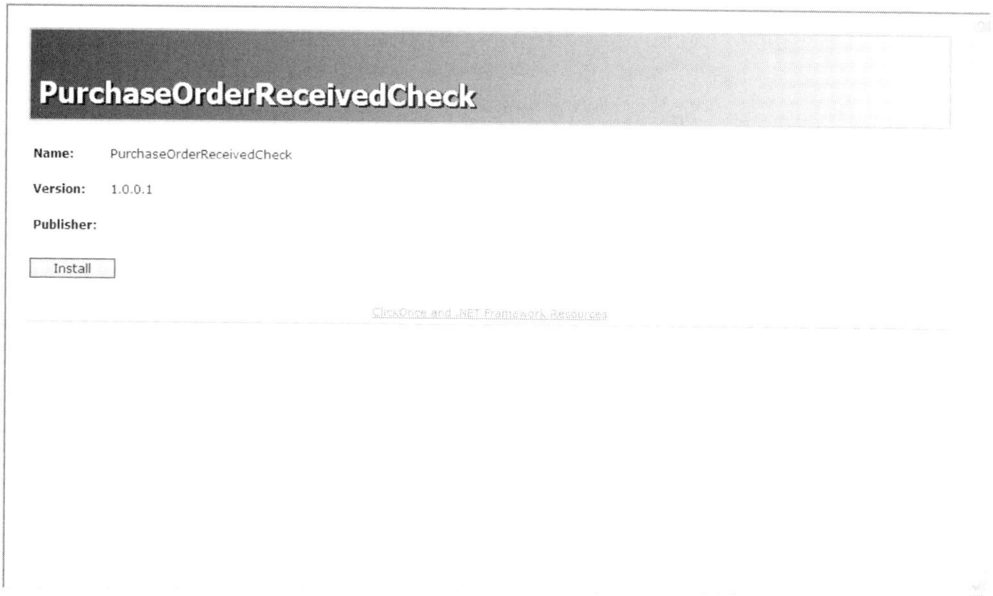

Name: PurchaseOrderReceivedCheck

Version: 1.0.0.1

Publisher:

Install

ClickOnce and .NET Framework Resources

Figure 9-3. *Publish.html to install the ClickOnce package*

To demonstrate how the updates work, add a Code activity to the PurchaseOrderReceivedCheck workflow. Leave the name the default. Generate the Handlers for the Code activity and add the following code to the Handlers created:

```
msgbox("I'm here")
```

Publish the application again. This constitutes an update to the application. When the Web browser appears at the end of the publishing just close it; don't install from the Web browser. Instead, click the Start menu and find the PurchaseOrderReceivedCheck application in the Start menu and click it. You receive a message that an update is available, and you're asked if you want to install the update. Click OK. Once you click OK, the update is installed and the application is executed. The necessary e-mails are sent, and the message box with "I'm here" appears. This shows that the update was installed and is being used. As you can see, the ClickOnce technology provides an easier way to install and update Windows applications than in the past.

SQLPersistenceService

So far the workflow that we've worked with has been rather simple, and in most cases completes immediately. However, real-world workflow usually doesn't work that way. This is especially true when dealing with business processes that require approvals. For example, a document management business process might require multiple approvals before the process is considered complete. If the author of the document sends the document to a reviewer and that reviewer is on vacation, the business process must wait for the reviewer to return. The same can be said for the workflow attempting to facilitate this process. The instance of the workflow that was created by the author would need to wait until the reviewer returned to continue the workflow. This keeping of workflows in memory would take up a lot of memory. Consider a workflow that's a document management workflow deployed as a Web service. The workflow is used by a company of only 100 people. If this is an employee performance review process, each employee would need to create a document. Therefore, there would be at least 100 instances of the workflow loaded in the server's memory. Also, what happens if the server is rebooted for patching, or for any other reason? The workflow wouldn't know that instances existed when the server was rebooted. It would be as if the workflow wasn't executed. WF addresses this with the Persistence Service.

When installing WF, the SQL services that the WF provides aren't installed by default. However, the SQL scripts for creating and configuring the database are provided. The SQL scripts work on Microsoft SQL Server 2005 Express, Microsoft SQL Server 2000 or later, and Microsoft SQL Server 2000 Desktop Engine. You can find the scripts at C:\[windows directory]\\Microsoft.NET\Framework\v3.0\Windows Workflow Foundation\SQL\[language]\ in most installs. Two files for SQL Persistence are in this folder. The first is SQLPersistenceService_Schema. This creates the tables necessary for the service to work. The other script is SQLPersistenceService_Logic. This script creates the stored procedures needed by the SQL Persistence Service.

Create a new database called SqlPersistenceService. Open the schema file (SQLPersistenceService_Schema.sql) either in Query Analyzer (SQL Server 2000) or within the Management Studio (SQL Server 2005). Execute the SQL file into the SqlPersistenceService database. Refresh the table list, if necessary, and you'll see two tables have been created: CompletedScope and InstanceState. Open the logic file (SQLPersistenceService_Logic.sql) and execute the file into the SQLPersistenceService database. You'll see there are now stored procedures in the database.

Implementing Persistence in VB

Create a new VB Sequential Workflow Console Application called VBPersistence in the Chapter 9 folder. There are two ways to tie the SQLWorkflowPersistenceService to your workflow. You can either add it to the runtime as a service, or you can define it within the app.config file. I'll show both ways here, but only the app.config approach will be used. Within the Sub Main() in Module1.vb after the AddHandler lines, add the following lines of code:

```
workflowRuntime.AddService(New SqlWorkflowPersistenceService("Initial Catalog=
SqlPersistenceService;Data Source=localhost;Integrated Security=SSPI;"))
```

These lines add an instance of the SQLWorkflowPersistenceService to the workflow runtime. The parameter provided is the connection string to the SQLPersistenceService database.

You can make changes to this as necessary. Add the following code as Handlers to the Module1.vb code file:

```
Shared Sub UnloadInstance(ByVal workflowInstance As Object)
    CType(workflowInstance, WorkflowInstance).TryUnload()
End Sub
Shared Sub OnWorkflowCompleted(ByVal sender As Object, ByVal e As
WorkflowCompletedEventArgs)
    WaitHandle.Set()
End Sub
Shared Sub OnWorkflowTerminated(ByVal sender As Object, ByVal e As
WorkflowTerminatedEventArgs)
    Console.WriteLine(e.Exception.Message)
WaitHandle.Set()
End Sub
Shared Sub OnWorkflowLoaded(ByVal sender As Object, ByVal e As WorkflowEventArgs)
    Console.WriteLine("Workflow was loaded.")
End Sub

Shared Sub OnWorkflowUnloaded(ByVal sender As Object, ByVal e As WorkflowEventArgs)
    Console.WriteLine("Workflow was unloaded.")
End Sub
Shared Sub OnWorkflowPersisted(ByVal sender As Object, ByVal e As WorkflowEventArgs)
    Console.WriteLine("Workflow was persisted.")
End Sub
Shared Sub OnWorkflowIdled(ByVal sender As Object, ByVal e As WorkflowEventArgs)
    Console.WriteLine("Workflow is idle.")
    ThreadPool.QueueUserWorkItem(New WaitCallback(AddressOf UnloadInstance),
    e.WorkflowInstance)
End Sub
```

Make sure the following Handlers are defined within the Sub Main():

```
AddHandler workflowRuntime.WorkflowCompleted, AddressOf OnWorkflowCompleted
AddHandler workflowRuntime.WorkflowIdled, AddressOf OnWorkflowIdled
AddHandler workflowRuntime.WorkflowPersisted, AddressOf OnWorkflowPersisted
AddHandler workflowRuntime.WorkflowUnloaded, AddressOf OnWorkflowUnloaded
AddHandler workflowRuntime.WorkflowLoaded, AddressOf OnWorkflowLoaded
AddHandler workflowRuntime.WorkflowTerminated, AddressOf OnWorkflowTerminated
```

Add a Code activity to the workflow, leaving the name the default and generating the Handlers. Within the Handler, add the following:

```
msgbox("First activity: " & now())
```

Next, add a Delay activity with a timeout duration property set to 30 seconds. Add another Code activity to the workflow, leaving the name the default and generating the Handlers. Within the Handler add the following:

```
msgbox("Second activity: " & now())
```

Execute the workflow, and you'll see the workflow going idle, persisting its data, unloading, loading again, and displaying the correct time. Using a Delay activity is the first way to force a workflow to go idle and persist its data. The other way is to call the Unload method of the workflow instance. By default, this method uses the Persistence Service associated with the workflow to take the workflow instance out of memory and save the state of the workflow. You can then use the GetWorkflow method of the workflow runtime and the Load method of the workflow instance to load the correct instance of the workflow up again.

To see how this might work, add a Suspend activity after the Delay activity but before the second Code activity. Execute the workflow. You'll see the workflow get unloaded, persist, and load up again. Then the workflow will stop. Open a new query into the SQLPersistenceDatabase and execute `Select * from instancestate`. You'll see there's a uidinstanceid column that has a GUID representing the workflow instance. How can you use this to your advantage? When you have an application that's using a workflow that will take some time, such as a document review process, you can store the GUID of the workflow instance that's taking care of that document. We'll use this to expand the purchase order example.

Implementing Persistence in C#

Create a new C# Sequential Workflow Console Application called CPersistence in the Chapter 9 folder. Within the void `Main` in Program.cs after the AddHandler lines, add the following lines of code:

```
workflowRuntime.AddService(new SqlWorkflowPersistenceService("Initial Catalog=
SqlPersistenceService;Data Source=localhost;Integrated Security=SSPI;"));
```

These lines add an instance of the SQLWorkflowPersistenceService to the workflow runtime. The parameter provided is the connection string to the SQLPersistenceService database. You can make changes to this as necessary. Add the following code as Handlers to the Program.cs code file:

```
static void OnWorkflowTerminated(object sender, WorkflowTerminatedEventArgs e)
{
    Console.WriteLine(e.Exception.Message);
    waitHandle.Set();
}
static void OnWorkflowLoaded(object sender, WorkflowEventArgs e)
{
    Console.WriteLine("Workflow was loaded.");
}
static void OnWorkflowUnloaded(object sender, WorkflowEventArgs e)
{
    Console.WriteLine("Workflow was unloaded.");
}
static void OnWorkflowPersisted(object sender, WorkflowEventArgs e)
{
    Console.WriteLine("Workflow was persisted.");
}
```

```
static void OnWorkflowIdled(object sender, WorkflowEventArgs e)
{
    Console.WriteLine("Workflow is idle.");
    ThreadPool.QueueUserWorkItem(UnloadInstance, e.WorkflowInstance);
}
static void UnloadInstance(object workflowInstance)
{
    ((WorkflowInstance)workflowInstance).TryUnload();
}
static void OnWorkflowCompleted(object sender, WorkflowCompletedEventArgs instance)
{
    waitHandle.Set();
}
```

Make sure the following Handlers are defined within the void `Main`:

```
workflowRuntime.WorkflowCompleted += OnWorkflowCompleted;
workflowRuntime.WorkflowIdled += OnWorkflowIdled;
workflowRuntime.WorkflowPersisted += OnWorkflowPersisted;
workflowRuntime.WorkflowUnloaded += OnWorkflowUnloaded;
workflowRuntime.WorkflowLoaded += OnWorkflowLoaded;
workflowRuntime.WorkflowTerminated += OnWorkflowTerminated;
```

Add a Code activity to the workflow, leaving the name the default and generating the Handlers. Within the Handler add the following:

```
Console .Write ("First Activity: " + DateTime .Now);
```

Next, add a Delay activity with a timeout duration property set to 30 seconds. Add another Code activity to the workflow, leaving the name the default and generating the Handlers. Within the Handler add the following:

```
Console .Write ("Second Activity: " + DateTime .Now);
```

Execute the workflow, and you'll see the workflow going idle, persisting its data, unloading, loading again, and displaying the correct time. Using a Delay activity is the first way to force a workflow to go idle and persist its data. The other way is to call the Unload method of the workflow instance. By default, this method uses the Persistence Service associated with the workflow to take the workflow instance out of memory and save the state of the workflow. You can then use the GetWorkflow method of the workflow runtime and the Load method of the workflow instance to load the correct instance of the workflow up again.

To see how this might work, add a Suspend activity after the Delay activity but before the second Code activity. Execute the workflow. You'll see the workflow get unloaded, persist, and load up again. Then the workflow will stop. Open a new query into the SQLPersistenceDatabase and execute `Select * from instancestate`. You'll see there's a uidinstanceid column that has a GUID representing the workflow instance.

Conclusion

This chapter has covered how to deploy a workflow application, and also how to persistent the workflow data. The next chapter will use all the knowledge learned in the previous chapters to build a real-world application. The application will be an ASP.NET-based employee performance review application that uses workflow.

■ ■ ■

CHAPTER 10

Employee Performance Review Application

The previous chapters first introduced you to workflow, then described the various activities that can be added to a workflow, and finally discussed custom activities. The previous chapters also covered how to interact with workflow from other applications. This chapter will bring together all the concepts learned in the previous chapters to build a real-world application: an Employee Performance Review workflow application.

Workflow Design

As with any software development project, the first step is to understand the requirements of the system. The first step in understanding the requirements is to understand the business process. In general, a workflow application models a business process. You must define that process so it can be modeled. Once you define the business process, you can create a model to show the project stakeholders—those that use the process—to make sure the process was captured correctly. After the process is modeled, you need to determine which type of workflow to use (Sequential or State Machine). Finally, you need to select and model all the activities that will be used. At the end of this process, a model will exist that models the process and also allows you to begin immediately with constructing the necessary activities.

Employee Performance Review Business Process

The first step in developing a workflow application is to define the business process. Here's the business process this application facilitates:

1. Employee begins a self-review. For each review, the employee's name, location, supervisor, title, and department must be known.

2. Employee provides a summary of activities for the previous year.

3. Employee rates himself or herself on various criteria, and provides a summary for each criterion.

4. Employee provides overall rating of self.

5. Employee provides goals for the coming year.

6. Employee provides a self-review to the supervisor.

7. Supervisor reviews the self-review.

8. Supervisor makes any necessary changes to the summary of activities.

9. Supervisor makes any necessary changes to the criteria ratings and summaries.

10. Supervisor provides an overall rating.

11. Supervisor makes any necessary revisions to the coming year goals.

12. Supervisor can submit the review back to the employee for further review or can submit the review to human resources.

13. Employee can receive the review back for further review or final submission.

14. Employee receiving the review back for further review can make changes and resubmit to the supervisor.

15. Employee receiving the review for final submission cannot make edits, and can either approve or disapprove.

16. Approved reviews are submitted to human resources and closed.

17. Disapproved reviews are submitted to human resources for review.

This is the business process to be modeled. However, the system needs to facilitate additional requirements. These requirements aren't part of the business process, but must exist in the system for the system to be more user friendly. The additional non-business–process requirements are as follows:

- Human resources must maintain a hierarchy of employees and supervisors.

- The system must determine the supervisor for any employee; the employee doesn't determine the supervisor when sending the review.

- The system must store the supervisor, location, title, and department for each employee. This is maintained by the human resources department.

- Supervisors must be able to see a list of all their reports and the status of their Employee Performance Reviews. A supervisor must also be able to see a read-only copy of an Employee Performance Review of any of his or her direct reports. This would be for reviews already completed.

- Human resources must be able to see the status of all reviews at all times.

Although these additional requirements aren't part of the business process, any system that facilitates this process must provide these features. The workflow doesn't provide most of these features; instead, the host application provides them, in this case an ASP.NET application. Figure 10-1 displays a flow chart showing the business process flow (it doesn't include the non-business–process requirements listed earlier).

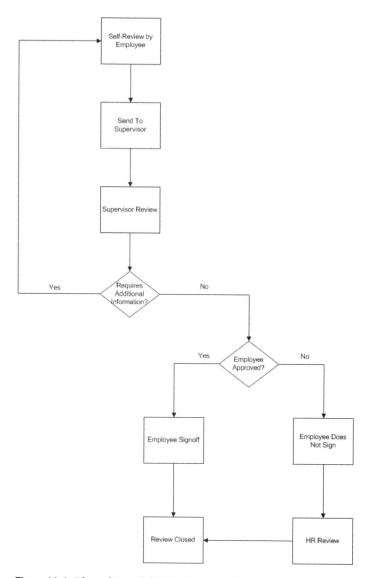

Figure 10-1. *Flow chart of the Employee Performance Review business process*

Translating Model into Workflow

Now that you've modeled the business process with a flow chart, you'll use this flow chart to lay out the workflow. As you can see in Table 10-1, an Employee Performance Review can be in a variety of statuses or states at any time.

Table 10-1. *Statuses Within Workflow*

Status	Description
New	Employee creates a new self-review
Submitted to Supervisor	Employee has submitted self-review to supervisor
Supervisor Approved	Supervisor approves the review
Return to Employee	Supervisor wants employee to make changes; returns to employee
Resubmitted to Supervisor	Employee makes changes and resubmits to supervisor
Employee Approved	Employee approves of final review
Employee Disapproved	Employee does not approve of final review

The first determination that needs to be made is which workflow to use. Because this workflow includes a variety of statuses or states, the best workflow to use is a State Machine workflow. The main reason for using a State Machine workflow in this case is because there's lots of human interaction with the workflow. Also, a single performance review can sit at a specific state for any given amount of time. For example, it's not difficult to see that it's possible for a review to sit at supervisor review for days or weeks.

Unfortunately, there aren't many design tools that exist for designing workflows. Even Microsoft Visio doesn't do a good job. Visio has a workflow template, but that's more for showing the workflow at a high level, not for designing a workflow system. I'm sure, as Microsoft gets WF to market, there will be better tools for designing workflows within WF. For now, I'm going to write out the description of each state within the State Machine.

- *State 1: New Self-Review.* The employee is submitting the self-review. This is the first step in the workflow. The employee can provide all the necessary information and save the information as many times as he or she wants before even activating the workflow. Once the self-review is submitted, then the workflow takes over the business process. Within this state, the supervisor must be found for the employee, and the review's current approver sent to the supervisor. Also, an e-mail notification must go out to the supervisor letting the supervisor know the employee has submitted the self-review. The state is changed to Supervisor Review.

- *State 2: Supervisor Review*. The employee has submitted the self-review and the supervisor has received the review notification. The supervisor chooses to view the review. The workflow provides the information about the review to the application. The supervisor provides any changes. The supervisor either approves or requests further information. If the supervisor approves, then the state changes to Supervisor Approved. If the supervisor requests additional information, then the state changes to Return to Employee.

- *State 3: Supervisor Approved*: The supervisor has approved the review. An e-mail is sent to the employee telling the employee the review has been approved. The current approver for the review is set to the employee. The workflow provides the application with information about the review. The employee either signs the review or doesn't sign. The state changes to either Employee Approved or Employee Disapproved.

- *State 4: Return to Employee*: The supervisor has asked the employee for more information. An e-mail is sent to the employee requesting additional information. The employee is the approver of the review. The employee provides additional information and sends it back to the supervisor for review. The state is changed to Supervisor Review.

- *State 5: Employee Approved*: The employee has approved the review. The date and time are recorded. The status is changed to Completed. The current approver is set to HR. The state is changed to Workflow Complete.

- *State 6: Employee Disapproved*: The employee has disapproved the review. The status is changed to Not Approved. An e-mail notification is sent to human resources. The state is changed to Workflow Complete.

Application Details

The Employee Performance Review (EPR) system will be an ASP.NET application that uses a workflow created with WF. Both the ASP.NET application and the workflow will use a SQL Server database called EPR. The workflow will also use the SQLPersistenceService database that will be used to keep persistence information about the workflow. You'll create both the ASP.NET application and the workflow using VB. Finally, the workflow will use the SendEmail and ExecuteSQL activities that were created in Chapter 8. Following are the steps that will be taken to develop this application:

1. Create the EPR database and the necessary tables.

2. Create the SQLPersistenceService SQL Server database.

3. Create a new ASP.NET Web site.

4. Build all ASP.NET Web pages that don't interact with the workflow.

5. Build the complete workflow and test with a simple console application first.

6. Connect the ASP.NET Web pages and the workflow together.

Of course, these tasks are rather high level, but they give you an idea of what needs to be completed to build this application. The completed application has been provided in the code samples with this book (you can download the samples from Source Code/Download area of the Apress Web site at http://www.apress.com).

Create the EPR Database and Tables

The first task to be completed is to create the EPR database. Nothing special needs to be done when creating this database; simply create a new SQL Server database called EPR. After the database is created, you must add a new SQL Server login. Both the Web application and the workflow will use this to communicate with the SQL Server. Click the Security folder on the database server, right-click Logins, and choose New Login. When the Login-New window appears, enter **EPRUser** as the Login Name and choose SQL Server authentication. Enter **EmployeeReview99** as the password (or you can use your own—just remember what it is). Choose EPR as the Default Database and click the User Mapping link on the left. Click the check box next to EPR to map the login to the EPR database, and click OK. The next step is to create the necessary tables. The following tables will be included:

- *tblDepartment*: Lists all the departments within the organization

- *tblEmployees*: Lists all the employees within the organization

- *tblLocation*: Lists all the employee locations within the organization

- *tblQuestions*: Lists the questions to be asked during the review

- *tblReview*: Main table that holds all reviews

- *tblReviewGoal*: Holds the goals for each review

- *tblReviewQuestion*: Links the Review and Questions tables together and provides the response to each question

This list was determined by looking at the business process and the flow chart of the process, along with the description of each step in the workflow. The Employees table is needed because HR, by business process, must maintain a list of all employees. The Location and Department tables are also necessary because HR must maintain the department and location of each employee. Creating separate tables for this data makes the database in third normal form. If you aren't familiar with third normal form as it relates to database design, a number of excellent database design books are available for more information.

The Questions table allows HR to create a list of questions to be used for reviews. The questions can be activated or deactivated from year to year. By storing the questions in a table and displaying them dynamically, the application becomes more flexible, as HR can control the questions. The Review table is the main table and contains information about each review that's created. This table links (via primary key and foreign key relationships) to the Employees table. The ReviewGoal table contains a list of goals for each review. The employee and supervisor can enter multiple goals for each review, so they need to be stored in a separate table. This table links (via primary key and foreign key relationships) to the Review table. Finally, the ReviewQuestion table contains a list of questions and the response to each question. For each question, the user needs to choose one of four possible answers. This table keeps a list of all the questions for a review, because there will be multiple questions per review. This table also links back to the Review table. Figure 10-2 shows a SQL Server 2005 database diagram of the tables and includes the relationships.

Figure 10-2. *SQL Server 2005 diagram of EPR database tables*

Within the code folder provided with this book, there's a folder called VBEmployeePerformanceReview. Within that folder is a file called EPR_Schema.sql. You can use this file to create the tables mentioned earlier; it's been created to work on either SQL Server 2005 or SQL Server 2000. Following are the contents of that file so you can create the tables if you don't have the code.

```
CREATE TABLE [dbo].[tblEmployees](
    [IntEmployeeID] [int] IDENTITY(1,1) NOT NULL,
    [StrFirstName] [varchar](50) NULL,
    [StrLastName] [varchar](50) NULL,
    [StrLogin] [varchar](20) NULL,
    [StrPassword] [varchar](20) NULL,
    [IntLocationID] [int] NULL,
    [StrTitle] [varchar](255) NULL,
    [IntDepartmentID] [int] NULL,
    [IntSupervisorID] [int] NULL,
    [blnHR] [bit] NULL CONSTRAINT [DF_tblEmployees_blnHR] DEFAULT ((0)),
    [blnActive] [bit] NULL CONSTRAINT [DF_tblEmployees_blnActive] DEFAULT ((1)),
    CONSTRAINT [PK_tblEmployees] PRIMARY KEY CLUSTERED
(
    [IntEmployeeID] ASC
    )WITH (IGNORE_DUP_KEY = OFF) ON [PRIMARY]
) ON [PRIMARY]
GO
CREATE TABLE [dbo].[tblLocation](
    [IntLocationID] [int] IDENTITY(1,1) NOT NULL,
    [StrLocation] [varchar](50) NULL,
    [blnActive] [bit] NULL CONSTRAINT [DF_tblLocation_blnActive] DEFAULT ((1)),
    CONSTRAINT [PK_tblLocation] PRIMARY KEY CLUSTERED
```

```
(
    [IntLocationID] ASC
    )WITH (IGNORE_DUP_KEY = OFF) ON [PRIMARY]
) ON [PRIMARY]
CREATE TABLE [dbo].[tblDepartment](
    [IntDepartmentID] [int] IDENTITY(1,1) NOT NULL,
    [StrDepartment] [varchar](50) NULL,
    [blnActive] [bit] NULL CONSTRAINT [DF_tblDepartment_blnActive]  DEFAULT ((1)),
    CONSTRAINT [PK_tblDepartment] PRIMARY KEY CLUSTERED
(
    [IntDepartmentID] ASC
    )WITH (IGNORE_DUP_KEY = OFF) ON [PRIMARY]
) ON [PRIMARY]
GO
CREATE TABLE [dbo].[tblReview](
    [IntReviewID] [int] IDENTITY(1,1) NOT NULL,
    [IntEmployeeID] [int] NULL,
    [IntSupervisorID] [int] NULL,
    [DteDateCreated] [datetime] NULL CONSTRAINT
        [DF_tblReview_DteDateCreated] DEFAULT (getdate()),
    [StrSummaryOfActivities] [text] NULL,
    [StrCareerInterests] [text] NULL,
    [StrEmployeeComments] [text] NULL,
    [DteEmployeeSignatureDate] [datetime] NULL,
    [DteSupervisorSignatureDate] [datetime] NULL CONSTRAINT
        [DF_tblReview_DteSupervisorSignatureDate]  DEFAULT ((0)),
    [blnComplete] [bit] NULL,
    [dteDateCompleted] [datetime] NULL,
    [IntInstanceID] [int] NULL,
    CONSTRAINT [PK_tblReview] PRIMARY KEY CLUSTERED
(
    [IntReviewID] ASC
    )WITH (IGNORE_DUP_KEY = OFF) ON [PRIMARY]
) ON [PRIMARY] TEXTIMAGE_ON [PRIMARY]
GO
CREATE TABLE [dbo].[tblReviewGoal](
    [IntGoalID] [int] IDENTITY(1,1) NOT NULL,
    [IntReviewID] [int] NULL,
    [StrGoal] [text] NULL,
    [StrActionPlan] [text] NULL,
    [StrTargetCompletionDate] [varchar](50) NULL,
    [StrPriority] [varchar](50) NULL,
    CONSTRAINT [PK_tblReviewGoal] PRIMARY KEY CLUSTERED
(
    [IntGoalID] ASC
    )WITH (IGNORE_DUP_KEY = OFF) ON [PRIMARY]
) ON [PRIMARY] TEXTIMAGE_ON [PRIMARY]
GO
```

```
CREATE TABLE [dbo].[tblReviewQuestion](
    [IntReviewID] [int] NOT NULL,
    [IntQuestionID] [int] NOT NULL,
    [blnResponse1] [bit] NULL CONSTRAINT [DF_tblReviewQuestion_IntResponse1]
        DEFAULT ((0)),
    [blnResponse2] [bit] NULL CONSTRAINT [DF_tblReviewQuestion_IntResponse2]
        DEFAULT ((0)),
    [blnResponse3] [bit] NULL CONSTRAINT [DF_tblReviewQuestion_IntResponse3]
        DEFAULT ((0)),
    [blnResponse4] [bit] NULL CONSTRAINT [DF_tblReviewQuestion_IntResponse4]
        DEFAULT ((0)),
    [StrComments] [text] NULL,
    CONSTRAINT [PK_tblReviewQuestion] PRIMARY KEY CLUSTERED
(
    [IntReviewID] ASC,
    [IntQuestionID] ASC
    )WITH (IGNORE_DUP_KEY = OFF) ON [PRIMARY]
) ON [PRIMARY] TEXTIMAGE_ON [PRIMARY]
GO
CREATE TABLE [dbo].[tblQuestions](
    [IntQuestionID] [int] IDENTITY(1,1) NOT NULL,
    [StrQuestion] [text] NULL,
    [IntOrder] [int] NULL,
    [blnActive] [bit] NULL CONSTRAINT [DF_tblQuestions_blnActive]  DEFAULT ((1)),
    CONSTRAINT [PK_tblQuestions] PRIMARY KEY CLUSTERED
(
    [IntQuestionID] ASC
    )WITH (IGNORE_DUP_KEY = OFF) ON [PRIMARY]
) ON [PRIMARY] TEXTIMAGE_ON [PRIMARY]
```

This application also uses a number of stored procedures within the EPR database. Stored procedures within SQL Server are similar to functions within VB code, in that they can accept parameters or not, and perform some type of action. The majority of this application isn't related to the actual workflow. For example, HR must maintain employees. There's no tie into the workflow with this part of the process. This is a maintenance function that is to be performed via the application. You handle this type of functionality by connecting the ASP.NET application with stored procedures housed in the EPR database. You handle the actions that need to be taken within the workflow via SQL statements within the workflow, using the ExecuteSQL activity that was created in Chapter 8.

Because there are stored procedures to be created, you can create them now. Within the same VBEmployeePerformanceReview folder in which you found the EPR_Schema.sql file, there's a file called EPR_Logic.sql. Either open this file into SQL Query Analyzer (SQL Server 2000) or just open the file (SQL Server 2005) and execute the file. This creates all the necessary stored procedures. Following is all the stored procedure logic.

```
CREATE PROCEDURE [dbo].[usp_UpdateReviewQuestion]
    @IntReviewID int,
    @IntQuestionID int,
    @IntResponse int,
    @StrComments text
AS
BEGIN
    update tblreviewquestion
    set IntResponse=@IntResponse,
    strComments = @Strcomments
    where IntReviewId = @IntReviewId
    and intQuestionId = @IntQuestionID
END
CREATE PROCEDURE [dbo].[usp_UpdateCriteriaComment]
    @IntReviewID int,
    @IntQuestionID int,
    @StrComments text
AS
BEGIN
    update tblReviewQuestion
    set strcomments = @StrComments
    where intreviewid=@intreviewid
    and intquestionid = @intquestionid
END
CREATE PROCEDURE [dbo].[usp_RetrieveEmployeeID]
    @StrLogin varchar(20)
AS
BEGIN
    select intemployeeid
    from tblemployees
    where strlogin = @strlogin
END
CREATE PROCEDURE [dbo].[usp_RetrieveEmployeeInformation]
    @IntEmployeeID int
AS
BEGIN
    SELECT tblEmployees.IntEmployeeID, tblEmployees.StrFirstName,
    tblEmployees.StrLastName, tblEmployees.StrLogin, tblEmployees.StrPassword,
    tblEmployees.IntLocationID, tblLocation.StrLocation, tblEmployees.StrTitle,
    tblEmployees.IntDepartmentID, tblDepartment.StrDepartment,
    tblEmployees.IntSupervisorID, sup.StrFirstName + ' ' + sup.StrLastName
    AS Supervisor,
    tblEmployees.blnHR, tblEmployees.blnActive
    FROM tblEmployees LEFT OUTER JOIN
    tblLocation ON tblEmployees.IntLocationID = tblLocation.IntLocationID
    LEFT OUTER JOIN
    tblEmployees AS sup ON tblEmployees.IntSupervisorID = sup.IntEmployeeID
```

```
        LEFT OUTER JOIN
        tblDepartment ON tblEmployees.IntDepartmentID = tblDepartment.IntDepartmentID
        where tblemployees.intemployeeid=@intemployeeid
END
CREATE PROCEDURE [dbo].[usp_AddReview]
        @IntEmployeeID int,
        @StrSummaryOfActivities text,
        @StrCareerInterests text
AS
BEGIN
        Declare @IntSupervisorID int
        select @IntSupervisorId = IntSupervisorID
        from tblemployees
        where intemployeeid = @IntEmployeeID
        insert into tblReview(IntEmployeeID,IntSupervisorID,
        StrSummaryOfActivities,StrCareerInterests)
        values (@IntEmployeeID,@IntSupervisorID,
        @StrSummaryOfActivities,@StrCareerInterests)
        declare @NextID int
        set @NextID=@@Identity
        insert into tblReviewQuestion(IntReviewID,
        IntQuestionID)
        select @NextID,IntQuestionID
        from tblQuestions
        where blnactive=1
        order by intorder
        select @NextID
END
CREATE PROCEDURE [dbo].[usp_RetrieveReviewsForEmployee]
        @IntEmployeeID int
AS
BEGIN
        SELECT     tblreview.intreviewid,Supervisor.StrFirstName +
        Supervisor.StrLastName AS SupervisorName, tblReview.DteDateCreated,
        tblReview.dteDateCompleted
        FROM tblEmployees AS Supervisor RIGHT OUTER JOIN
        tblReview ON Supervisor.IntEmployeeID = tblReview.IntSupervisorID
        WHERE (tblReview.IntEmployeeID = @IntEmployeeID)
END
CREATE PROCEDURE [dbo].[usp_AddEmployee]
        @StrFirstName varchar(50),
        @StrLastName varchar(50),
        @StrLogin varchar(20),
        @StrPassword varchar(20),
        @IntLocationID int,
        @StrTitle varchar(255),
        @IntDepartmentID int,
```

```
        @IntSupervisorID int,
        @blnHR bit
AS
BEGIN
        Insert into tblemployees(StrFirstName,StrLastName,
        StrLogin,StrPassword,IntLocationID,StrTitle,
        IntDepartmentID,IntSupervisorID,blnHR)
        values(@StrFirstName,@StrLastName,@StrLogin,
        @StrPassword,@IntLocationID,@StrTitle,
        @IntDepartmentID,@IntSupervisorID,@blnHR)
END
CREATE PROCEDURE [dbo].[usp_UpdateEmployee]
        @IntEmployeeID int,
        @StrFirstName varchar(50),
        @StrLastName varchar(50),
        @StrLogin varchar(20),
        @StrPassword varchar(20),
        @IntLocationID int,
        @StrTitle varchar(255),
        @IntDepartmentID int,
        @IntSupervisorID int,
        @blnHR bit,
        @blnActive bit
AS
BEGIN
        update tblemployees
        set StrFirstName = @StrFirstName,
        StrLastName = @StrLastName,
        StrLogin = @StrLogin,
        StrPassword = @StrPassword,
        IntLocationID = @IntLocationID,
        StrTitle = @StrTitle,
        IntDepartmentID = @IntDepartmentID,
        IntSupervisorID = @IntSupervisorID,
        blnHR = @blnHR,
        blnActive = @blnActive
        where IntEmployeeID = @IntEmployeeID
END
CREATE PROCEDURE [dbo].[usp_DeleteEmployee]
        @IntEmployeeID int
AS
BEGIN
        update tblEmployees
        set blnActive=0
        where intemployeeid = @IntEmployeeID
END
```

```
CREATE PROCEDURE [dbo].[usp_RetrieveEmployeeListForLocation]
     @IntLocationId int
AS
BEGIN
     Select StrFirstName, StrLastName
     from tblEmployees
     where IntLocationID = @IntLocationID
END
CREATE PROCEDURE [dbo].[usp_RetrieveEmployeesForSupervisor]
     @IntSupervisorID int
AS
BEGIN
     select StrFirstName,StrLastName
     from tblEmployees
     where IntSupervisorID = @IntSupervisorID
END
CREATE PROCEDURE [dbo].[usp_AddLocation]
     @StrLocation varchar(50)
AS
BEGIN
     insert into tbllocation(StrLocation)
     values(@StrLocation)
END
CREATE PROCEDURE [dbo].[usp_UpdateLocation]
     @IntLocationId int,
     @StrLocation varchar(50),
     @blnActive bit
AS
BEGIN
     Update tblLocation
     set StrLocation = @StrLocation,
     blnActive=@blnActive
     where IntLocationID = @IntLocationID
END
CREATE PROCEDURE [dbo].[usp_RetrieveLocationList]
AS
BEGIN
     select IntLocationID,StrLocation
     from tbllocation
     where blnactive=1
END
```

```
CREATE PROCEDURE [dbo].[usp_DeleteLocation]
    @IntLocationID int
AS
BEGIN
    update tbllocation
    set blnactive=0
    where intlocationid = @intlocationid
END
CREATE PROCEDURE [dbo].[usp_RetrieveFullLocationList]
AS
BEGIN
select IntLocationID,StrLocation,blnactive
from tbllocation
END
CREATE PROCEDURE [dbo].[usp_DeleteDepartment]
    @IntDepartmentID int
AS
BEGIN
    update tbldepartment
    set blnactive=0
    where intdepartmentid = @intdepartmentid
END
CREATE PROCEDURE [dbo].[usp_RetrieveFullDepartmentList]
AS
BEGIN
    select IntDepartmentID,StrDepartment,blnactive
    from tblDepartment
END
CREATE PROCEDURE [dbo].[usp_AddDepartment]
    @StrDepartment varchar(50)
AS
BEGIN
    insert into tbldepartment(StrDepartment)
    values (@StrDepartment)
END
CREATE PROCEDURE [dbo].[usp_UpdateDepartment]
    @IntDepartmentID int,
    @StrDepartment varchar(50),
    @blnActive bit
AS
BEGIN
    update tbldepartment
    set StrDepartment = @StrDepartment,
    blnActive=@blnActive
    where intdepartmentid = @intdepartmentid
END
```

```
CREATE PROCEDURE [dbo].[usp_RetrieveDepartmentList]
AS
BEGIN
    select IntDepartmentID,StrDepartment,blnactive
    from tblDepartment
    where blnactive=1
END
CREATE PROCEDURE [dbo].[usp_UpdateReview]
    @IntReviewID int,
    @StrSummaryOfActivities text,
    @StrCareerInterests text,
    @StrEmployeeComments text
AS
BEGIN
    update tblreview
    set StrSummaryofActivities = @StrSummaryOfActivities,
    StrCareerInterests = @StrCareerInterests,
    StrEmployeeComments = @StrEmployeeComments
    where IntReviewID = @IntReviewID
END
CREATE PROCEDURE [dbo].[usp_CompleteReview]
    @IntReviewID int
AS
BEGIN
    update tblreview
    set blncomplete=1,
    dtedatecompleted=getdate()
    where intreviewid = @intreviewid
END
CREATE PROCEDURE [dbo].[usp_EmployeeSignature]
    @IntReviewId int
AS
BEGIN
    update tblReview
    set dteEmployeeSignatureDate = getdate()
    where intreviewid = @intreviewid
END
CREATE PROCEDURE [dbo].[usp_SupervisorSignature]
    @IntReviewID int
AS
BEGIN
    update tblreview
    set dtesupervisorsignaturedate=getdate()
    where intreviewid = @intreviewid
END
```

```
CREATE PROCEDURE [dbo].[usp_RetrieveReview]
    @IntReviewID int
AS
BEGIN
    select IntReviewID,IntEmployeeID,
    intsupervisorID,dtedatecreated,
    strsummaryofactivities,strcareerinterests,
    stremployeecomments,dteemployeesignaturedate,
    dtesupervisorsignaturedate,
    blncomplete,dtedatecompleted
    from tblreview
    where intreviewid=@intreviewid
END
CREATE PROCEDURE [dbo].[usp_AddGoal]
    @IntReviewID int,
    @StrGoal text,
    @StrActionPlan text,
    @StrTargetCompletionDate varchar(50),
    @StrPriority varchar(50)
AS
BEGIN
    insert into tblReviewGoal(IntReviewID,
    StrGoal,StrActionPlan,StrTargetCompletionDate,
    StrPriority)
    values(@IntReviewID,@StrGoal,@StrActionPlan,
    @StrTargetCompletionDate,@StrPriority)
END

CREATE PROCEDURE [dbo].[usp_UpdateGoal]
    @IntGoalID int,
    @StrGoal text,
    @StrActionPlan text,
    @StrTargetCompletionDate varchar(50),
    @StrPriority varchar(50)
AS
BEGIN
    update tblReviewGoal
    set StrGoal = @StrGoal,
    StrActionPlan = @StrActionPlan,
    StrTargetCompletionDate = @StrTargetCompletionDate,
    StrPriority = @StrPriority
    where IntGoalID =@intGoalID
END
```

```
CREATE PROCEDURE [dbo].[usp_RetrieveGoalsForReview]
    @IntReviewID int
AS
BEGIN
    Select IntGoalID,StrGoal,StrActionPlan,StrTargetCompletionDate,
    StrPriority
    from tblReviewGoal
    where IntReviewID = @IntReviewID
END
CREATE PROCEDURE [dbo].[usp_RetrieveReviewQuestions]
    @IntReviewID int
AS
BEGIN
    SELECT tblReviewQuestion.IntReviewID, tblReviewQuestion.IntQuestionID,
    tblReviewQuestion.blnResponse1, tblReviewQuestion.blnResponse2,
    tblReviewQuestion.blnResponse3, tblReviewQuestion.blnResponse4,
    tblReviewQuestion.StrComments, tblQuestions.StrQuestion
    FROM tblReviewQuestion INNER JOIN
    tblQuestions ON tblReviewQuestion.IntQuestionID = tblQuestions.IntQuestionID
    WHERE (tblReviewQuestion.IntReviewID = @Intreviewid)
    ORDER BY tblReviewQuestion.IntQuestionID
END
CREATE PROCEDURE [dbo].[usp_RetrieveFullQuestionList]
AS
BEGIN
    select IntQuestionId,StrQuestion,blnactive,intorder
    from tblQuestions
    order by IntOrder
END
CREATE PROCEDURE [dbo].[usp_DeleteQuestion]
    @IntQuestionID int
AS
BEGIN
    update tblquestions
    set blnactive=0
    where intquestionid = @intquestionid
END
CREATE PROCEDURE [dbo].[usp_AddQuestion]
    @StrQuestion text,
    @IntOrder int
AS
BEGIN
    insert into tblQuestions(StrQuestion,IntOrder)
    values(@StrQuestion,@IntOrder)
END
```

```
CREATE PROCEDURE [dbo].[usp_UpdateQuestion]
     @IntQuestionID int,
     @StrQuestion text,
     @IntOrder int,
     @blnActive bit
AS
BEGIN
     update tblQuestions
     set StrQuestion = @StrQuestion,
     IntOrder = @IntOrder,
     blnActive = @blnActive
     where IntQuestionId = @IntQuestionID
END
CREATE PROCEDURE [dbo].[usp_RetrieveQuestionList]
AS
BEGIN
     select IntQuestionId,StrQuestion
     from tblQuestions
     where blnactive=1
     order by IntOrder
END
```

Create the SQLPersistenceService SQL Server Database

After you create the EPR database, tables, and stored procedures, the next task is to create the SQLPersistenceService database. You might have installed this database for Chapter 9; if so, you can skip the rest of this section and go on to create the ASP.NET Web site.

WF includes two scripts to add tables and logic to the persistence database. You can find the scripts at C:\[windows directory]\Microsoft.NET\Framework\v3.0\Windows Workflow Foundation\SQL\[language]\ in most installs. Two files for SQL persistence are in this folder. The first is SQLPersistenceService_Schema. This creates the tables necessary for the service to work. The other script is SQLPersistenceService_Logic. This script creates the stored procedures needed by the SQL Persistence Service.

Create a New ASP.NET Web Site

After you've created the EPR and SQLPersistenceService databases, you can create the ASP.NET Web site. Open Visual Studio 2005 and click File ➤ New ➤ Web Site. When the New Web Site screen appears, click the Browse button. This allows you to create a Web site but point to the file location. The folder VBEmployeePerformanceReview that was included with the book's downloadable code includes a folder called EPRWeb. That's the folder you want to find. When the Choose Location screen appears, click File System and find the folder mentioned earlier, as shown in Figure 10-3.

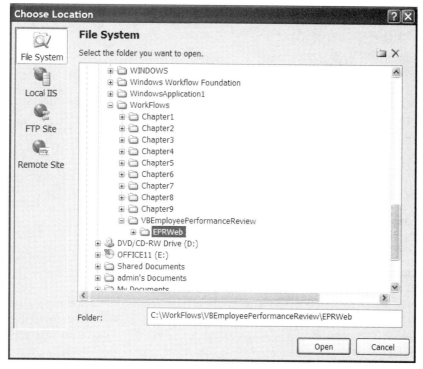

Figure 10-3. *Choose File System and EPRWeb to create the Web site.*

Build All ASP.NET Web Pages That Don't Interact with the Workflow

After you've created the Web site, you can build the Web pages. This application contains the following Web pages:

- *Default.aspx:* The home page of the application

- *DepartmentMaintenance.aspx:* Allows for maintenance of departments

- *EmployeeMaintenance.aspx:* Allows for maintenance of employees

- *Goals.aspx:* User enters goals in this page

- *LocationMaintenance.aspx:* Allows for maintenance of locations

- *MaintenanceHome.aspx:* A page with a menu linking to all the maintenance pages

- *MyReviews.aspx:* A page with all reviews for the user; if the user is a supervisor, contains the reviews of all the user's direct reports

- *PerformanceCriteria.aspx:* User selects a response to a specific question here

- *QuestionMaintenance.aspx:* Allows for maintenance of questions

- *Review.aspx:* All information for the review

Build the Complete Workflow and Test with a Simple Console Application First

Now that you've built all the ASP.NET pages, you need to build the workflow. Create a new State Machine Workflow Library called EPRWorkflow, and place the project within a folder called EPRWorkflow inside the VBEmployeePerformanceReview folder. When the project opens, rename the workflow from Workflow1 to EPR by right-clicking and choosing Rename within the Solution Explorer.

Following are the highlights of the first state again:

1. Employee sends a self-review to the supervisor

2. System finds the supervisor for the employee

3. System changes the current approver of the review to be the supervisor

4. System generates an e-mail notification to the supervisor

5. State is changed to Supervisor Review

Remember the nature of a State Machine workflow is that the workflow is waiting for events to happen. The first State activity (Initial State) must wait for an event to occur. In this case, the event is called EmployeeToSupervisor. Remember that in the business process, the review could potentially go between the employee and the supervisor several times. The supervisor could ask for changes, or make changes that the employee is to review. Therefore, this state and event may be used multiple times. Previous chapters have covered the use of the HandleExternalEvent activity. This is the activity that's used to listen for the external event EmployeeToSupervisor and to perform the necessary actions.

Click the Initial State activity that's created by default within the workflow. Change the name of the state to ReviewToSupervisor and change the description to "Send review to the supervisor." Also, while on the Properties page, click the Set as Initial State link at the bottom of the Properties page. This sets this State activity as the initial state. Add an EventDriven activity to the ReviewToSupervisor activity. Change the name of this EventDriven activity to EmployeeToSupervisor and change the description to "Employee sends to supervisor." Double-click the EmployeeToSupervisor activity and add a HandleExternalEvent activity to the EmployeeToSupervisor activity. Change the name of this activity to HandleToSupervisor and the description to "Handle the ToSupervisor event." At the moment, don't worry about the event type or interface type; you're just going to lay out the various states. However, you'll create a sub that will be executed when the EmployeeToSupervisor event is encountered. Before that occurs, you'll set up the connection string that the workflow will use to communicate with the database. Because this workflow is going to be specific to this application, you'll add an app.config file to the workflow and add the database connection string to that.

Click the My Project folder within the Solution Explorer and click the Settings tab. You'll see a message that there's no default configuration file for this project; you need to click the link if you want to create it. Click the link to create the new configuration file. From the drop-down under the Type column, choose (ConnectionString) and change the name to ConnString, as shown in Figure 10-4.

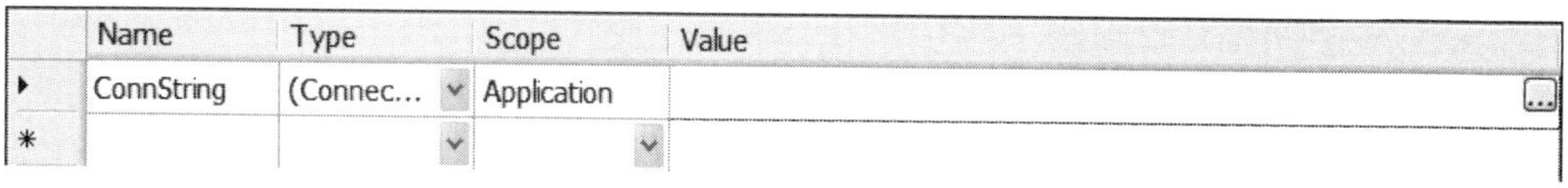

	Name	Type	Scope	Value
▶	ConnString	(Connec... ∨	Application	[...]
✱		∨	∨	

Figure 10-4. *Setting the name and type of the first setting*

Next, click the ellipse at the far right of the Value column. Set the server name—I'm using (local). Then choose SQL Server Authentication, enter **EPRUser** as the user name, and enter the password that you entered when adding the user to the server. The completed connection properties appear in Figure 10-5. Click OK when done.

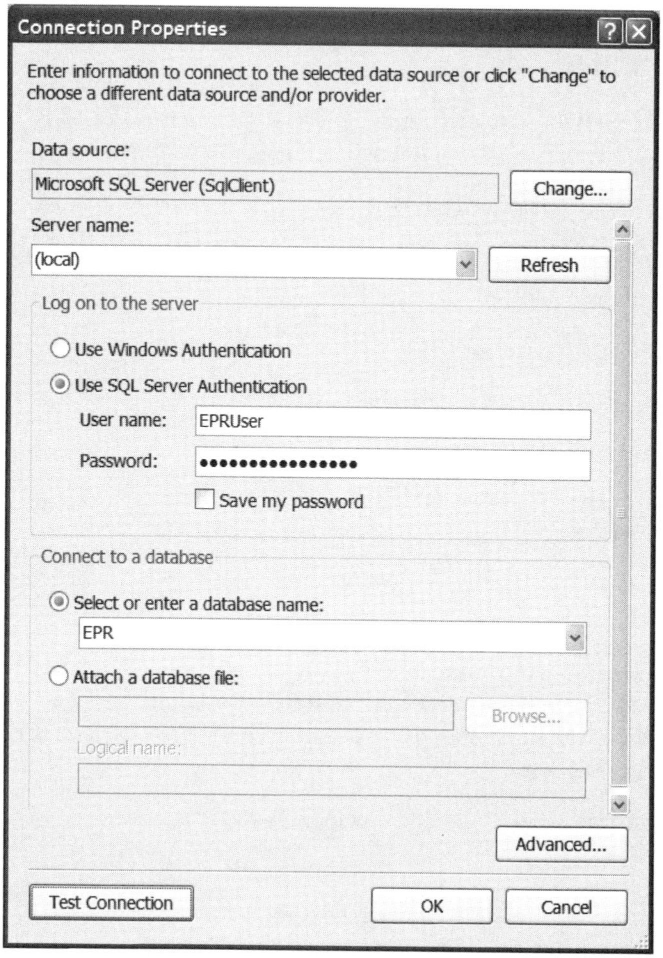

Figure 10-5. *Completed connection properties for the EPRWorkflow*

Save the settings, then open the EPR.vb Workflow Designer file if it isn't already opened. Right-click the design area and choose View Code. Add the following code to the EPR workflow code page:

```
Private Sub ProcessToSupervisor(ByVal sender As System.Object, ByVal e As
    System.Workflow.Activities.ExternalDataEventArgs)
End Sub
```

Next, to be able to work with data, you need to add some code. While in the code of the workflow, add `Imports System.Data.SQLClient` to the top of the code page. Also, you need to add a couple private variables to handle the Connection and Command objects. The beginning of the EPR class looks like the following:

```
Imports System.Data.SqlClient
Public Class EPR
    Inherits StateMachineWorkflowActivity
    Private Local_Conn As New SqlConnection
    Private Local_Comm As New SqlCommand
    Private Local_Parameter As SqlParameter
```

Next, you need to add a sub to allow you to add parameters to stored procedures. Most of the work will be done with the stored procedures mentioned earlier in this chapter.

```
Public Sub AddInputParameter(ByVal ParameterName As String, ByVal Value As String)
    Local_Parameter = New SqlParameter
    Local_Parameter.Direction = ParameterDirection.Input
    If InStr(ParameterName, "@") = 0 Then
        Local_Parameter.ParameterName = "@" & ParameterName
    Else
        Local_Parameter.ParameterName = ParameterName
    End If
    Try
        Local_Comm.Parameters.Add(Local_Parameter)
    Catch newexception As Exception
        Throw newexception
    End Try
End Sub
```

After you add parameters for a stored procedure (if they're required), then the stored procedure must be executed. The following code executes the stored procedure. Based on the parameter SPName, the code provides either a True or False success status based on the number of rows affected by the transaction.

```
Private Function ExecuteNonQuerySP(ByVal SPName As String) As Boolean
    Dim Local_NumberReturned As Long
    Try
        If Not Local_Conn.State = ConnectionState.Open Then
            Local_Conn.ConnectionString = My.Settings.ConnString
            Local_Conn.Open()
            Local_Comm.CommandText = SPName
            Local_Comm.CommandType = CommandType.StoredProcedure
            Local_Comm.Connection = Local_Conn
            Local_NumberReturned = CInt(Local_Comm.ExecuteNonQuery)
```

```
                If Local_NumberReturned > 0 Then
                    Return True
                Else
                    Return False
                End If
                Local_Comm.Dispose()
            End If
        Catch newexception As SqlException
            Throw newexception
        Finally
            Local_Conn.Close()
            Local_Conn.Dispose()
            Local_Comm.Dispose()
        End Try
    End Function
```

There will also be times that a single string value needs to be returned from a stored procedure (that is, return the e-mail address of the supervisor). Add the following function to execute a stored procedure and return just a single string value:

```
Private Function ReturnSingleStringSP(ByVal SPName As String) As String
    Dim Local_StringReturned As String
    Try
        If Not Local_Conn.State = ConnectionState.Open Then
            Local_Conn.ConnectionString = My.Settings.ConnString
            Local_Conn.Open()
            Local_Comm.CommandText = SPName
            Local_Comm.CommandType = CommandType.StoredProcedure
            Local_Comm.Connection = Local_Conn
            Local_StringReturned = CStr(Local_Comm.ExecuteScalar)
            If Not IsDBNull(Local_StringReturned) Then
                Return Local_StringReturned
            Else
                Return String.Empty
            End If
            Local_Comm.Dispose()
        End If
    Catch newexception As SqlException
        Throw newexception
    Finally
        Local_Conn.Close()
        Local_Conn.Dispose()
        Local_Comm.Parameters.Clear()
        Local_Comm.Dispose()
    End Try
End Function
```

When the employee chooses to send the review to the supervisor, the system must change the current approver of the review to be the supervisor, and an e-mail notification must go to the supervisor. The ProcessToSupervisor sub created earlier does this. First, you must add a property to the workflow so the review ID can be provided to the workflow. That's so the workflow knows which review to deal with. Add a private integer variable called IntReviewID and a public property called Review ID. Also, add a private string variable called StrEmailAddress to hold the e-mail address of the supervisor:

```
Private IntReviewID As Integer
Private StrEmailAddress As String
Public Property ReviewID() As Integer
    Get
        Return IntReviewID
    End Get
    Set(ByVal value As Integer)
        IntReviewID = value
    End Set
End Property
```

Add the following code to ProcessToSupervisor:

```
Private Sub ProcessToSupervisor(ByVal sender As System.Object,
    ByVal e As System.Workflow.Activities.ExternalDataEventArgs)
    Try
        Local_Conn = New SqlConnection
        Local_Comm = New SqlCommand
        AddInputParameter("@IntReviewID", IntReviewID)
        If ExecuteNonQuerySP("usp_ReviewToSupervisor") Then
            AddInputParameter("@IntReviewID", IntReviewID)
            StrEmailAddress =
            ReturnSingleStringSP("usp_RetrieveSupervisorEmailAddress")
        End If
    Catch ex As Exception
    End Try
End Sub
```

The first two lines of this code declare new instances of the SQLConnection and SQLCommand objects. Next, a parameter is added for the review ID to the Command object. Then a call is made to ExecuteNonQuerySP, which then executes the stored procedure called usp_ReviewToSupervisor. This stored procedure changes the current approver of the review denoted by IntReviewID to be the supervisor of the employee the review is for. If that update is successful (it affects at least one row), then a new parameter is added to the Command object (note at the end of each sub or function, the Parameters collection is cleared). Next, a call is made to the function ReturnSingleStringSP, which uses the review ID to find the supervisor of the employee the review is for and get the e-mail address of that supervisor. That e-mail address is stored in the local variable StrEmailAddress and will be used shortly.

Now it's time to begin creating the interface class that will be between the workflow and the ASP.NET application. This interface class will define the interface for the workflow and include the events that the ASP.NET application can call and that the workflow will

handle. Create a new VB Class Library project called EPRService, placing this within the
VBEmployeePerformanceReview folder. When the project is added, change the name of
Class1.vb to IEPRService.vb within the Solution Explorer. Next, add a reference to System.
Workflow.Activities by right-clicking the EPRService project in the Solution Explorer and
choosing Add Reference. When the Add Reference form appears under the .NET tab (the default
tab), find and select System.Workflow.Activities and click OK. Open the IEPRService.vb file
and change the code to the following:

```
Imports System
Imports System.Workflow.Activities
<ExternalDataExchange()> _
Public Interface IEPRService
End Interface
```

The first two lines import the necessary namespaces. Remember the
<ExternalDataExchange()> _ line defines this as an interface that exchanges data with other
applications. Add a new class to the EPRService project called EPREventArgs. Open the new
class and replace the default code with the following:

```
Imports System
Imports System.Workflow.Activities
<Serializable()> _
Public Class EPREventArgs
    Inherits ExternalDataEventArgs
    Private IntReviewID As Integer
    Public Property ReviewID() As Integer
        Get
            Return IntReviewID
        End Get
        Set(ByVal value As Integer)
            IntReviewID = value
        End Set
    End Property
    Public Sub New(ByVal InstanceID As Guid, ByVal ReviewID As Integer)
        MyBase.New(InstanceID)
        IntReviewID = ReviewID
    End Sub
End Class
```

Again, the first two lines just import the necessary namespaces. The <Serializable()> _
attribute tells the .NET Framework to serialize this class. This class also inherits from External-
DataEventArgs and must have a New sub within it. That New sub must call the New sub of the
base class (ExternalDataEventArgs). The New sub for this class accepts two parameters. The
first is the instance ID of the workflow that is to be used, and the second is the ReviewID of the
review this instance of the workflow is to work with.

Now you need to define the events for the interface file. There will be four events representing the four different state shifts that can occur. The first is EmployeeToSupervisor,
which is called anytime the review is sent from the employee to the supervisor. The second is
SupervisorToEmployee, which is called anytime the review is sent from the supervisor to the

employee. The third is EmployeeApproved, which is called when the employee approves the
review. Finally, EmployeeNotApproved is called if the employee doesn't approve the final
version of the review. Open IEPRService if it isn't already opened. Add the following code to
the interface so the interface code looks like this:

```
Imports System
Imports System.Workflow.Activities
<ExternalDataExchange()> _
Public Interface IEPRService
    Event EmployeeToSupervisor As EventHandler(Of EPREventArgs)
    Event SupervisorToEmployee As EventHandler(Of EPREventArgs)
    Event EmployeeApproved As EventHandler(Of EPREventArgs)
    Event EmployeeNotApproved As EventHandler(Of EPREventArgs)
End Interface
```

Now you must create the actual class that implements the interface. Add a new class
called EPRService to the EPRService project. On the next line after the class declaration for
EPRService, add Implements IEPRService. This automatically generates an event handler for
each of the events defined in the interface. The resulting EPRService class looks like this:

```
Public Class EPRService
    Implements IEPRService
    Public Event EmployeeToSupervisor(ByVal sender As Object,
        ByVal e As EPREventArgs) Implements IEPRService.EmployeeToSupervisor
    Public Event EmployeeApproved(ByVal sender As Object,
        ByVal e As EPREventArgs) Implements IEPRService.EmployeeApproved
    Public Event EmployeeNotApproved(ByVal sender As Object,
        ByVal e As EPREventArgs) Implements IEPRService.EmployeeNotApproved
    Public Event SupervisorToEmployee(ByVal sender As Object,
        ByVal e As EPREventArgs) Implements IEPRService.SupervisorToEmployee
End Class
```

After you've defined the events, you need to create subs to raise the events to the workflow.
Add the following code immediately after Implements IEPRService (before the previous code):

```
Private e As EPREventArgs
Public Sub RaiseEmployeetoSupervisor(ByVal ReviewID As Integer,
    ByVal InstanceId As Guid)
    e = New EPREventArgs(InstanceId, ReviewID)
    RaiseEvent EmployeeToSupervisor(Me, e)
End Sub
Public Sub RaiseSupervisorToEmployee(ByVal ReviewID As Integer,
    ByVal InstanceID As Guid)
    e = New EPREventArgs(InstanceID, ReviewID)
    RaiseEvent SupervisorToEmployee(Me, e)
End Sub
```

```
Public Sub RaiseEmployeeApproved(ByVal ReviewID As Integer,
    ByVal InstanceID As Guid)
    e = New EPREventArgs(InstanceID, ReviewID)
    RaiseEvent EmployeeApproved(Me, e)
End Sub
Public Sub RaiseEmployeeNotApproved(ByVal ReviewID As Integer,
    ByVal instanceid As Guid)
    e = New EPREventArgs(instanceid, ReviewID)
    RaiseEvent EmployeeNotApproved(Me, e)
End Sub
```

Now that the interface and events are defined, go back to the Workflow Designer and open the ReviewToSupervisor activity that was created earlier. Right now you should have an activity called HandleToSupervisor, but with a red exclamation mark in the upper-right corner of the activity. This is because the interface and event properties haven't been set. Before the connection between this activity and the interface can be established, you must make a connection between the two projects. Within the Solution Explorer, double-click the My Project folder within the EPRWorkflow project. Click the References tab and click the Add button in the middle of the form. The Add Reference screen appears. Click the Projects tab and choose EPRService (the only one listed) as shown in Figure 10-6, and click OK.

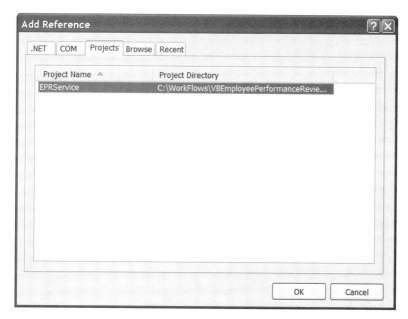

Figure 10-6. *Add a reference to the EPRService project.*

There's one final step before the interface can be linked to the activity. Right-click the EPRService project within the Solution Explorer and choose Build. This builds the project and creates an EPRService.dll file that the HandleToSupervisor activity points to. Click the HandleToSupervisor activity and open the Properties window. Click the ellipse next to the InterfaceType property. Under Referenced Assemblies, click the EPRService assembly, then click the EPRService namespace, and finally click the IEPRService interface, as shown in Figure 10-7. Click OK.

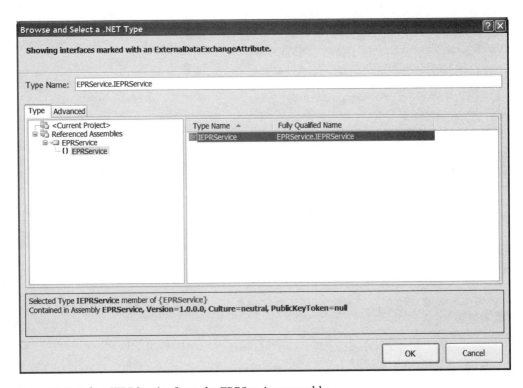

Figure 10-7. *Select IEPRService from the EPRService assembly.*

On the Properties window for the HandleToSupervisor activity, click the EventName property and choose EmployeeToSupervisor. The Properties for HandleToSupervisor will look like Figure 10-8.

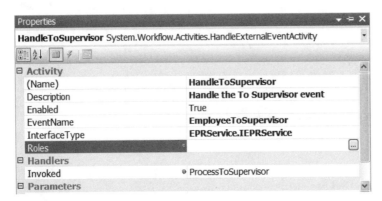

Figure 10-8. *Properties of the HandleToSupervisor activity*

Now the connection between the ASP.NET application and this workflow is ready to be used. You need to complete the rest of the ReviewToSupervisor activity. So far, only the HandleToSupervisor activity is within the ReviewToSupervisor activity. Remember the HandleToSupervisor activity only changes the status of the review and the current approver of the review. The next step is to use the supervisor's e-mail address that was retrieved as part of the HandleToSupervisor activity to send an e-mail to the supervisor.

Previously in this chapter, you added the ExecuteSQL activity built in Chapter 8 to the Toolbox. Now you need to add the SendEmail activity to the Toolbox. Right-click the Toolbox and click Choose Items. When the Choose Toolbox Items window appears, click the Activities tab and the Browse button. Browse to the Chapter8 folder and the SendEmail folder. Within the Bin folder, you'll find the SendEmail.dll file. Click it to add the SendEmail activity to the Toolbox. When the activity is available in the Toolbox, drag a SendEmail activity just after the HandleToSupervisor activity. Change the name of the new SendEmail activity to SendEmailToSupervisor. Once the status and current approver of the review is changed via the HandleToSupervisor activity, the SendEmailToSupervisor activity will send the necessary e-mail. Before adding more code, open the Solution Explorer and click the My Project folder within the EPRWorkflow project. Click the Settings tab, add a new setting called SMTP, and enter the IP address of the SMTP server you'll use.

View code for the workflow again and find the ProcessToSupervisor sub. Add code to provide a value for each of the properties of the SendEmailToSupervisor activity (ToAddress, FromAddress, Subject, Body, SMTPHost). The completed ProcessToSupervisor sub follows:

```
Private Sub ProcessToSupervisor(ByVal sender As System.Object,
    ByVal e As System.Workflow.Activities.ExternalDataEventArgs)
    Try
        Local_Conn = New SqlConnection
        Local_Comm = New SqlCommand
        AddInputParameter("@IntReviewID", IntReviewID)
        If ExecuteNonQuerySP("usp_ReviewToSupervisor") Then
            AddInputParameter("@IntReviewID", IntReviewID)
            StrEmailAddress =
            ReturnSingleStringSP("usp_RetrieveSupervisorEmailAddress")
            SendEmailToSupervisor.ToAddress = StrEmailAddress
            SendEmailToSupervisor.From = "Notifications@yourcompany.com"
            SendEmailToSupervisor.Body =
            "An Employee Review has been sent to you"
            SendEmailToSupervisor.Subject = "Employee Review Notification"
            SendEmailToSupervisor.SmtpHost = My.Settings.SMTPAddress.ToString
        End If
    Catch ex As Exception

    End Try
End Sub
```

Add a new State activity to the workflow called SupervisorToEmployee. Within this State activity, add a new EventDriven activity and call it HandleSupervisorToEmployee. Double-click the HandleToSupervisor EventDriven activity within the ReviewToSupervisor State activity. Within this activity, after the SendEmailToSupervisor activity, add a SetState activity called TransitionToSupervisor. Set the TargetStateName property to SupervisorToEmployee. The completed ReviewToSupervisor activity will look like Figure 10-9.

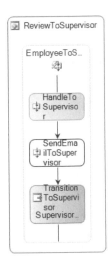

Figure 10-9. *ReviewToSupervisor completed activity*

Right-click the Workflow Designer and choose View Code. Create a stub for the sub called ProcessToEmployee. It's similar to the ProcessToSupervisor sub, but changes the review to the employee, not the supervisor:

```
Private Sub ProcessToEmployee(ByVal sender As System.Object, ByVal e As
System.Workflow.Activities.ExternalDataEventArgs)
End Sub
```

View the Workflow Designer again and double-click the SupervisorToEmployee activity. Add a new HandleExternalEvent activity to the SupervisorToEmployee activity, calling it HandleToEmployee. Just as with the HandleToSupervisor activity, click the ellipse next to the Interface Type property and choose IEPRService from the EPRService assembly. Choose SupervisorToEmployee as the EventName property, and ProcessToEmployee as the Invoked property. The completed properties for HandleToEmployee will look like Figure 10-10.

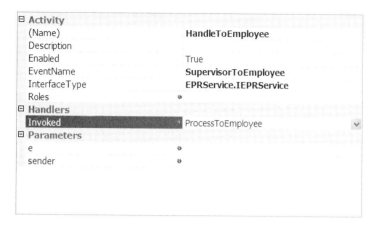

Figure 10-10. *HandleToEmployee properties*

Add a SendEmail activity to the SupervisorToEmployee activity called
SendEmailToEmployee. View the code for the workflow again and fill in the
ProcessToEmployee sub that was created earlier. The code is similar to the
ProcessToSupervisor sub, but changes supervisor to employee, and uses the
SendEmailToEmployee activity:

```
Private Sub ProcessToEmployee(ByVal sender As System.Object, ByVal e As
    System.Workflow.Activities.ExternalDataEventArgs)
    Try
        Local_Conn = New SqlConnection
        Local_Comm = New SqlCommand
        AddInputParameter("@IntReviewID", IntReviewID)
        If ExecuteNonQuerySP("usp_ReviewToEmployee") Then
            AddInputParameter("@IntReviewID", IntReviewID)
            StrEmailAddress = ReturnSingleStringSP
                ("usp_RetrieveEmployeeEmailAddress")
            SendEmailToEmployee.ToAddress = StrEmailAddress
            SendEmailToEmployee.From = "Notifications@yourcompany.com"
            SendEmailToEmployee.Body = "An Employee Review has been sent to you"
            SendEmailToEmployee.Subject = "Employee Review Notification"
            SendEmailToEmployee.SmtpHost = My.Settings.SMTPAddress.ToString
        End If
    Catch ex As Exception

    End Try
End Sub
```

Return to the main Workflow Designer and add a State activity to the workflow called EmployeeChoice. Double-click the SupervisorToEmployee activity and add a SetState activity after the SendEmailToEmployee activity. Call this activity TransitionToEmployeeChoice and set the TargetStateName to EmployeeChoice. The completed SupervisorToEmployee activity will look like Figure 10-11.

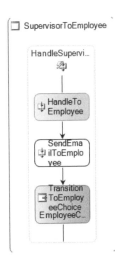

Figure 10-11. *Completed SupervisorToEmployee activity*

Return to the main EPR Workflow Designer and add an EventDriven activity to the EmployeeChoice State activity. Change the Name property to EmployeeApproves. Add a second EventDriven activity to the same State activity, this time with a name of EmployeeDoesNotApprove. These two State activities represent what the employee decides, either to approve or not approve. Each has its own actions to be taken. While still on the main EPR Workflow Designer page, add another State activity and change the Name property to Completed. Right-click this State activity and choose Set as Completed State. Doing this sets the Completed State activity as the last state within the workflow. When this State activity is reached, the workflow is considered completed.

Double-click the EmployeeApproves EventDriven activity within the EmployeeChoice State activity. Add a HandleExternalEvent activity and change the name to HandleEmployeeApproved. As with the previous EventDriven activities, choose IEPRService from the `EPRService` assembly for the Interface Type property and choose EmployeeApproved as the EventName. Next, add a SendEmail activity after the HandleEmployeeApproved activity and change the name to SendApprovedEmailToHR. Finally, add a SetState activity after the SendEmail activity. Change the name of this SetState activity to TransitionToCompleted and the Target State Name property to Completed. The completed EmployeeApproved activity is shown in Figure 10-12.

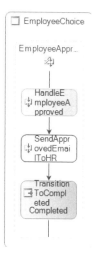

Figure 10-12. *EmployeeApproved EventDriven activity within the EmployeeChoice activity*

Return to the main EPR Workflow Designer and double-click the
EmployeeDoesNotApprove activity. Add a HandleExternalEvent activity and change the name
to HandleEmployeeDoesNotApprove. As with the previous EventDriven activities, choose
IEPRService from the `EPRService` assembly for the Interface Type property and choose
EmployeeNotApproved as the EventName. Next, add a SendEmail activity after the
HandleEmployeeDoesNotApprove activity and change the name to
SendNotApprovedEmailToHR. Finally, add a SetState activity after the SendEmail activity.
Change the name of this SetState activity to TransitionToCompleted2 (you can't have two
activities with the same name within the same workflow) and the Target State Name property
to Completed. The completed EmployeeDoesNotApprove activity is shown in Figure 10-13.

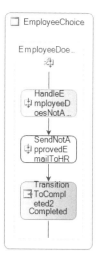

Figure 10-13. *EmployeeDoesNotApprove EventDriven activity within the EmployeeChoice activity*

The completed EPR workflow is shown in Figure 10-14.

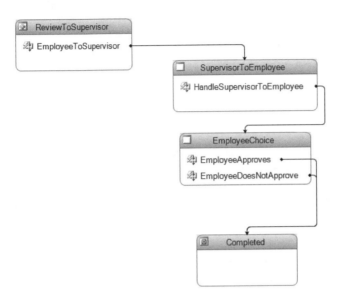

Figure 10-14. *Completed EPR workflow*

The workflow code isn't completed yet. The EmployeeApproves and EmployeeDoesNotApprove activities still need code to be invoked when the respective events are handled. View the code for the workflow and add the following two subs:

```vb
Private Sub ProcessApproved(ByVal sender As System.Object, ByVal e As
System.Workflow.Activities.ExternalDataEventArgs)
    Try
        Local_Conn = New SqlConnection
        Local_Comm = New SqlCommand
        AddInputParameter("@IntReviewID", IntReviewID)
        If ExecuteNonQuerySP("usp_ReviewApproved") Then
            AddInputParameter("@IntReviewID", IntReviewID)
            StrEmailAddress = ReturnSingleStringSP("usp_RetrieveHREmailAddress")
            SendEmailToSupervisor.ToAddress = StrEmailAddress
            SendEmailToSupervisor.From = "Notifications@yourcompany.com"
            SendEmailToSupervisor.Body = "An Employee Review has
                been Approved and Completed"
            SendEmailToSupervisor.Subject = "Employee Review Notification"
            SendEmailToSupervisor.SmtpHost = My.Settings.SMTPAddress.ToString
        End If
    Catch ex As Exception
    End Try
End Sub
```

```
Private Sub ProcessNotApproved(ByVal sender As System.Object,
ByVal e As System.Workflow.Activities.ExternalDataEventArgs)
     Try
          Local_Conn = New SqlConnection
          Local_Comm = New SqlCommand
          AddInputParameter("@IntReviewID", IntReviewID)
          If ExecuteNonQuerySP("usp_ReviewNotApproved") Then
               AddInputParameter("@IntReviewID", IntReviewID)
               StrEmailAddress = ReturnSingleStringSP("usp_RetrieveHREmailAddress")
               SendEmailToSupervisor.ToAddress = StrEmailAddress
               SendEmailToSupervisor.From = "Notifications@yourcompany.com"
               SendEmailToSupervisor.Body =
                    "An Employee Review has been NOT Approved"
               SendEmailToSupervisor.Subject = "Employee Review Notification"
               SendEmailToSupervisor.SmtpHost = My.Settings.SMTPAddress.ToString
          End If
     Catch ex As Exception
     End Try
End Sub
```

Finally, return to the Workflow Designer and double-click the EmployeeApproves activity. Click the HandleEmployeeApproves activity and change the Invoked property to ProcessApproved. Return to the main EPR workflow, double-click the EmployeeDoesNotApprove activity, and click the HandleEmployeeDoesNotApprove activity. Change the Invoked property to ProcessNotApproved.

Now the EPR workflow is complete and can be added to the Web site.

Connect the ASP.NET Web Pages and the Workflow

The first task that must be completed when integrating a Web site and workflow is to add the necessary references. Open the previously created EPRWeb Web site. Right-click the project name within the Solution Explorer and choose Add Reference. When the Add Reference dialog box appears, find System.Workflow.Activities, System.Workflow.ComponentModel, and System.Workflow.Runtime under the .NET tab. Select each of these and click OK. This adds a reference to the necessary workflow base classes.

Next, you need to add the EPRService and EPRWorkflow projects to the Web site. Choose File ➤ Add ➤ Existing Project. Navigate to the EPRService project file and choose it. Then repeat this process for the EPRWorkflow project. Now you need to reference these projects from the Web site project. Again, right-click the EPRWeb project within the Solution Explorer and choose Add Reference. Under the Projects tab, you should see EPRService and EPRWorkflow. Choose both of these as shown in Figure 10-15, then click OK.

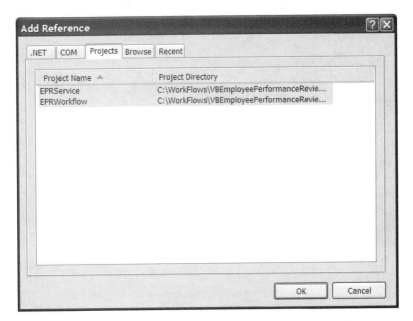

Figure 10-15. *Choose EPRService and EPRWorkflow as project references.*

Open the Review.aspx page from the EPRWeb project. At the top, add the following code:

```
Imports System.Workflow.Runtime
Imports System.Workflow.Runtime.Hosting
Imports System.Workflow.Activities

Partial Class Review
    Inherits System.Web.UI.Page
    Private clsEPR As EPR
    Private workflowruntime As WorkflowRuntime
    Private workflowinstance As WorkflowInstance
    Private workflowinstanceid As Guid
    Private eprservice As New EPRService.EPRService
```

Create a new sub called InitiateWorkflow and add the following code:

```
Private Sub InitiateWorkflow()
    Try
        workflowruntime = New WorkflowRuntime
        Dim dataExchangeService As New
            ExternalDataEventArgs(Session("WorkflowInstanceID"))
        workflowruntime.AddService(dataExchangeService)
        workflowruntime.AddService(eprservice)
        HttpContext.Current.Cache("WorkflowRuntime") = workflowruntime
        workflowruntime.StartRuntime()
    Catch ex As Exception
    End Try
End Sub
```

Add another sub called StartWorkflow that creates the workflow and starts it:

```
Private Sub StartWorkflow()
    workflowinstanceid = System.Guid.NewGuid
    workflowinstance = workflowruntime.CreateWorkflow(GetType(EPR))
    workflowinstanceid = workflowinstance.InstanceId
    workflowinstance.Start()
    Session("WorkflowInstanceID") = workflowinstanceid
End Sub
```

Finally, on the click event of btnSubmit, add the following code:

```
InitiateWorkflow()
StartWorkflow()
eprservice.RaiseEmployeetoSupervisor(Trim(txtReviewID.Text), workflowinstanceid)
```

This creates the workflow, starts the runtime, and makes a call to the RaiseEmployeetoSupervisor event that the workflow will handle. You can continue to use this code within the application when you want to interact with the workflow.

Conclusion

This chapter has shown an extensive real-world application that you can use as a model for other applications you want to build with ASP.NET and WF. The next chapter will cover how to integrate Office 2007, WF, and SharePoint Server 2007.

CHAPTER 11

■■■

Integration with Office 2007

This chapter will show you how to integrate workflow created with WF with the new Office 2007 suite. This integration will allow more end users to use workflow. You can publish documents with built-in workflows and allow users to activate the workflow via easy options within Word 2007.

Requirements

The integration between WF and Office 2007 requires a middleman, Microsoft SharePoint. This can be either Microsoft SharePoint Services or Microsoft SharePoint Portal. SharePoint will host the workflow that you've developed and thus facilitate the actions of the workflow. Both SharePoint Portal and SharePoint Services must be run on a Windows 2003 Server. This chapter uses a beta of Microsoft SharePoint Server 2007. This chapter also requires the Enterprise Content Management Starter Kit (ECM) for Microsoft 2007 Office System.

Setup

You need to take a couple steps before you can begin creating workflow for SharePoint. The first step is to install SharePoint Portal or SharePoint Services on a Windows 2003 server and configure it, if you haven't already done that. You need to copy the following DLL files from the server with SharePoint installed to your development computer before you can create a workflow for SharePoint:

- Microsoft.Office.Server.dll

- Microsoft.Office.Workflow.Tasks.dll

- Microsoft.SharePoint.dll

- Microsoft.Sharepoint.Portal.dll

- Microsoft.SharePoint.Security.dll

- Microsoft.SharePoint.Publishing.dll

- Microsoft.Sharepoint.WorkflowActions.dll

If you plan to build multiple SharePoint workflow projects, you should install these files into the Global Assembly Cache (GAC). To do this, open the Visual Studio 2005 Command Prompt from the Start ➤ Programs menu. Type the following command, replacing [path] with the path to where you placed the DLL files:

```
gacutil /i "c:\[path]\microsoft.sharepoint.workflowactions.dll"
```

After you enter the command, hit Enter, and you should get a message "Assembly successfully added to the cache." Continue this for the other DLL files as well. To test out the new project templates that were installed with the ECM, open Visual Studio 2005 and choose File ➤ New ➤ Project. When the New Project dialog box appears, click VB on the left and choose SharePoint Sequential Workflow Library. Enter **VBSharePointSequential** as the name. The New Project dialog box will look like Figure 11-1.

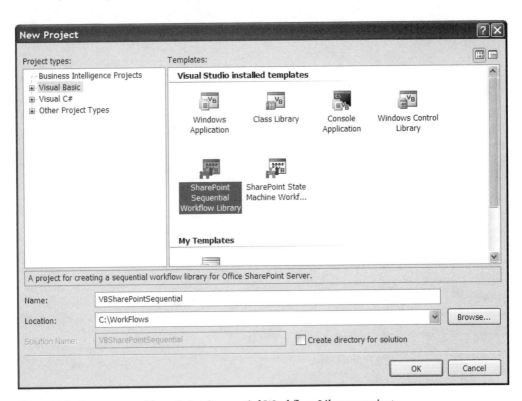

Figure 11-1. *Create a new SharePoint Sequential Workflow Library project.*

When this project is opened, notice there are a few new files in the Solution Explorer, as shown in Figure 11-2.

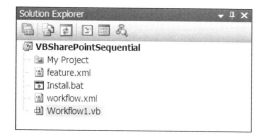

Figure 11-2. *Files in Solution Explorer for the SharePoint workflow*

All three new files (feature.xml, Install.bat, and Workflow.xml) are necessary to publish the workflow directly from this project to the SharePoint server. Double-click the Workflow1.vb file. When it opens, you'll notice there is already an activity within the workflow, as shown in Figure 11-3.

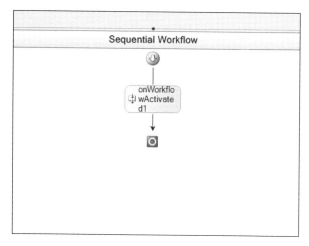

Figure 11-3. *Default activity on SharePoint Sequential Workflow*

While still on the Designer, open the Toolbox. Scroll down the Toolbox and you'll see a much larger number of activities in the Toolbox. This is because the file Microsoft.Sharepoint.WorkflowActions.dll was added to the GAC. If you hadn't added this file to the GAC, you'd need to choose this file each time to add items to the Toolbox. Figure 11-4 gives you a partial showing of the new activities within the Toolbox.

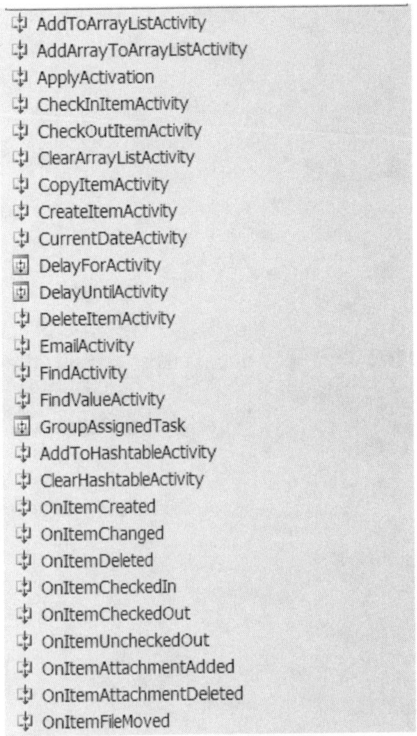

Figure 11-4. *Partial list of new activities*

Right-click the workflow and choose View Code. Following is the default code for this type of workflow:

```
Imports Microsoft.SharePoint
Imports Microsoft.SharePoint.Workflow
Imports Microsoft.SharePoint.WorkflowActions
Imports Microsoft.Office.Workflow.Utility

Public Class Workflow1
    Inherits SequentialWorkflowActivity
    Public Sub New()
        MyBase.New()
        InitializeComponent()
    End Sub
    Public workflowProperties As SPWorkflowActivationProperties =
        New Microsoft.SharePoint.Workflow.SPWorkflowActivationProperties
End Class
```

Notice the first four lines import various SharePoint libraries and also a workflow library from Office. Also, notice that although this is a SharePoint workflow library, the workflow still inherits from SequentialWorkflowActivity just like all other workflows created in this book have. The only difference between the SharePoint workflow and any other workflow created in this book is the last line of code that associates SharePoint Workflow Activation Properties (SPWorkflowActivationProperties) with the properties of the workflow so this workflow takes on the necessary properties.

Real-World Example

You need to do a few things to integrate Office 2007, SharePoint, and WF. You'll take the following steps:

- Model the workflow in VS

- Create the InfoPath form

- Deploy to the SharePoint Server

- Test

Note the use of InfoPath. InfoPath is a product that has been included with Office since Office 2003 that gives you a compact development environment for forms. You can't add code to these forms, but you can use preexisting buttons and boxes to mock up or build forms quickly.

Model Workflow in VS

The first step in the process of creating a workflow that can be used in SharePoint is to model that workflow in VS. Create a new VB SharePoint Sequential Workflow Library project called ShareDocumentExample. This example will show how to create a workflow, and then use that workflow within SharePoint to request approvals for a document and also gather some comments (via InfoPath).

Within the Toolbox, find the CreateTask activity. This activity creates a task for a user within SharePoint. After a task is created, you need to wait for that task to change. For this, first add a While activity to wait until a condition is satisfied, then add an OnTaskChanged activity within the While activity. Finally, the task will be completed, so add a TaskCompletion activity last. Once all those activities are added to the workflow, the workflow will look like Figure 11-5.

If you click any of the red exclamation points in the upper-right corner of the activities, you'll see an error related to the CorrelationToken property. The CorrelationToken property allows you to tie various activities together so the action they perform is performed on the same item. Because you want all the actions within the workflow to be performed on the same task or item, the CorrelationTask property for each activity needs to be the same. Click the createTask1 activity and add TaskToken to the CorrelationToken property. After you add the CorrelationToken, there's a plus sign next to the property. Click it and the OwnerActivityName property appears. Choose Workflow1, as shown in Figure 11-6.

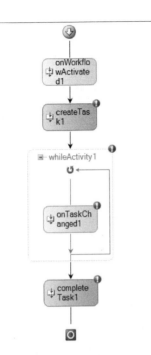

Figure 11-5. *Workflow model to share a document in SharePoint*

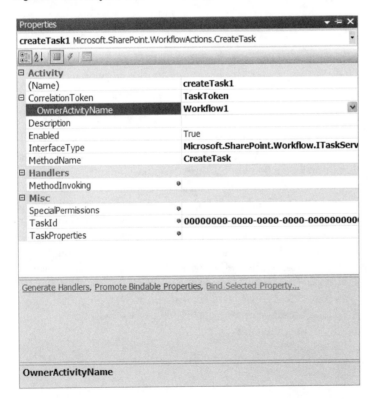

Figure 11-6. *CorrelationToken and OwnerActivityName properties*

Next, click the ellipse next to the TaskProperties property. When the Bind Task Properties dialog box appears, enter **TaskProp** as the name and choose Create Field, as shown in Figure 11-7.

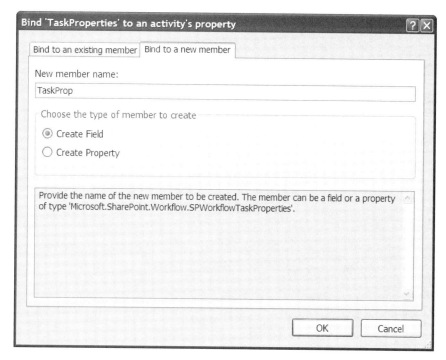

Figure 11-7. *Add TaskProp as a property.*

After the TaskProp property is added, click the ellipse again, and this time add a field called TaskGUID. After adding these properties to the CreateTask1 activity, add the CorrelationToken property to the OnTaskChanged1 and CompleteTask1 activities. You do this by choosing TaskToken from the drop-down list for the CorrelationTask property on each activity. The set of activities is defined by a Sequence activity. You should place all the existing activities inside a Sequence activity. The new workflow is shown in Figure 11-8.

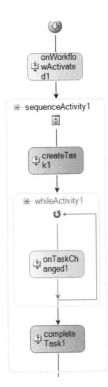

Figure 11-8. *Workflow after adding Replicator and Sequence activities*

Create InfoPath Form

This example will use three different types of InfoPath forms: Association, Initiation, and Task Completion. The Association form sets default, initial data for the workflow. The Initiation form gives the workflow initial data to use. The Task Completion form allows users to modify tasks they've been assigned.

Open InfoPath, and when the Getting Started dialog box appears, choose Design a Form Template. When the Design a Form dialog box appears, choose Blank, and make sure to check the "Enable browser-compatible features only" check box, as shown in Figure 11-9.

When the blank form appears, click the Controls link on the right side of the form. Drag a text box control onto the form in the upper-left corner of the form. Just before the text box control, add **Instructions**. Enlarge the text box so it can accept several sets of instructions. The form should look like Figure 11-10.

Now you need to name the text box. Double-click the text box, and when the Text Box Properties dialog box appears, enter **Instructions for the Field Name**. Add another text box, calling it **Assignee**, and add a label of Assignee before it.

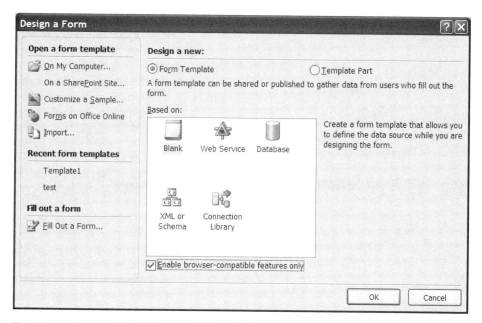

Figure 11-9. *Create a blank form with "Enable browser-compatible features only" checked.*

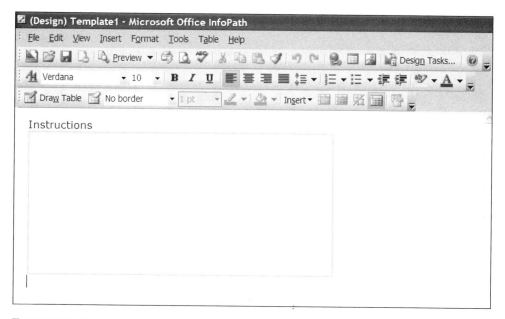

Figure 11-10. *New form with Instructions text box*

Click Design Tasks again and choose Controls from Design Tasks. Drag a button from the Controls area to the form after the Instructions text box. Double-click the button and change the label to Submit. Click the Rules button on the Button Properties dialog box. When the Rules dialog box appears, click Add. Then, when the Rules dialog box appears, click Add Action. Finally, when the Action dialog box appears, choose "Submit using a data connection" from the drop-down list. Click Add to add a connection. The Data Connection Wizard dialog box appears again. Choose Create a New Connection and Submit Data, then click Next. Click "To the hosting environment" when asked where to submit the data, as shown in Figure 11-11. Click Next. Leave Submit as the name of the connection and click Finish.

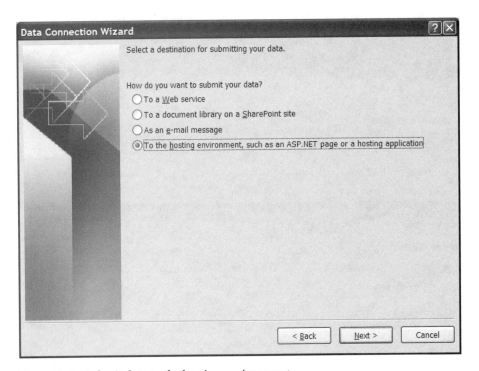

Figure 11-11. *Submit data to the hosting environment.*

Click OK on the Action dialog box. Click the Add Action button, and when the Action dialog box appears, choose Close the Form from the drop-down box and click OK. This will close the form when the user has submitted the data. Then click OK through the remaining open forms.

Click File ➤ Publish to publish the form. Save the template any place you'd like. When the Publishing Wizard appears, click To a Network Location as the location to publish the template and click Next. When prompted for the network location, click the Browse button, browse to the location of the workflow project (SharedDocument), change the name of the template to InitialForm, and click Next. Remove the contents of the Alternative Path screen and click Next. Finally, click Finish.

Create a new template as you did with the last one. Add a text box with the same name, and a submit button with the same rules. Then, between the text box and the submit button, add a check box. Set the name of the check box to isFinished. Change the text next to the check box to "I am finished." Publish this template to the same location, but with a name of FinalSubmission.

Now you need to return to the workflow. Open the workflow project if it isn't already open and click the OnWorkflowActivated1 activity (the default activity that was already on the workflow when it was created). Within the Properties window, click the Invoked property, type **OnWorkflowActivated**, and then click off that property. This creates a sub called OnWorkflowActivated. Add the following declarations to the class (just below the class declaration):

```
Public Assignee As String
Public Instructions As String
Public Comments As String
Public CurrentUser As Integer
public IsFinished as Boolean
Public TaskID As Guid
```

Return to the OnWorkflowActivated sub. This sub takes the values of the various properties from the form just created and populates a hash table (a type). Add code to this sub so the sub looks like the following code:

```
Private Sub OnWorkflowActivated(ByVal sender As System.Object,
ByVal e As System.Workflow.Activities.ExternalDataEventArgs)
    Assignee=formdata("Assignee").ToString
    Instructions = formdata("instructions").ToString
End Sub
```

Now you need to worry about what occurs when the task is created by the CreateTask activity. View the Workflow Designer again and click the CreateTask activity. Click the Properties window and the TaskId property. Click the ellipse next to the TaskID property and choose TaskID. Next, choose the MethodInvoking property. Enter **CreateTask**, which creates a new sub called CreateTask. Add the following code to this sub:

```
Private Sub CreateTask(ByVal sender As System.Object,
ByVal e As System.EventArgs)
    TaskID = Guid.NewGuid
    TaskProp.AssignedTo = "bmyers"
    TaskProp.Title = "Please review this document"
    TaskProp.Description = Instructions
End Sub
```

Return to the Workflow Designer and click the OnTaskChanged1 task and the AfterProperties property. Click the ellipse next to this property and add AfterProps as a property. Click the Invoked property, add **OnTaskChanged**, and move off. This creates a sub called OnTaskChanged. Add the following code:

```
Private Sub OnTaskChanged(ByVal sender As System.Object,
ByVal e As System.Workflow.Activities.ExternalDataEventArgs)
    IsFinished = Boolean.Parse(AfterProps.ExtendedProperties("isFinished").
    ToString)
End Sub
```

Return to the Workflow Designer to address the While activity. Click the While activity and the Condition property. Choose Code Condition and enter **NotFinished** as the Code, which creates a sub called NotFinished:

```
Private Sub NotFinished(ByVal sender As System.Object,
ByVal e As System.Workflow.Activities.ConditionalEventArgs)
        e.Result = Not IsFinished
        IsFinished=False
End Sub
```

Deploy to SharePoint Server

Once the workflow and InfoPath forms have been created, you need to deploy them. This requires a few steps:

- Generate Feature and Workflow XML files

- Install and activate the feature

- Use IISReset.exe to load the assembly into SharePoint server memory

- Associate the workflow to the SharePoint list or library

Open the Feature.xml file. You case use code snippets to populate this file. To do this, right-click Insert Snippet ➤ SharePoint Server Workflow ➤ Feature.xml Code, as shown in Figure 11-12.

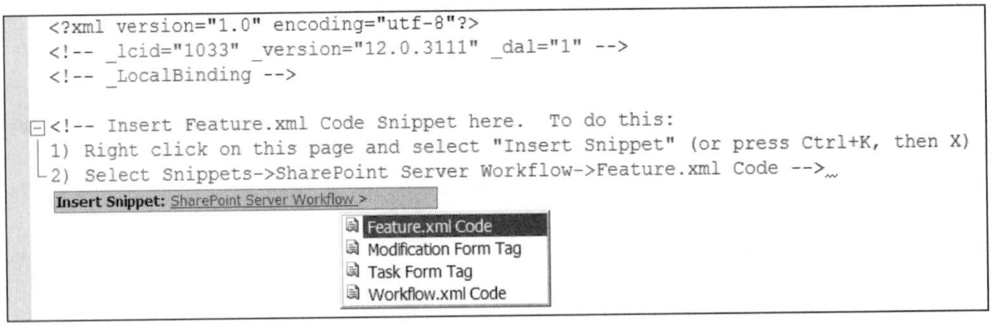

Figure 11-12. *Insert the Feature.xml Code snippet.*

The snippet fills in all the required XML with green areas denoting changes that you need to make. The inserted XML is shown in Figure 11-13.

You need to provide a GUID for ID. To do this, select Tools ➤ Create GUID. Click the Registry Format radio button and then the New GUID button. Next, click the Copy button, go to the XML file, and paste the new GUID in place. Next, provide a title and a description for the feature. Save the Feature.xml file and then open the Workflow.xml file. Again, right-click and choose Insert Snippet ➤ SharePoint Server Workflow ➤ Workflow.xml Code.

```
<?xml version="1.0" encoding="utf-8"?>
<!-- _lcid="1033" _version="12.0.3111" _dal="1" -->
<!-- _LocalBinding -->

<!-- Insert Feature.xml Code Snippet here.  To do this:
1) Right click on this page and select "Insert Snippet" (or press Ctr
2) Select Snippets->SharePoint Server Workflow->Feature.xml Code -->
<Feature   Id="GUID"
           Title="Default Title"
           Description="This feature is a workflow that ..."
           Version="12.0.0.0"
           Scope="Site"
           ReceiverAssembly="Microsoft.Office.Workflow.Feature, Versio
           ReceiverClass="Microsoft.Office.Workflow.Feature.WorkflowFe
           xmlns="http://schemas.microsoft.com/sharepoint/">
    <ElementManifests>
        <ElementManifest Location="workflow.xml" />
    </ElementManifests>
    <Properties>
        <Property Key="GloballyAvailable" Value="true" />

        <!-- Value for RegisterForms key indicates the path to the fo
        <!-- if you don't have forms, use *.xsn -->
        <Property Key="RegisterForms" Value="*.xsn" />
    </Properties>
</Feature>
```

Figure 11-13. *Snippet for Feature.xml*

Enter the name you want to see within SharePoint for this workflow as the Name. Enter a description and create another GUID, which can't be the same as the one used in the Feature.xml file. For the CodeBesideClass, enter the name of your project and the workflow name (in my case, ShareDocumentExample.Workflow1).

Next, you need to provide the ID for the InfoPath forms. To do this, open the InitialForm template and make sure you're designing the form (Tools ➤ Design This Form). Choose File ➤ Properties, and when the Form Template Properties dialog box appears, copy the contents of the ID box. Paste this into the associationFormURN and instantiationFormURN tags within the XML file. Finally, remove the modificationURN tags; you don't need them, as you aren't using a modification form.

Open the install.bat file within the Solution Explorer and replace MyFeature with the name of your feature (in my case, ShareDocumentExample). Change the http://localhost to the site you want to use the workflow with. After you save, then copy the folder to the server and run the bat file. This installs the workflow DLL file in the GAC, and also performs the necessary associations and installs the feature.

Open the SharePoint site and click the Shared Documents link on the left. Click Settings ➤ Document Library Settings. Click Workflow Settings under the Permissions and Policies area. If you haven't added a workflow before, you'll automatically come to the Add a Workflow form. If you have workflows already defined in your SharePoint server, you'll need to click Add a Workflow first. On the Add Workflow page, you'll see your workflow name at the top with other default workflows. If you don't see your workflow in the list, then the installation of the feature didn't complete correctly. Enter a name for the workflow and take the default of the other options.

Click Next to move to the next page. When the next page appears, choose "One participant at a time" under "Assign tasks to, do not assign reviewers."

To test the workflow out, create a new document in Word 2007 and add some text. Save the document as workflowtest. Go to your Shared Document area within SharePoint and choose Upload. This allows you to update the document. Browse to the document and click it. Once the document is available in the Shared Document area, click the drop-down box that appears when you click the document. From that drop-down box, choose Workflows. When the Workflows page appears, choose the workflow that you added earlier. Enter the login name of the person to assign the document to and click Submit. When you return to the Shared Document area, you'll see a listing for the document, and a column to the right with the name of the workflow and a listing of the workflow status (In Progress). If you click that In Progress link, you'll get a status of the workflow and see the history of that document and workflow. If you're the approver of the workflow, you can choose Edit Item from the drop-down list and get the final submission form. If you want to complete the task, click the check box next to I'm Finished and click Submit. This completes the workflow.

Conclusion

This chapter has shown how you can integrate Microsoft Office 2007, InfoPath 2007, Share-Point Server 2007, and WF to create a document review process using WF and hosted inside SharePoint Server.

Index

Find it faster at http://superindex.apress.com

Find it faster at http://superindex.apress.com

Find it faster at http://superindex.apress.com

Find it faster at http://superindex.apress.com

forums.apress.com

FOR PROFESSIONALS BY PROFESSIONALS™

JOIN THE APRESS FORUMS AND BE PART OF OUR COMMUNITY. You'll find discussions that cover topics of interest to IT professionals, programmers, and enthusiasts just like you. If you post a query to one of our forums, you can expect that some of the best minds in the business—especially Apress authors, who all write with *The Expert's Voice*™—will chime in to help you. Why not aim to become one of our most valuable participants (MVPs) and win cool stuff? Here's a sampling of what you'll find:

DATABASES
Data drives everything.

Share information, exchange ideas, and discuss any database programming or administration issues.

INTERNET TECHNOLOGIES AND NETWORKING
Try living without plumbing (and eventually IPv6).

Talk about networking topics including protocols, design, administration, wireless, wired, storage, backup, certifications, trends, and new technologies.

JAVA
We've come a long way from the old Oak tree.

Hang out and discuss Java in whatever flavor you choose: J2SE, J2EE, J2ME, Jakarta, and so on.

MAC OS X
All about the Zen of OS X.

OS X is both the present and the future for Mac apps. Make suggestions, offer up ideas, or boast about your new hardware.

OPEN SOURCE
Source code is good; understanding (open) source is better.

Discuss open source technologies and related topics such as PHP, MySQL, Linux, Perl, Apache, Python, and more.

PROGRAMMING/BUSINESS
Unfortunately, it is.

Talk about the Apress line of books that cover software methodology, best practices, and how programmers interact with the "suits."

WEB DEVELOPMENT/DESIGN
Ugly doesn't cut it anymore, and CGI is absurd.

Help is in sight for your site. Find design solutions for your projects and get ideas for building an interactive Web site.

SECURITY
Lots of bad guys out there—the good guys need help.

Discuss computer and network security issues here. Just don't let anyone else know the answers!

TECHNOLOGY IN ACTION
Cool things. Fun things.

It's after hours. It's time to play. Whether you're into LEGO® MINDSTORMS™ or turning an old PC into a DVR, this is where technology turns into fun.

WINDOWS
No defenestration here.

Ask questions about all aspects of Windows programming, get help on Microsoft technologies covered in Apress books, or provide feedback on any Apress Windows book.

HOW TO PARTICIPATE:
Go to the Apress Forums site at **http://forums.apress.com/**.
Click the New User link.

You Need the Companion eBook

Your purchase of this book entitles you to its companion eBook for only $10.

We believe this Apress title will prove so indispensable that you'll want to carry it with you everywhere, which is why we are offering the companion eBook for $10 to customers who purchase this book now. Convenient and fully searchable, the eBook version of any content-rich, page-heavy Apress book makes a valuable addition to your programming library. You can easily find, copy, and apply code—and then perform examples by quickly toggling between instructions and the application. Even simultaneously tackling a donut, diet soda, and complex code becomes simplified with hands-free eBooks!

Once you purchase this book, getting the $10 companion eBook is simple:

❶ Visit **www.apress.com/promo/tendollars/**.

❷ Complete a basic registration form to receive a randomly generated question about this title.

❸ Answer the question correctly in 60 seconds and you will receive a promotional code to redeem for the $10 eBook.

2560 Ninth Street • Suite 219 • Berkeley, CA 94710

eBookshop

Offer valid through 4/23/07.